The Image
of
BAR KOKHBA
in
Traditional Jewish
Literature

Hermeneutics: Studies in the History of Religions
Kees W. Bolle, Editor

Joanne Punzo Waghorne, The Raja's Magic Clothes:
 Re-visioning Kingship and Divinity in England's India
Devin DeWeese, Islamization and Native Religion in the
 Golden Horde: Baba Tükles and Conversion to Islam in
 Historical and Epic Tradition

Richard G. Marks

The Image of BAR KOKHBA in Traditional Jewish Literature

False Messiah and National Hero

The Pennsylvania State University Press
University Park, Pennsylvania

Library of Congress Cataloging-in-Publication Data

Marks, Richard Gordon.
   The Image of Bar Kokhba in traditional Jewish literature : false messiah and national hero / Richard G. Marks.
         p.   cm.
   Includes bibliographical references and index.
   ISBN 0-271-00939-X (cloth). — ISBN 0-271-00940-3 (pbk.)
   1. Bar Kokhba, d. 135. 2. Jews—History—Bar Kokhba Rebellion, 132–135—Historiography. 3. Rabbinical literature—History and criticism. 4. Jewish historians. I. Title.
   DS122.9.M3   1993
   956.94′02′092—dc20   92-34744
                                                                    CIP

Copyright © 1994 The Pennsylvania State University
All rights reserved
Printed in the United States of America

Published by The Pennsylvania State University Press, Suite C, Barbara Building, University Park, PA 16802-1003

It is the policy of The Pennsylvania State University Press to use acid-free paper for the first printing of all clothbound books. Publications on uncoated stock satisfy the minimum requirements of American National Standard for Information Sciences—Permanence of Paper for Printed Library Materials, ANSI Z39.48–1984.

*For my parents
Leon and Jay Marks*

Contents

Acknowledgments	ix
List of Abbreviations	xi
Hebrew Transliteration	xiii
INTRODUCTION: FREEDOM FIGHTER, RECKLESS THUG, HERO-SAINT	**1**
The Modern Historian's Picture	4
Three Ideas about the Image of Bar Kokhba in Jewish Thought	9
The Argument of This Book	10
1 BAR KOKHBA IN RABBINIC LITERATURE	**13**
The Messianic Claimant	14
The Legends in the Jerusalem Talmud and Midrash Rabbah	22
The Great Gibbor	26
Literary Elements in the Story	31
Implications of the Story	43
The Two Traditions	56

2 BAR KOKHBA IN THE WRITINGS OF IBN DAUD AND MAIMONIDES 57
Ibn Daud's Image of Bar Kokhba 59
Bar Kokhba in the *Mishneh Torah* of Maimonides 81
Changes in the Image of Bar Kokhba 95

3 ABRAVANEL'S IMAGE OF BAR KOKHBA 99
The Polemical Context 100
The Problem of Bar Kokhba's Story 103
Abravanel's Solution: The Yearning for Redemption 107
The False Messiah 114
Agent of Divine Vengeance 118
Changes in Abravanel's Image of Bar Kokhba 126

4 BAR KOKHBA IN SIXTEENTH-CENTURY HISTORICAL WRITINGS 135
Samuel Usque: *Consolation for the Tribulations of Israel* (1553) 137
Yosef Ha-Kohen: *The Vale of Tears* (1575) 149
Abraham Zacuto: *Book of Genealogies* (1504) 155
Azariah de' Rossi: *Light to the Eyes* (1573) 160
Gedaliah ibn Yahya: *The Chain of Tradition* (1587) 169
David Gans: *Sprout of David* (1592) 173
Persecutions, Eschatology, and History 181

5 BAR KOKHBA IN THE LATER KABBALAH 185
Sefer Ha-Gilgulim 187
Nathan's Letters 194
The Kabbalistic Image of Bar Kokhba 199

Conclusion 201

Appendix: Roman and Christian Writings on the Jewish Rebellion of 116–117 and the War of Bar Kokhba 209

Bibliography 215

Index 223

Acknowledgments

This book depended upon the work and kind words of many people. That includes the scholars upon whose previous labors and insights it relies throughout. Of the people who have directly helped me in many various ways, I wish to name the following:

Amos Funkenstein, my adviser at UCLA, helped conceive this project and guided my initial, and essential, work upon the Jewish writers studied in this book, as well as their social settings. I have tried to model much of my teaching and research on what I learned from him.

I have always felt inspired by another of my professors at UCLA, Kees Bolle, and am pleased that after many years, my book can find a place in his new Hermeneutics series.

Lewis Barth taught me to read rabbinic midrash and gave me an enduring admiration for its delights and mysteries. I would have wished my exegetical and literary analyses in Chapter 1 to have approached the subtlety of his own work.

Michael Meyer encouraged me to revise my dissertation and offered many kind and valuable suggestions.

David Ruderman made an incisive, knowledgeable critique of the entire manuscript in an earlier form. I am especially grateful for his help with Chapters 3 and 4.

My student Eve Mullen, through an R. E. Lee Research Grant from Washington and Lee University, investigated some of the topics related to European history in Chapters 3 and 4 during the summer of 1990.

Washington and Lee University subsidized four summers of research and revision on this book through John M. Glenn Grants.

Colleagues at Washington and Lee University have encouraged my work, read portions of the manuscript, and helped me solve some of its problems. I thank Herman Taylor, John Elrod (vice-president for academic affairs), Ken White and Arlene White, Hugh Blackmer, Winston Davis, Alexandra Brown, and particularly Harlan Beckley, who was department chair during much of my work on this book and gave frequent advice about final revisions. I wish that our dear friend and mentor, Minor Lee Rogers, could have read this expression of my gratitude. I also appreciate the hard work of Karen S. Lyle, secretary of my department.

Philip Winsor at Penn State Press saw merit in the latest form of the manuscript and guided it toward publication with grace and patience. Eric Schramm edited the manuscript with sincere interest, meticulous care, and wise advice, saving me from numerous errors. The book is more clearly written and documented because of him.

All translations of the Hebrew passages are my own unless otherwise indicated.

I dedicate this book to my parents, who love good stories and distant places (even Virginia) and have always encouraged me in my own stories and travels, both inner and outer.

My family—Walapa, Danny, Teera, and Ariya—continued to be the soul of my life during the several summers and many late nights that I worked on the latest revision of this book. My son Danny, critiquing my list of people to thank, penciled in: "Espically Mommy"—which is true. Especially Walapa.

Tu Bi-Shevat 5753

List of Abbreviations

Biblical Books

Cant.	Song of Songs
Dan.	Daniel
Deut.	Deuteronomy
Eccl.	Ecclesiastes
Exod.	Exodus
Gen.	Genesis
Isa.	Isaiah
Jer.	Jeremiah
Lam.	Lamentations
Lev.	Leviticus
Neh.	Nehemiah
Num.	Numbers
Obad.	Obadiah
Ps.	Psalms
Sam.	Samuel
Zech.	Zechariah

Rabbinic Writings

Avod. Zar.	Avodah Zarah
b.	Babylonian Talmud
b.	bar, ben
B. Bat.	Baba Batra

	Bekh.	Bekhorot
	Ber.	Berakhot
	Giṭ.	Gittin
	m.	Mishnah
	Ma'as.	Ma'asot
	Ma'as. Sh.	Ma'aser Sheni
	Menaḥ.	Menaḥot
	Midr.	Midrash
	Nedar.	Nedarim
	Pesiq. R.	Pesiqta Rabbati
	Pesiq. Rab. Kah.	Pesiqta de Rab Kahana
	Qidd.	Qiddushin
	R.	Rabbi
	Rab.	Rabbah
	Sanh.	Sanhedrin
	Shab.	Shabbat
	Ta'an.	Ta'anit
	Tg.	Targum
	t.	Tosefta
	y.	Jerusalem Talmud

Other

EJ	*Encyclopedia Judaica*
JJS	*Journal of Jewish Studies*
JQR	*Jewish Quarterly Review*

Hebrew Transliteration

This book follows generally the transliteration scheme adopted by the *Association for Jewish Studies Review* (see 3 [1978]: ix–x). The main exceptions are names that have become widely recognized in other transliteration patterns, such as Akiba, Kokhba, and Gans.

The transliteration of the more problematic Hebrew letters and vowels appears below:

א	ʾ
quiescent א	not transliterated
בּ	b
ב	v
ו	v (where not a vowel)
ח	ḥ
ט	t
כּ	k
כ	kh
ע	ʿ
פּ	p
פ	f
צ	ṣ
ק	q
ת, תּ	t
ֵ	ei
vocal *sheva*	e
quiescent *sheva*	not transliterated

Introduction:
Freedom Fighter, Reckless Thug, Hero-Saint

Children still play a game called "Bar Kokhba and the Romans," and I have talked with adults who recall playing it in their youth, in New York, Eastern Europe, or Palestine. "It became traditional," wrote Yigael Yadin about the custom, "for children of Jewish communities in eastern Europe to go into the fields at the festival of Lag Ba'omer and play 'Bar Kokhba and the Romans' with makeshift bows and arrows, as Western children played cowboys and indians or Robin Hood."[1]

In the State of Israel there are streets and sports teams named after Bar Kokhba, and kindergarten children learn a song by Levin Kipnis:

> There was a man in Israel named Bar Kokhba,
> A man young and tall with eyes that shone.

---

1. Yigael Yadin, *Bar Kokhba* (New York, 1971), 27.

2   Introduction

> He was brave, and called for liberty.
> The people all loved him because he was brave.

Similarly, the Israeli children's encyclopedia *Tarbut* teaches its young readers that Bar Kokhba bequeathed a "legacy of supreme heroism." Indeed, many Israelis today admire Bar Kokhba as a great national hero, a symbol of self-sacrificing courage in the service of national liberation and revival.[2]

But Bar Kokhba has long been a hero of the political right in Zionist thought, and the name of the Betar organization, a militant Zionist youth movement begun in 1923, alludes to the fortress where Bar Kokhba made his last stand. As head of the organization in the 1930s, Vladimir Jabotinsky, founder of Zionist Revisionism, shaped it to teach Jewish youth not only martial skills, but pride and nobility of spirit. He told them they were "heirs to . . . the proud heroic tradition of the Maccabees and Bar Kokhba."[3]

Menachem Begin, as commander of Irgun, the Revisionist paramilitary organization in British Palestine, called up the figure of Bar Kokhba in a public radio address of 1948. In this speech he declared that the "spirit of our ancient heroes," including "the rebels of Judea" (the Maccabees and Bar Kokhba), will go with Israel's fighters into battle as they "smite the enemy and bring freedom" to the suffering Jewish people.[4]

In *The Chains*, a novel by Gerald Green (1981), the story of Bar Kokhba is cited by Jewish members of an American labor union to justify employing Jake Chain as a Jewish "tough" to defend them in the picket line. But Paul Breines, author of *Tough Jews* (1990), expresses dismay over the new trend he finds among American Jews, evidenced by *The Chains* and many other recent novels, of admiring "tough Jews" over the older, traditional stereotype of "gentle Jews."[5]

---

2. Yehoshafat Harkabi, *The Bar Kokhba Syndrome*, trans. Max Ticktin (New York, 1983), 103–4; Jonathan Frankel, "Bar Kokhba and All That," *Dissent* 31 (1984): 192–202.

3. The name "Betar" is an abbreviation for *"Brit Trumpedor"* (covenant of Trumpedor). Joseph Trumpedor exemplified the ideals of pioneering, military defense, and self-sacrifice espoused by the Betar movement. But the word so formed, "Betar," alludes to Bar Kokhba's fortress. The sites of this fortress and of Yodefet, a stronghold of Bar Kokhba's soldiers in the Galilee, became places of pilgrimage for Betar members. Ehud Sprinzak, *The Ascendance of Israel's Radical Right* (New York, 1991), 26; Walter Laqueur, *A History of Zionism* (New York, 1976), 357–61; Joseph Schechtman, *The Jabotinsky Story*, vol. 2, *Fighter and Prophet* (New York, 1961), 411; Charles Liebman and Eliezer Don-Yehiya, *Civil Religion in Israel* (Berkeley and Los Angeles, 1983), 79.

4. Robert Rowland, *The Rhetoric of Menachem Begin: The Myth of Redemption through Return* (Lanham, Md.: 1985), 256–57. In the same speech, Begin proclaimed the "wonderful youth" of the reborn Hebrew army equal to the great soldiers of Bar Kokhba (252).

5. Paul Breines, *Tough Jews* (New York, 1990), 116–17; Gerald Green, *The Chains* (New York, 1981), 62. Breines also discusses the rise of the Zionist ideal of toughness during the last century,

In the historical romance *If I Forget Thee* (1985), by Brenda Lesley Segal, Bar Kokhba is an emotionally scarred warrior needing a woman's love.

In the complex theological novel by Arthur Cohen, *In the Days of Simon Stern* (1972), Bar Kokhba appears under a different guise, as something of an existentialist hero enacting a redemptive role as Messiah of his time.[6]

These are a few of the ways in which Bar Kokhba is remembered today. He lives on in games and street signs, in novels, and in our political and historical consciousness. And, like all significant figures of the past, Bar Kokhba presents us with a variety of faces; his life, as in these examples, reveals different meanings to different people.

Who was Bar Kokhba? That, in a sense, is the subject of this book. It is a history of the perceptions that Jewish writers of the fourth through the seventeenth centuries, many of them famous and influential, formed of this military leader. Studying the writings of this period, containing what can be called traditional or premodern images of Bar Kokhba, allows us to compare the classical (rabbinic) images of him with several later patterns of their modification, some of which, especially in the sixteenth century, seem to lead toward his picture in modern secular historiography.

My procedure will be to examine the literary passages that speak of Bar Kokhba and try to understand them in the context of the books in which they appear and the authors' other writings. Sometimes literary strands that make up a particular image can be traced. I then ask several questions about each image: how is it related to the author's political and philosophical ideas and the social and political setting in which he lived? What attitudes or messages are expressed in each account of Bar Kokhba? What, in particular, are its political and religious implications? Each new image of Bar Kokhba can then be compared with relevant older images to identify significant distinctions. In this way, I build up a history of images and look for larger patterns in the changes.

What we are seeking, then, is a history of perceptions and meanings—the varied perceptions that Jewish writers formed of Bar Kokhba and the changing contemporary meanings his story revealed as it was told and retold over the centuries. Specialized period studies, with their intensive research into

---

and in doing so, points to the establishment of "Bar Kokhba Gymnastic Clubs" in Europe around 1900 in response to an appeal by the Zionist leader Max Nordau, that Jews build hardy athletic bodies as part of their national revival. "Let us once again become deep-chested, sturdy, sharp-eyed men," proclaimed Nordau, and Bar Kokhba's name became connected with this effort (142–43).

6. Arthur Cohen, *In the Days of Simon Stern* (New York, 1972); Bar Kokhba appears throughout the book and as the historical figure on 462–63. The name "Simon Stern" is itself a play on the full Hebrew name "Shim'on Bar Kokhba": the German word "stern" = kokhba ("star" in Aramaic).

single cultural settings and literatures, cannot offer us this kind of perspective upon changes occurring over a long span of time. We must employ the broader and less exact tools of a comparative history examining documents from diverse cultural settings and historical periods. As much as possible, I follow the guidance of specialized studies in interpreting particular periods and documents, but my subject is both more limited (the image of Bar Kokhba) and more inclusive (a history of images extending beyond any one period).

This is political and religious history revealed in the changing garb of a legendary hero-villain and his story. The changes that occur in that story over time, reflecting changing features of Jewish life, open windows onto some of the various worlds and crises of Jewish history.

The Modern Historian's Picture

So who was Bar Kokhba? In the literature we shall study, ideas about who he was were based on legends told about him in rabbinic literature and on reports found in Greek and Latin chronicles. These legends and reports will occupy our attention in the first two chapters of this book. But first, to provide readers with a familiar type of image, and for purposes of comparison, I summarize what modern historians say about Bar Kokhba.

They base their ideas about him on several different sources of information, to which they give differing degrees of credence. They place the most trust in archaeological evidence: letters, coins, inscriptions, habitations, roads, and other remains from the first and second centuries C.E. Somewhat less credence is given to the Roman and Greek references to the events, the longest and most important being that of Dio Cassius in the Byzantine epitome of Xiphilinus. Secondary evidence is accepted, with reservations, from the writings of the church fathers and, with greater reservations, from rabbinic traditions about Bar Kokhba, but only if logic and external evidence support a tradition. (There are, of course, good reasons for evaluating the sources in this order. But these reasons assume different values, almost a mirror-opposite concept of authority, from that found in most of the Jewish literature we shall study.)

Several new and important studies of the revolt led by Bar Kokhba have been published in the last twenty years. Benjamin Isaac and Aharon Oppenheimer attribute this surge of interest to a new appreciation for the historical importance of the revolt, to spectacular new archaeological discoveries from the time of Bar Kokhba, including letters written by the man himself, and to the tendency of contemporary Israelis to identify with ancient Jews who fought heroic battles against foreign empires.[7]

By the standards of modern historiography, the most important of the recent writings about Bar Kokhba are Geza Vermes and Fergus Millar's 1973 revision of Emil Schürer's classic, *The History of the Jewish People in the Age of Jesus Christ;* Shimon Applebaum's *Prolegomena to the Study of the Second Jewish Revolt* (1976); various essays by Aharon Oppenheimer, as well as his anthology of older scholars, *The Bar Kokhba Revolt* (1980), and his collection (with Uriel Rappaport) of recent Israeli scholarship, *The Bar Kokhba Revolt: New Studies* (1984)—both in Hebrew; and Peter Schäfer's *Der Bar Kokhba-Aufstand* (1981). The Israeli scholarship shows the clear influence of the historians Gedaliah Alon and Shmuel Yeiven, whose work in the 1950s on the revolt began to use a combination of rabbinic, archaeological, and classical sources in a sophisticated way.

Isaac and Oppenheimer, reviewing the recent scholarship in their essay, "The Revolt of Bar Kokhba: Ideology and Modern Scholarship" (1985), discover that the pictures of the revolt presented by modern scholars reflect their personal conceptions of "the Roman empire, the Jewish people, Greek and Roman culture, and Jewish religion." Israeli historians, for example, "often see the result as an heroic struggle against Roman oppression." Other scholars, taking a Roman viewpoint, see Bar Kokhba as "a pious thug."[8] Even estimates of Bar Kokhba's military achievements imply ideological viewpoints: if he succeeded in controlling Jerusalem and a large area of land for a considerable time, his revolt appears heroic; but if he failed to capture land beyond the Judean hills, then his cause appears to have been rash and hopeless from the beginning.[9]

---

7. Benjamin Isaac and Aharon Oppenheimer, "The Revolt of Bar Kokhba: Ideology and Modern Scholarship," JJS 36 (1985): 34–35. The right-wing Israeli politician and writer Israel Eldad found a "sublime" meaning in Yigael Yadin's discovery in 1960 of actual letters written by Bar Kokhba. To Eldad, these letters from the last commander of an organized Jewish army had been waiting to be read by the first commander of the Jewish army of today. (Yadin was Operational Commander during Israel's War of Independence.) This was a miraculous sign "proving" that the Jewish nation and army had been destined to be reborn in our time. Eldad, *The Jewish Revolution: Jewish Statehood*, trans. Hannah Schmorak (New York, 1971), 84–87, 106–7.

8. G. W. Bowerstock, "A Roman Perspective on the Bar Kokhba Revolt," *Approaches to Ancient Judaism* 2, ed. William S. Green (Chico, Cal., 1980), 131–41. See Shimon Applebaum's critique, "Points of View on the Second Jewish Revolt," *Scripta Classica Israelica* 7 (1983/84): 77–87.

9. Isaac and Oppenheimer, "Revolt of Bar Kokhba," 35–36, 55.

Modern scholarship thus disagrees over many aspects of Bar Kokhba's life and the revolt he led, and important questions remain unsolved. Isaac and Oppenheimer open their essay with the minimal picture of the revolt that nearly all scholars agree upon:

> Jewish armed resistance against Roman rule in Judea reached its culmination and exhausted itself in the Revolt of Bar Kokhba. Great numbers of rebels participated in the insurrection, employing guerilla-tactics, and large reinforcements were needed to suppress it. The rebels were united under the leadership of one man: Bar Kokhba. The revolt resulted in the emergence of a kind of independent state, marked by the organization of local authorities, the issue of coinage and the leasing of state-land.[10]

Almost everything else about Bar Kokhba and the revolt is problematic. The following picture of it summarizes the views of a majority of scholars while also indicating areas of disagreement. I follow in particular the account by Vermes and Millar and the essay by Isaac and Oppenheimer.[11]

Bar Kokhba, then, was the leader of this last Judean revolt against Rome, lasting from around 132 to 135 C.E. The recently discovered letters show that his given name was Shim'on bar Kosiva. The name "Bar Kokhba," which is a messianic allusion, was bestowed on him by people who believed that he was the promised king who would free Israel and rebuild the Temple that had been destroyed sixty years earlier. Just how many people believed this about him is unclear. Most scholars, on the basis of a rabbinic legend, think that one man who believed it was Rabbi Akiba ben Joseph, the foremost rabbinic authority of the day; but scholars disagree as to how many other sages shared Rabbi Akiba's opinion. In any case, large numbers of Judean Jews joined the revolt, apparently in hope of gaining freedom from Rome and rebuilding the Temple—which are messianic hopes.

Gedaliah Alon, applying modern political concepts, considers the revolt "a war of national liberation" that took the form of a messianic movement.[12] Peter Schäfer, however, warns us that the Jewish thought of that time did not distinguish a "messianic" war from any other "political" war, and that there

---

10. Ibid., 33.
11. Ibid., 33–60. Emil Schürer, *The History of the Jewish People in the Age of Jesus Christ*, rev. and ed. Geza Vermes and Fergus Millar (Edinburgh, 1973), 1:534–57, 606.
12. Gedaliah Alon, *Toldot Ha-Yehudim Be'Ereṣ Yisra'el Bitequfat Ha-Mishnah Ve-ha-Talmud* (Tel Aviv, 1956), 2:33, 36.

is no way to corroborate the rabbinic tradition connecting Rabbi Akiba with Bar Kokhba or the revolt. Furthermore, Schäfer conceives of the war along the pattern of the earlier Hasmonean uprising: a small number of strictly pious Jews begin a guerrilla war against the objections of a majority who prefer the status quo under the Roman government. Hence, he views the revolt as smaller in scope and consequence than do other scholars.[13]

Coins minted by the revolutionaries, as well as their letters, show that Bar Kokhba's official title was *Nesi Yisrael,* "Prince of Israel." Some of the coins bear the image of a star above the figure of a temple. Some bear the inscriptions, "For the Freedom of Jerusalem," "Year I of the Liberation of Israel," "Year II of the Freedom of Israel." These coins, while not proof that Bar Kokhba's forces captured Jerusalem, do show what Bar Kokhba fought for. Further information is provided by newly found documents, from which we learn, for example, that his government was strong, centralized, and authoritarian, that he imposed harsh discipline on his forces, and that he made efforts to observe religious rituals strictly, particularly rituals relating to the land, such as *sukkot* (booths) and tithing.

Scholars remain divided in their explanations of the revolt's cause. Some argue that the underlying cause was the Jews' desire to regain independence and rebuild the Temple; this hope had burned in the people's hearts for sixty years, igniting incidents of local unrest until it finally flamed into active revolt. It has been suggested that the Pharisees fanned this hope by instituting prayers for the rebuilding of the Temple, or that a priestly leadership actively incited the hope. Alternatively, Shimon Applebaum views the revolt as primarily a peasant uprising "engendered by expropriation and oppressive tenurial conditions."[14] The immediate cause of the revolt is likewise problematic. Most scholars think that a general Roman ban against circumcision had first angered the Jews, and then this anger erupted into active military preparations when Hadrian began to transform Jerusalem into a pagan city or announced plans to found a Roman temple to Jupiter Capitolinus on the site

---

13. Peter Schäfer, *Der Bar Kokhba-Aufstand* (Tübingen, 1981), 45–50, chap. 3, 168–69; Schäfer, "Rabbi Aqiva and Bar Kokhba," *Approaches to Ancient Judaism* 2, 113–30; Schäfer, "The Causes of the Bar Kokhba Revolt," *Studies in Aggadah, Targum and Jewish Liturgy in Memory of Joseph Heinemann,* ed. Jakob Petuchowski and Ezra Fleischer (Jerusalem, 1981), 74–94. See also the critiques by Oppenheimer, JJS 14:217–20, and Harry Sysling, *Bibliotheca Orientalis* 40(1983): 717–22, both of whom question Schäfer's "atomistic" methodology and his comparison of the Bar Kokhba revolt with the Hasmonean revolt.

14. Isaac and Oppenheimer, *Revolt of Bar Kokhba,* 45. See Applebaum, *Prolegomena to the Study of the Second Jewish Revolt* (Oxford, 1976), 9–17; Applebaum, "The Second Jewish Revolt (A.D. 131–35)," *Palestine Exploration Quarterly* 116 (1984): 35–37.

where the Jewish temple had stood. Other scholars look for the revolt's cause more in what they consider "Jewish fanaticism" than in any particular actions of Hadrian, which they view as prudent and cosmopolitan.

Most of the fighting took place in Judea proper. There is no consensus about whether the war spread to the Galilee or whether Jerusalem was captured by the Jews. Schäfer and Bowerstock think the city remained in Roman hands, but many scholars think it was indeed captured although never rebuilt. The rebels achieved dramatic victories at first. Through guerrilla tactics they defeated the Roman army stationed in Judea and then organized an independent state. Hadrian had to bring in large numbers of troops from other provinces as reinforcements. According to Dio Cassius, he assigned command of these forces to Julius Severus, one of his best generals. Severus then began the task of suppressing the revolt by hunting out the rebels a few at a time, cutting off their supplies and fighting them in long and costly individual battles. Slowly he succeeded. The rebels lost ground and had to concentrate their forces in the mountain stronghold of Betar, which stood near the present site of Bittir, six miles southwest of Jerusalem. After a long, stubborn resistance, the fortress was conquered in the eighteenth year of Hadrian (134/135). Rabbinic traditions (supported only by Eusebius) assert that this was where Bar Kokhba died, along with his soldiers and the town's civilian population. Vermes and Millar describe the revolt as "an uprising that in scope, dynamic power and destructive consequences was at least as violent as that of the time of Vespasian. It is only due to the relative poverty of the sources that it has seemed less important."[15]

Casualties were enormous on both sides. According to Dio, Roman losses were so great that Hadrian, writing to the Senate, omitted the usual opening formula, "I and the legions are in health." As to Jewish losses, Dio reported that "the whole of Judea was made desolate": 580,000 Jews had fallen in battle and innumerable others had died of starvation and illness.[16] Most of the survivors were sold as slaves and sent to Gaza or Egypt. (Applebaum finds archaeological correlation for these figures.)[17] In the end, Jerusalem was turned into a Roman colony and the temple to Jupiter was built as planned. Heavy Roman taxes, as well as the devastation, brought on a grave economic crisis in Judea, which forced many of the remaining Jews

15. Vermes and Millar, eds., in Schürer, *History of the Jewish People*, vol. 1, 542–43.
16. Dio Cassius, *Roman History*, trans. E. Cary, Loeb Classical Library, 1925, 8:447–51. See Benjamin Isaac, "Cassius Dio on the Revolt of Bar Kokhba," *Scripta Classica Israelica* 7 (1983/84): 68–76.
17. Applebaum, "The Second Jewish Revolt (A.D. 131–35)," 40.

to emigrate. Most went to Babylonia, furthering its growth as a new center of Jewish life and learning. In the Land of Israel (now renamed "Palestine" by the Romans), the Jewish community was rehabilitated in Galilee, which now took over the institutions of Jewish leadership formerly residing in Judea. But Judea itself never completely recovered from the war.

Such is the uncertain history of Bar Kokhba at which modern scholarship has arrived. It provides one way of speaking about him—but not the only way. Perhaps this book should not have begun with the modern historiographical image so as not to prejudice the reader's response to the earlier literature. My purpose is not to judge the historical accuracy of that literature but to learn how premodern writers constructed "history" (defined as perceptions of the past) and how the "history" of Bar Kokhba grew and changed over time. Such a study heightens our awareness of the circumstances shaping our own historical perceptions—the motivations for our study, the resources available to us, the kind of knowledge we hold authoritative, and the worldview by which we judge what is real and important.

Three Ideas about the Image of Bar Kokhba in Jewish Thought

Israelis today debate the political meaning of the story. In 1982 Yehoshafat Harkabi, an Israeli professor of international relations and a past Chief of Military Intelligence, wrote *Vision, Not Fantasy*, which became a controversial best-seller in Israel and appeared in American bookstores translated as *The Bar Kokhba Syndrome*. In it, Harkabi compared Menachem Begin's political policies with what he saw as the irresponsible zealotry of Bar Kokhba, whom Harkabi charged with dragging the nation into a war of bravado, political fantasy, and "national suicide." He asserted that too many Israelis today exhibit an admiration for "heroism and rebelliousness detached of responsibility for their consequences," an admiration he termed "the Bar Kokhba syndrome," since it often accompanies an unreflective admiration for Bar Kokhba himself.[18] Here, then, are two modern images of

---

18. Harkabi, *Bar Kokhba Syndrome*, 105 and chap. 4; Frankel, "Bar Kokhba and All That." See also the American Zionist view of Joseph Sternstein, *Judaism* 33 (1984): 490–96. Paul Breines, in *Tough Jews*, takes Harkabi's side and extends the attack to American-Jewish novels that glorify toughness over compassion and humanitarian values.

Bar Kokhba—the popular Israeli image of a glorious national defender and Harkabi's image of an irresponsible zealot.

This book seeks to add historical depth to the debate over the use of military force in the pursuit of Jewish security. Harkabi claims that traditional Jewish literature harshly condemned Bar Kokhba and tried to suppress all memory of him, but Harkabi's evidence is scant and superficially analyzed. He refers briefly to my own research, but my studies suggest that Jewish literature expresses rather a variety and complexity of attitudes toward Bar Kokhba, often holding condemnation and admiration of him together in a complex ambivalence that reflected the ambivalence Jews often felt about political and military power.

To my knowledge, only two modern scholars other than Harkabi have written about the image of Bar Kokhba in Jewish thought, and they did so only in brief remarks. Gershom Scholem asserted, "Popular tradition did not subscribe to the rabbinic disparagement of Bar Kokhba's memory. He remained a kind of hero-saint."[19] Yigael Yadin identified a different image of Bar Kokhba in popular memory, that of a fighter for national independence: "It was centuries of persecution of the Jews and their yearning for national rehabilitation that turned Bar Kokhba into a people's hero—an elusive hero they clung to because he had demonstrated, and was the last to demonstrate, that Jews could fight to win spiritual and political independence."[20] The evidence we shall examine, however, supports neither of these generalizations.

Who, then, was Bar Kokhba in Jewish literature—before he became, in our time, the hero of a nationalist movement, a children's game, and an existentialist novel?

The Argument of This Book

Early rabbinic literature remembered Bar Kokhba in two ways: as an imposter claiming to be the Messiah and as a glorious military leader whose successes led Rabbi Akiba, one of the great rabbinic authorities of Jewish tradition, to acclaim him the Messiah. These earliest images of Bar Kokhba in Jewish literature formed the core of most later perceptions of him, so that

---

19. Gershom Scholem, *Sabbatai Ṣevi* (Princeton, 1973), 285.
20. Yadin, *Bar Kokhba*, 27.

he became the prototypical false messiah and one of the great rebels of Jewish history.

As such, Bar Kokhba attracted the attention of important Jewish teachers and writers over the centuries because his story touched deeply some of their dearest hopes, their hopes for the Messiah and for national redemption, challenging these hopes as well as strengthening them. His story also interested them for the crucial religious and political issues it raised: questions of messianic doctrine, of rabbinic authority, and of political policy, the problem of identifying the Messiah, and lessons about the people's relationship with God. The story further spoke to them about specific events occurring in their own day—messianic movements, acts of persecution by Gentiles (especially the expulsion from Spain), and polemical attacks on rabbinic authority and Jewish messianic doctrine.

The story of Bar Kokhba sometimes raised political and ethical issues about the use of force—whether war had been the proper course of action, whether Bar Kokhba had used military power responsibly and wisely. The opinions expressed in Jewish literature about Bar Kokhba, who is portrayed by the rabbinic legends as a powerful warrior, offer insight into how premodern Jews conceived of the role of warriors in Jewish society and how they assessed the value of physical strength and military might.

The images of Bar Kokhba that appear in these writings exhibit fascinating features and changes over time. Two early rabbinic works, the Jerusalem Talmud and Midrash Lamentations, portray Bar Kokhba with the miraculous powers and the virtues and vices characteristic of the rabbinic image of mighty warriors called *gibborim*. This image of Bar Kokhba resembles biblical warriors such as Samson and may also have been influenced by Greek and Near Eastern legends about heroes such as Heracles. In the books of two twelfth-century writers, Ibn Daud and Maimonides, on the other hand, Bar Kokhba assumes the features of a human king acting through natural (Aristotelian) political processes. At the end of the fifteenth century, when Bar Kokhba had become an issue in Jewish-Christian debate, Isaac Abravanel discovers in him a divinely appointed agent of vengeance wielding miraculous powers, perhaps something like the avenging knights of God portrayed in chivalric romances. The six Jewish historians of the sixteenth century who write about Bar Kokhba give him, variously, the features of a Faustian scholar-magician, the ruler of an expanding city-state, a military power in world history, and (in reference to the Spanish expulsion) an avenger upon the Gentiles. From a very different perspective, two kabbalists of the sixteenth and seventeenth centuries perceive Bar Kokhba as one embodiment of the messianic soul during the long course of its rebirths leading toward full messianic stature.

The story has functioned differently in its different contexts. For example, in the Babylonian Talmud, it clarified messianic doctrine and warned against false messiahs. In Midrash Lamentations, the story warned against the political sins of military activism and of rejecting rabbinic leadership. It was recounted on the fast day of the Ninth of Av to call for repentance, especially from the sins of overconfidence and distrusting God. Nathan of Gaza (b. 1644), however, the kabbalist prophet of the Shabbatean messianic movement, used the story to prove the authenticity of the messianic claims of Shabbatai Sevi and to urge Jews to believe in him. Yet the primary lesson that premodern Jews drew from the story was that of political quietism. To most writers the story conveyed a warning not to seek national power by one's own political and military efforts and a plea to wait for God to initiate redemptive action. At the same time, the story often represented a glorious memory of Israel's past greatness or a promise of messianic triumph and power in the future.

The story of Bar Kokhba has also conveyed several kinds of religious teachings. Not only was it used to clarify messianic doctrine, defend rabbinic authority, and call for repentance, but nearly all the writers told it in such a way as to console readers and reply to doubts about messianic redemption. If Bar Kokhba had failed despite mighty efforts and apparent victory and the support of Rabbi Akiba, with terrible consequences, why should Jews ever trust the messianic promise and its rabbinic promoters? Yet writers succeeded in telling the story in such a way as to neutralize the effects of Bar Kokhba's failure and even to turn it into cause for new faith. For example, Bar Kokhba's defeat not by the Romans but by God was offered by Midrash Lamentations as a sign that God is still active and ready to redeem Jews when the time is right. Or, according to the kabbalists, Bar Kokhba's failure meant only that the messianic soul had not as yet fully matured, so that its very incompleteness implied growth and final completion in a full Messiah of later days.

This literature does not ignore the dark side of Bar Kokhba—his failure, falsehood, or the disastrous consequences of his rebellion and Rabbi Akiba's mistake. But it shows us how a people struggled to come to terms with this man, and through him, some of the sins, sorrows, and disappointed hopes of the past.

1
Bar Kokhba in Rabbinic Literature

Bar Kokhba's war against Rome had failed. The nation had suffered terribly. Legends arose to tell the story and explain what had gone wrong. Those legends found their way into the writings of the rabbinic sages, becoming the first stories about Bar Kokhba to appear in Jewish literature.

The rabbinic legends convey two distinct images of the man, expressing two distinct but related memories Jews formed of him. One group of legends portrays him in the image of a false messiah, another group as a glorious if flawed warrior. All the images of Bar Kokhba that will follow in later Jewish literature reflect these two prototypical perceptions of the man, sometimes stressing one over the other, sometimes merging them together. The Bar Kokhba legends of rabbinic literature provided the raw material of character, plot, and setting out of which later writers fashioned their own visions of the story.

The Messianic Claimant

One of the legends that aroused the greatest interest and consternation among later generations portrays Rabbi Akiba, one of the most revered sages of traditional Judaism, proclaiming Bar Kokhba the messianic king. Rabbinic literature contains two versions of this legend.

Jerusalem Talmud

R. Shim'on b. Yoḥai taught: Akiba my teacher would expound *A star shall step forth from Jacob* (Num. 24:17) thus: Koziva shall step forth from Jacob.

R. Akiba, when he saw Bar Koziva, would say, "This is the King Messiah" (*malka meshiḥa*).

R. Yoḥanan b. Torta said to him, "Akiba, grass will grow up from your jaws and the son of David will not yet have come."[1]

Midrash Lamentations Rabbah

R. Yoḥanan said: Rabbi would expound *A star shall step forth from Jacob* thus: do not read "star" (*kokhav*) but "liar" (*kozav*).

R. Akiba, when he saw this Bar Koziva, would say, "This is the King Messiah."

R. Yoḥanan b. Torta said to him, "Akiba, grass will grow up from your jaws and the son of David will not yet have come."[2]

"Bar Koziva" is the name by which Bar Kokhba was known in traditional Jewish literature. From the recent discovery of the Bar Kokhba letters in the Judean Desert, we have now learned that the man's given name was Shim'on bar Kosiva. But he appears throughout rabbinic literature—and in all of Jewish literature until the sixteenth century—under the name of Bar Koziva or Ben Koziva (or Kozba). Justin and Eusebius, on the other hand, call him Bar Kokhba ("Barchochebas" in Greek).[3] How are these three names related? Vermes and Millar offer an explanation based on evidence from the archaeological finds:

> The spelling displayed in the new documents is כוסבא, כוסבה or כסבה, pronounced no doubt as Kosiba, as its Greek transliteration

---

1. Y. Ta'an. 4.8 (24a).
2. Lam. Rab. 2.5.
3. Justin, 1 *Apol.* 31, 6; Eusebius, *Eccl. Hist.* IV, 6.

(Χωσιβα) indicates. From this it would follow that both Christian and rabbinic forms represent puns. The former—Bar Kokhba, Son of the Star—was coined by R. Akiba and alluded to the leader's messianic dignity; the latter—Bar Koziba, Son of the Lie = Liar—was probably invented by his opponents, and those of Akiba, and was regularly used by later writers only too aware of his failure and its disastrous consequences.[4]

This explanation of the names is plausible, although it tries to be too exact: we cannot ascertain when the taunting name Bar Koziva was invented, nor whether it was coined by Bar Kokhba's opponents or, as Schäfer prefers, by later generations remembering his failure.[5]

Moreover, we shall discover that not all later writers necessarily understood "Bar Koziva" as a reference to the man's lies. That meaning of the name fits only those rabbinic traditions that portray him as a false messiah; and since oral transmission does not easily preserve such slight distinctions as between "Kosiva" and "Koziva," writers living just a few generations after Shim'on Bar Kosiva may not have known his original name. Nor does R. Judah Ha-Nasi's interpretation of Num. 24:17 (replacing *kokhav*, "star," with *kozev*, "liar") imply that "Koziva" was not the original name; his exegesis merely emphasizes the relationship of *Koziva* with *kozev*. Later writers seem to have accepted "Bar Koziva" as the man's given name (however appropriate the hint of lying), and not until the sixteenth century do they even suggest that "Koziva" might be something else.

It would therefore be wrong to read every mention of "Bar Koziva" in rabbinic literature as a taunting attack on his "falsehood." When the legend in Y. Ta'anit has R. Akiba proclaim, "Koziva shall step forth from Jacob," it does not assert that R. Akiba knew that Bar Kosiva was a false hope—although later readers may certainly have perceived the irony in the man's name.[6]

---

4. Vermes and Millar, eds., in Schürer, *History of the Jewish People*, 1:543–44. Cf. Shmuel Abramsky, *Bar Kokhva: Nesi Yisra'el* (Tel Aviv, 1961), 53–54, for a similar explanation.

5. Schäfer, "Rabbi Aqiva and Bar Kokhba," 118–19.

6. Contrary to C. G. Montefiore and H. Loewe, *A Rabbinic Anthology* (New York, 1962), 262, Abramsky, *Bar Kokhba: Nesi Yisra'el*, 53–54, and Jacob Neusner, *Our Sages, God, and Israel* (Chappaqua, N.Y., 1984), 14, who read R. Akiba's exegesis as a condemnation of Bar Kokhba, translating "Koziva" as "liar."

Solomon Buber's manuscript of Midr. Lam. (Vilna, 1899), 101, records a different version of the passage: "When R. Akiba saw Ben Koziva, he would say, *A star shall step forth from Jacob*: Bar Kokhba shall step forth from Jacob." Indeed, both Buber and Jacob Levy, *Worterbuch über die*

These two texts thus draw a picture of R. Akiba telling people that Bar Koziva was the messianic king and that Balaam's fourth oracle (Num. 24:15–19), interpreted as a messianic prophecy, pointed specifically to him. The only reported opposition to R. Akiba comes from R. Yoḥanan b. Torta, an insignificant sage whose name is hardly known otherwise in rabbinic literature.[7] Bar Koziva appears in these legends as a man whom a highly respected rabbi, one of the leaders of his generation, proclaimed the Messiah.

R. Akiba's words about Bar Kokhba are few, appear in the form of legend and midrash (scriptural exegesis), and offer no historical references. We cannot even determine whether R. Akiba did in fact proclaim Bar Kokhba the Messiah. Even if we could accept the legends as historical evidence, we would still learn very little from them about the image R. Akiba actually held of Bar Kokhba—although contemporary scholars have tried to do so.[8] The relevant question for us, however, is what the legends themselves mean as literature, as a memory—what image they convey of Bar Kokhba. In this matter, the scriptural verse applied to Bar Koziva can guide us.

The Image in Numbers 24:17

"Koziva shall step forth from Jacob": this sentence attributed to R. Akiba means that he has substituted the word "koziva" for *kokhav* (star) in Num. 24:17, the verse he is expounding. How are we to understand this substitution?

Talmudim und Midrashim (Berlin, 1924), 2:312, believed that the name "Kokhba" had also appeared in the original version of the corresponding passage in y. Ta'an. 4.8, as follows: "Akiba my teacher would expound Num. 24:17 thus: Kokhba shall step forth from Jacob." The name "Koziva" found in the present versions of the passage is, they thought, a later substitution by scribes influenced by R. Judah Ha-Nasi's reinterpretation of the verse. This theory of Buber and Levy, however, seems unlikely because R. Akiba's exegesis in the version they propose would have little purpose: it would merely translate "star" in Num. 24:17 from Hebrew to Aramaic. Moreover, with the discovery of the Bar Kokhba letters, "Kosiva" seems more likely to be the name that R. Akiba was (believed to be) identifying with the star in Num. 24:17. If scribal modification occurred, it was most likely a change from "kosiva" to "koziva."

7. See t. Menaḥ. 13.22, y. Yoma 1.1 (4b), b. Yoma 9a.
8. Louis Finkelstein, *Akiba: Scholar, Saint and Martyr* (New York, 1975), 369; George Foot Moore, *Judaism in the First Centuries of the Christian Era* (New York, 1971), 1:89, 2:116 and 329; Joseph Klausner, *The Messianic Idea in Israel from Its Beginning to the Completion of the Mishnah*, trans. W. F. Stinespring (New York, 1955), 397–99; Abramsky, *Bar Kokhba*, 61–62, 133–34; Ephraim Urbach, *The Sages: Their Concepts and Beliefs*, trans. I. Abrahams (Jerusalem, 1975), 1:673–76; Aharon Oppenheimer, "Meshiḥiyuto shel Bar Kokhba," in *Messianism and Eschatology*, ed. Zvi Baras (Jerusalem, 1983).

First, R. Akiba has given the verse a messianic meaning. This is shown by the following sentence identifying Bar Koziva as the King Messiah and also by R. Yoḥanan b. Torta's reply. (Although history is not our concern, we can notice that the verse had already been given a messianic meaning by the Septuagint, the Testaments of the Twelve Patriarchs, the Aramaic translations of Scripture, and one of the Dead Sea Scrolls.)[9] This verse is part of the fourth oracle of Balaam, which speaks of a future Israelite king who would conquer the surrounding nations (Num. 24:17–19):

> I see him, but not now;
> I behold him, but not near:
> A star shall step forth from Jacob,
> A comet [or sceptre] arise from Israel.
> He shall smite through the corners of Moab,
> And break down all the sons of Seth.
> Edom shall be a possession,
> And Seir, his enemy, shall be his.
> Israel shall do valiant deeds;
> Out of Jacob shall one have dominion,
> And shall destroy the remnant from the city.

It is easy to understand how later generations could interpret this oracle as an eschatological prophecy about a messianic king symbolized by the star and comet (or sceptre) of verse 17.

In the legends under consideration, R. Akiba has identified this star-Messiah: it is Koziva who has stepped forth from Jacob (that is, from the people Israel). This exegesis of the verse has some affinity with various attempts by other sages to uncover the name of the Messiah from clues found in messianic prophecies. They proposed names ranging from "Shalom" to "Ḥadrakh" to "Menaḥem b. Hezekiah," "Ṣemaḥ," and "David." Students even identified their teachers' names in the messianic verses (a form of praise)—suggesting that "Shiloh" (Gen. 49:10) referred to R. Shelah and "Yinnon" (Ps. 72:17) to R. Yannai.[10] The exegesis attributed to R. Akiba in our legends resembles this type of messianic speculation in both

---

9. Damascus Document (Genizah text) 7.18; Septuagint to Num. 24:17; Testament of the Twelve Patriarchs, Levi 18, Judah 24:1–6; Aramaic translations to be discussed.

10. R. Yosi in *Pereq Ha-Shalom*; R. Judah in Sifre, Deut. 1 (cited in Klausner, *Messianic Idea in Israel*, 461–63). For Amoraic opinions, see b. Sanh. 96b–97a, 98b; y. Ber. 2.3 (5a). On "Ḥivara," see Urbach, *Sages* 1:685, 2:n. 42. Also see Moore, *Judaism in The First Centuries* 2:348.

subject matter and function. The word *kokhav* (or *kokhva* in Aramaic) of Num. 24:17 was understood as the Messiah's name or a clue to it, hence pointing to the name "Koziva" (or "Kozva"), which is close to *kokhva* in sound and spelling. "Kokhva," considered as the Messiah's name, would be symbolic, like "Shalom," "Menaḥem" (Comforter), and "Ṣemaḥ" (Scion). "Kokhva" (usually written as "kokhba" in English) would signify a fiery or meteoric conqueror.

The Bar Koziva legends thus portray R. Akiba as believing that he has discovered the name "Koziva" hidden within the word *kokhva* of Num. 24:17. His exegesis was a form of decoding that unlocked the secret message contained within the prophecy of Balaam. In addition, the very choice of this particular prophecy implies a rather specific image of Bar Koziva within the context of rabbinic thought, because a fairly distinct set of meanings had attached itself to the verses, at least during the post-Mishnaic period, as we learn elsewhere in rabbinic literature.

The Aramaic translations of the Hebrew Bible—the Targumim—were recorded at a relatively late date (Bowker and Grossfeld suggest the early third century C.E. for Targum Onqelos, and later for the Targum Pseudo-Jonathan),[11] but they contain interpretations deriving from a much earlier time. Targum Onqelos and Targum Pseudo-Jonathan both interpret the oracle of Balaam as an eschatological vision of the Messiah destroying Rome, identified with Seir and Edom in the oracle. Onqelos, in comparison with the Hebrew text, expands the arena of battle into a universal war and emphasizes the finality of Rome's destruction. The Messiah is not only a warrior but he brings prosperity to Israel and "will reign over all mankind" as universal king. All these events are ascribed to the power of God acting at that time to punish the guilty. Targum Pseudo-Jonathan, more apocalyptic in mood, perceives in Balaam's oracle a great final battle, bloody and violent, against the amassed armies of Gog—that is, the armies of Rome and the other nations. The Messiah is pictured as a marvelous warrior hacking down the soldier of Gog: "their corpses shall fall before him," "these shall fall by the hand of the King Messiah." At the same time, the Memra of the Lord (God's "word") manifests itself "to punish the wicked and smite the nations and kings."[12]

Turning next to the Talmudim and Midrashim, we find four interpreta-

---

11. John Bowker, *The Targums and Rabbinic Literature* (Cambridge, 1969), 22–28; Bernard Grossfeld, "Bible: Aramaic Translations," EJ 4:841–45; Samson Levey, *The Messiah: An Aramaic Interpretation* (Cincinnati, 1974), 23–24.

12. Tg. Pseudo-Jonathan to Num. 24:17, 24, and 23.

tions of Num. 24:17 other than the one attributed to R. Akiba. The one exception to the general trend of the verse's exegesis is the midrash attributed to R. Yishma'el b. R. Yosi (late second century). Applying a system of dream analysis based on scriptural symbolism, R. Yishma'el learns from Num. 24:17 that a star in dreams signifies an Israelite.[13]

The second interpretation appears in an anonymous midrash of Pisḥa 12 in the Mekhilta. This midrash reads Num. 24:19, in association with Obad. 18, as a divine promise that the Messiah will destroy Rome (Esau) in the future, leaving no survivor. The eschatological force of this interpretation is augmented by its position alongside other verses interpreted also as eschatological promises spoken by God—promises to punish the wicked, save a remnant from Israel, resurrect the dead, bring peace to the world, and grant humanity a vision of the Shekhinah (the divine presence). The Messiah's role in these events of the redemption is, first of all, to conquer Rome.

Finally, there are two later interpretations of the verse. Most explicit in its reference to the Messiah is the exegesis attributed to R. Shmu'el b. Naḥman (third century), who discovers in Num. 24:17 a statement of when and how God will give Israel victory over Rome—namely, "when that one shall come of whom it is written, 'A star shall step forth from Jacob': this is the King Messiah." In the remainder of the midrash, R. Shmu'el develops the implications of this exegesis by citing verses from Obadiah. Verse 18 ("The house of Jacob shall be a fire ... and the house of Esau for stubble") describes, for R. Shmu'el, the fiery avenging star of Jacob destined to consume utterly the stubble that is Rome; or, as he puts it, "A star shall step forth from Jacob and devour the stubble of Esau." Obad. 19 ("They will inherit ... the mountain of Esau") defines the Messiah's work: "In the World to Come, you [Israel] will be redeemed ... and inherit it [Rome]." Then God will judge Rome and establish his kingdom, as promised by Obad. 21.[14]

The final interpretation of Num. 24:17, attributed to R. Aḥa (fourth century), follows the same pattern as the others. R. Aḥa interprets the star of Num. 24:17 as a reference to the messianic king who will end Rome's domination over this world and give Israel dominion over the World to Come.[15]

This brief examination of the rabbinic interpretations of Num. 24:17–19 has revealed what can be called a "tradition of meanings" attached to these verses through most of rabbinic literature. In all six messianic interpreta-

---

13. Y. Ma'as. Sh. 4.6 (27b).
14. Tanḥuma B, Devarim, on Deut. 2:15; Deut. Rab. 1.20.
15. Y. Nedar. 3.8 (12a).

tions, the "star" of Num. 24:17 signifies the Messiah; the Messiah is a warrior-king whose primary role is to conquer and destroy Rome; and this will occur within the framework of a transcendent process of judgment and redemption. Therefore, when the Bar Koziva legends have R. Akiba applying this same verse to Bar Koziva, the legend evokes from the verse's tradition of meanings a specific implication about what R. Akiba was saying—whether or not the original storyteller or R. Akiba himself actually intended this implication. R. Akiba's quotation of Num. 24:17 means (as legend, in the context of other rabbinic writings) that he thought Bar Koziva was a national warrior-king arisen to conquer and destroy Rome like a star of fire and ruin, and that R. Akiba saw the deeds of Bar Koziva as part of a larger movement of redemption deriving ultimately from beyond human history: God had begun to act, Rome was inexorably doomed, and Israel's redemption was at hand.

Another legend offers a similar explanation for R. Akiba's support for Bar Koziva. It first describes Bar Koziva catching catapult stones flung by the enemy's machines and hurling them back to kill great numbers of soldiers. "On account of this," the legend concludes, "R. Akiba said what he said."[16] The legend is asserting that Bar Koziva's astounding powers in battle were what convinced R. Akiba that he was the Messiah. Hence, R. Akiba saw Bar Koziva as a fierce military Messiah—which is what the citation of Num. 24:17 in the first legends implies.

As a whole, then, these legends assert that not only did R. Akiba think he had discovered the name "Koziva" hidden in the "*kokhva*" of Num. 24:17, but that he also thought he had discovered in the verse a description of the character of Bar Koziva—that of a fiery military Messiah who would conquer Rome and free Israel.

The Messianic Impostor

As mentioned, it is in a midrash attributed to R. Judah Ha-Nasi, called "Rabbi" (later second century), that the name "Koziva" is connected with *kazav*, falsehood.

> R. Yoḥanan said: Rabbi would expound *A star shall step forth from Jacob* thus: do not read "star" (*kokhav*) but "liar" [or "lie"] (*kozav*).[17]

---

16. Lam. Rab. 2.5.
17. Ibid.

Rabbi is alluding to R. Akiba's interpretation of Num. 24:17. Instead of the conquering messianic star whom R. Akiba saw, Rabbi discovers only a liar arisen out of Jacob, a false messiah. This exegesis of the verse, rejecting R. Akiba's, transforms the image of Bar Kokhba dramatically, as Shmuel Yeiven explains: "From a *ben kokhav*, a 'star,' who professes to bring light to the darkness of exile, he has turned into a *ben kozav*, a 'liar,' who has disillusioned the nation that followed after him."[18]

Judah Ha-Nasi's midrash is the first of the two passages in rabbinic literature that portray Bar Kokhba as a messianic impostor. The second passage, showing a further development of the theme, is the following story recorded in the Babylonian Talmud (b.Sanh. 93b):

> Vahariḥo *The fear of the Lord* (Isa. 11:3). . . . Rava said that he [the Messiah] smells (*moraḥ*) and judges, as it is written, *and not through the sight of his eyes shall he judge, nor through the hearing of his ears shall he decide, but he shall judge the poor with righteousness* (Isa. 11:3–4). Bar Koziva ruled for two and a half years. He said to the rabbis, "I am the Messiah." They said to him, "Of the Messiah it is written that he smells and judges [i.e., judges by smelling]. Let us see if he can judge by smelling." When they saw that he could not judge by smelling, they killed him.

Although this story may derive from an early tradition, its present form seems to be late because the test described in it relies on the scriptural proof and the phraseology of the preceding midrash of Rava, a sage of the early fourth century. The purpose of the story, too, is mainly to illustrate the character of the Messiah as it is defined by Rava. Essential to the Messiah's character is the ability to judge by smell alone, to discern a person's guilt through special powers of perception that would clearly distinguish the Messiah from other men. Bar Koziva's failure to meet this requirement, despite his political achievements, serves to reinforce Rava's exegesis by showing how truly wondrous the Messiah's powers will be.

The legend thus functions as a reply to doubts that Bar Kokhba's falsehood, the failure of a messianic movement, may have raised. Instead of evidence for the emptiness of messianic hope, Bar Kokhba's deficiencies are turned into evidence of the far greater powers of the Messiah yet to

---

18. Shmuel Yeiven, *Milḥemet Bar Kokhva* (Jerusalem, 1952), 63.

come. That is, Bar Kokhba failed because he was false, not because redemption is impossible.

The legend also teaches people to be wary of any man claiming to be the Messiah and it encourages them to trust the judgment of the sages in deciding a claimant's authenticity. The rabbis' role appears as that of vigilant protectors of the people and final arbiters of messianic claims.[19]

These two texts—the midrash in which Judah Ha-Nasi condemns Bar Koziva as a *kozav*, "liar," and the legend of the sages' response to Bar Koziva's messianic claim—constitute the rabbinic tradition that portrays Bar Kokhba as a false messiah. They represent one of the ways in which later generations explained his failure, one form of response to the disappointment and suffering associated with him. That response was to repudiate Bar Kokhba altogether, rejecting him as a worthless impostor. His failure was explained directly from his falsehood: not being the Messiah appointed by God, he could not possibly redeem Israel. Indeed, the repudiation of Bar Kokhba was necessary for affirming hope in a true Messiah yet to come.

We turn now to a series of legends in Midrash Lamentations, a collection of homiletic exegeses, and the Jerusalem Talmud. These legends portray Bar Kokhba as a flawed military hero; the question of his messianic identity goes almost unmentioned and is irrelevant to the outcome of the story.

The Legends in the Jerusalem Talmud and Midrash Rabbah

The story of Bar Kokhba as a mighty hero of Israel—a lengthy tale as rabbinic tales go—is told through a number of short legends woven together and attached to the longest piece, the legend of Bar Kokhba's downfall. Together, these legends compose a generally consistent story that begins with the Roman siege of Betar and concludes with the massacre of its population. The story is recorded in two versions that differ primarily in matters of style. In the Jerusalem Talmud the legend is sometimes crisper and more dramatic, in Midrash Lamentations, occasionally more abstract

---

19. The exact nature of Bar Koziva's crime, however, is unclear. Rabbi Menaḥem Ha-Meiri of the late thirteenth century compares it with the crime of the *nevi ha-sheqer*, the false prophet punished in the Mishnah by death (m. Sanh. 11.5).

and explanatory. Such differences, however, do not by themselves tell us which version is the older. In any case, most scholars think that the Jerusalem Talmud and Midrash Lamentations, which share much material in common, reached their literary form between 350 and 450 C.E.

In both texts the legends are attributed, apparently, to R. Yoḥanan (late third century). Because a number of other historical legends are also attributed to him,[20] it seems that R. Yoḥanan was interested in preserving legends from the recent past and so may indeed have been instrumental in collecting and transmitting these legends about Bar Kokhba. At the present stage of historical inquiry into rabbinic texts, however, we can say nothing concrete about the origin and transmission of these legends and must therefore consider them only as literary phenomena found in a final text.

Jerusalem Talmud

R. Yoḥanan said: eighty thousand pairs of trumpeters surrounded Betar, and each of them was set over many soldiers. And Ben Kozba (or Kozeba) [=Ben Koziva] was there, and he had two hundred thousand [soldiers] who had each cut off a finger. The sages sent word to him, saying, "How long will you go on making Israel into maimed men?" He said to them, "But how else would it be possible to test them?" They said to him, "Whoever cannot uproot a tree of Lebanon while riding a horse, let him not be enrolled in your army." So he had two hundred thousand of these and two hundred thousand of those.

When he would go out to battle, he would say, "Master of the World, neither help us nor shame us! *Do not, O God, cast us down and do not, O God, go forth against our enemies*" (Ps. 60:12).

For three and a half years, Hadrian besieged Betar, and R. El'azar of Modi'im would sit in sackcloth and ashes and would pray every day, saying, "Master of the World, do not sit in judgment today, do not sit in judgment today." Hadrian was about to leave, but a certain Cuthean said to him, "Do not leave, for I see what needs to be done, and I shall surrender [=deliver] the city to you." He entered through

---

20. See b. Git. 55b, y. Ta'an. 4.8 (24a), b. Shab. 63b.

a drainpipe of the city and found R. El'azar of Modi'im standing and praying. He [the Cuthean] made as though he were whispering in his ear. People of the city saw him and brought him to Ben Kozba. They said to him, "We saw this old man conversing with your friend [or uncle]." He asked him [the Cuthean], "What did you say to him and what did he say to you?" He replied, "If I tell you, the king will kill me, but if I do not tell you, you will kill me. It is better for me that the king kill me and you do not." He [the Cuthean] said to him, "He told me that I should surrender my city." He [Ben Kozba] came to R. El'azar of Modi'im and asked him, "What did this Cuthean say to you?" He replied to him, "Nothing at all." He [Ben Kozba] asked him, "What did you say to him?" He replied to him, "Nothing at all." He [Ben Kozba] gave him [R. El'azar of Modi'im] one kick and killed him. Immediately, a Bat Qol [echo from Heaven] went forth saying, "*Woe to the worthless shepherd who abandons the flock; the sword shall be upon his arm and upon his right eye; his arm shall be wholly withered and his right eye utterly blinded* (Zech. 11:17): you slew R. El'azar of Modi'im, the arm of all Israel and their right eye. Therefore, your own arm *shall be wholly withered* and your right eye *utterly blinded.*"

Immediately, Betar was captured and Ben Kozba was killed. They came carrying his head to Hadrian. He asked them, "Who killed this man?" A certain Cuthean replied, "I killed him." He [Hadrian] said to him, "Show me his corpse." He showed his corpse to him, and there was a snake coiled around it. He said, "If God had not killed him, who would have been able to do so?" And he applied to him the verse, *Not unless their rock had given them over, and the Lord had handed them over* (Deut. 32:30).[21]

Midrash Lamentations 2.5
The Lord has swallowed unsparingly all the dwellings of Jacob
(Lam. 2:2)

R. Yoḥanan said: eighty thousand trumpeters encircled Betar. And Ben Koziva was there, and he had two hundred thousand [soldiers] who had each cut off a finger. The sages sent word to him saying,

---

21. Y. Ta'an. 4.8 (24a–b) to m. Ta'an. 4.6. The translations in Neusner, *Our Sages, God, and Israel*, 14–16, and Schäfer, *Der Bar Kokhba-Aufstand*, 55, 136–51, were consulted.

"How long will you go on making Israel into maimed men?" He said to them, "But how else can they be tested?" They said to him, "Whoever cannot uproot a tree of Lebanon, let him not be enrolled in your army." So he had two hundred thousand of these and two hundred thousand of those.

When they would go out to battle, they would say, "Neither help us nor shame us! *Do not, O God, cast us down and do not, O God, go forth against our enemies*" (Ps. 60:12).

What would Ben Koziva do? He would catch the stones of the catapults on one of his knees and throw them back, killing many of them, and on account of this, R. Akiba said what he said.

For three and a half years, Hadrian Caesar besieged Betar, and R. El'azar of Modi'im was there, in sackcloth, engaged in fasting, and every day he would pray, saying, "Master of the World, do not sit in strict judgment today," so that finally he [Hadrian] thought of returning [to Rome]. A certain Cuthean came and found him and said to him, "So long as that old cock wallows in ashes, you will not conquer it. But wait for me, for I shall enable you to conquer it today." Immediately he entered through the drainpipe of the city and found R. El'azar standing and praying. He made as though he were whispering in the ear of R. El'azar of Modi'im and they [people of the city] went and said to Ben Koziva, "Your friend [or uncle] R. El'azar wants to surrender the city to Hadrian." He sent and had the Cuthean brought to him. He asked him, "What did you say to him?" He [the Cuthean] replied to him, "If I tell you, the king will kill me, but if I do not tell you, you will kill me. It is better for me to kill myself so that the secrets of the [Roman] government will not be divulged." Ben Koziva reasoned in his mind that he [R. El'azar of Modi'im] wanted to surrender the city. When R. El'azar finished his praying, he [Ben Koziva] sent and had him brought. He asked him, "What did this Cuthean say to you?" He replied to him, "I do not know what he whispered in my ear; I did not hear him at all, for I was standing in prayer and I do not know what he said." Ben Koziva was filled with anger and gave him one kick with his foot and killed him. A Bat Qol went forth saying, "*Woe to the worthless shepherd who abandons the flock; the sword shall be upon his arm and upon his right eye;*

his arm shall be wholly withered and his right eye utterly blinded" (Zech. 11:17). It said to him, "You bound the arm of all Israel and blinded their right eye. Therefore, your own arm *shall be wholly withered* and your right eye *utterly blinded.*"

Immediately, sins brought it to pass, and Betar was captured and Ben Koziva was killed. And they brought his head to Hadrian. He asked, "Who killed this man?" A certain Cuthean replied to him, "I killed this man." He [Hadrian] said to him, "Go and bring him to me." He went and brought him, and he found a snake coiled around his neck. He [Hadrian] said to him, "If his God had not killed this man, who would have been able to do so?" And he applied to him the verse, *Not unless their rock had given them over* (Deut. 32:30).

How do these legends portray Bar Kokhba? How do they explain his failure and the fall of Betar? What might be the intended effect on the reader's perceptions?

The Great Gibbor

One of the most striking features of the Ben Koziva of these legends is his extraordinary strength. He is portrayed as a glorious warrior, fierce in battle. He heads an army of powerful, fearless soldiers. He catches the huge stones flung from Roman catapults and hurls them back, killing great numbers of enemy soldiers. One kick from his foot kills instantly. He could not be conquered by men—as Hadrian acknowledges when he declares that only God could have brought him down.[22]

Legends attribute similar abilities to other Judean warriors who fought against the Romans. One named Bar Daroma is portrayed jumping a *mil* (about two-thirds of a mile) and killing numerous Roman soldiers single-handedly. Seeing him, the emperor fears that this man might conquer the whole Roman empire. Another legend tells of two brothers from Ḥaruva who kill every Roman soldier that passes through their village. They, too, are invincible and, like Ben Koziva, could be stopped only by God.[23]

---

22. See Richard G. Marks, "Dangerous Hero: Rabbinic Attitudes toward Legendary Warriors," HUCA 54 (1983): 181–94.
23. B. Git. 57a, y. Ta'an. 4.8 (24a), Lam. Rab. 2.5.

Biblical Warriors in Rabbinic Legend

Similar powers are ascribed in rabbinic legends to a number of biblical heroes. For example, a series of legends in Parasha 93 of Midrash Genesis Rabbah portrays the sons of Jacob as mighty warriors. The legends begin with Joseph, now viceroy of Egypt, threatening to make Benjamin his slave (Gen. 44:17). In Scripture Judah replies with humble entreaty, but in these legends he answers with threats of violence. Filled with rage, Judah chews iron bars into powder and roars like a lion. The roar carries all the way to the Land of Israel, where Dan's son, Hushim, hears it and comes to Judah's aid by jumping with one leap to Egypt. Together they roar so loudly that they almost turn Egypt upside down; and Judah's brothers, also enraged, stamp on the ground and make furrows. But when Joseph, not to be outdone, kicks a stone pillar into a heap of rubble, Judah finally quiets down.[24]

Seeing Joseph demolish the pillar in this way, Judah exclaims, "He is (a) *gibbor* like us!" Here the word *gibbor* describes a man who performs feats of extraordinary strength like those of Judah and his brothers. This is the meaning the word has elsewhere in rabbinic literature when it refers to such heroes as Samson, Abner, and Joab, who are expressly cited as exemplary representatives of the type.[25] Rabbinic legends ascribe to them the same astounding strength that Judah and his brothers exhibit. According to certain sages, Samson could uproot two mountains and grind them into dust, and he could traverse vast distances in a single step; his shoulders were one hundred feet wide.[26] The Samson of Scripture is a fierce and powerful warrior, but rabbinic legends picture him even stronger, larger, and more terrifying. As for Abner, a legend depicts his strength and size by comparing him to a wall eleven feet high by eleven feet thick: this wall would be easier to move than just one of Abner's feet.[27]

The Ben Koziva of the legends is never explicitly called a gibbor, but he and Bar Daroma are portrayed with the exceptional strength and fighting ability that characterize the biblical heroes as *gibborim*. Ben Koziva and Bar Daroma even exhibit some of the same abilities—a powerful kick, distant leaps—that the sons of Jacob do. I am speaking about a type of hero in rabbinic legend, and Ben Koziva fits that type. (The Hasmoneans and

---

24. Gen. Rab., ed. J. Theodor and C. Albeck, 93, 6–9.
25. B. Qidd. 49b; Lev. Rab., ed. M. Margolies, 5, 3.
26. Lev. Rab. 8, 2; b. Sotah 9b–10a.
27. Gen. Rab. Ms. V, 96. The word gibbor has other meanings in rabbinic usage. It can specify a particular type of soldier, such as a knight on horseback or a veteran soldier of high rank (b. Sanh. 95b, b. Ber. 53b).

Zealots, on the other hand, do not: rabbinic legend portrays them as kings and rebels but not as gibborim.) As is usual in rabbinic thought, recent history is understood through typologies perceived in Scripture. I contend that Ben Koziva is perceived through such a typology, including the particular virtues and vices of biblical gibborim, and that the legends understand his failure as a consequence of sins characteristic of gibborim.

Rabbinic legends and commentary express a variety of attitudes toward gibborim. The texts convey a sense of pleasure in telling the feats of the mighty heroes of Israel. This pleasure is evident in the way Judah's confrontation with Joseph is told: many of the details have no teaching value and function only to show off the heroes' strength. There is a tone of lighthearted sport to the story as brothers vie to outdo one another. But these feats of strength arouse pride, too. When Menasseh stamps his foot on the floor so hard that the entire palace shakes, Judah cries out, "Such a stamp could come only from my father's house!" The Jewish audience is expected to feel pride in the strength of its warrior-fathers. A legend in Midrash Leviticus Rabbah has a similar intent when it describes the nations of the world boasting that Goliath is the greatest gibbor of all and Israel replying that its own Samson is greater.[28]

In addition, the texts generally consider the gibbor's strength valuable insofar as he uses it properly. Judah's use of force to save Benjamin appears justified in the legend, and sages approve of the way Samson used his strength to protect Israel and punish the Philistines.[29]

However, in the same texts—even in the same sages—that express admiration for gibborim, we can detect also a sense of anxiety about them. Because gibborim possessed tremendous strength, how they used it became all the more important. There was all the more danger from what they could do wrong. The blessing could turn into a curse. In the rabbinic texts dealing with gibborim, this problem claims the greater portion of attention. Possessing strength to an extreme measure, these heroes served the sages as object lessons in the nature and use of force. Three themes stand out in particular.

First, the texts warn against putting too much faith in one's own powers, as gibborim are apt to do. Samson is criticized for boasting.[30] Abner is presented as an object lesson in overconfidence. His example proves that however strong one may become, one can never win the battle against death,

---

28. Lev. Rab. 5, 3.
29. B. Sotah 10a.
30. Gen. Rab. 98, 16.

since, as Scripture says (Eccl. 9:11), "The battle is not to the gibborim."[31] Ben Koziva and Bar Daroma, as we shall see, represent especially egregious examples of overconfidence.

Second, the texts teach from the examples of gibborim that God is the true source of strength and that the warrior's own strength is conditional, dependent upon his good relationship with God. The legend is careful to ground Joseph's strength in his "fear of heaven"; and sages teach that Samson lost his strength not through mere recklessness, but because he "rebelled" (*marad*) against God and for this suffered punishment.[32]

The third theme has to do with the proper exercise of force, and comes out of the fear, expressed often in the texts, that gibborim might use their strength in dangerous and sinful ways. We see this concern expressed most clearly in an exchange between two sages that has been included with the legends about Judah and his brothers. The text has R. Ḥama b. Ḥanina question Joseph's prudence in asking his guards to leave him alone with his brothers, since, as the sage says, just one kick from his brothers would have killed him instantly. But R. Samuel b. Naḥmani replies that Joseph, trusting in his brothers' righteousness (*ṣidqan shel eḥav*), thought to himself, "Heaven forbid! My brothers are not to be suspected of shedding blood!" The point is, however, that R. Ḥama does suspect Joseph's brothers of shedding blood and expresses concern as to what they might do with their enormous strength.[33] This same fear shows elsewhere in the legends with the various pictures of how terrifying Judah appears in his rage and how frightened Joseph and his guards become of him. In these legends, gibborim arouse the fear that they might lose control of their strength and commit serious crimes.

Abner did not lose control of his strength, but he did fail to use it responsibly. Expressing opinions about why Abner deserved his death at the hands of Joab, various sages suggest the following sins: Abner killed Asahel needlessly when wounding him would have sufficed; Abner made sport of human life by commanding young men to fight each other in a contest; he stirred up hostility between Saul and David; and he did not act to save the priests of Nob.[34] What all these sins suggest is an attitude dangerous in a gibbor—a disregard for human life resulting in needless bloodshed and strife. For this, Abner deserved his death.

---

31. Gen. Rab. V 96; Eccl. Rab. 9, 11.
32. B. Sotah 9b.
33. Gen. Rab. 93, 9.
34. Lev. Rab. 26, 2; b. Sanh. 20a, 49a; y. Peah 1:1 (4a); Pesiq. Rav Kah. 4, 2.

What we therefore find expressed in the various legends and opinions that make up the rabbinic texts dealing with gibborim is an ambivalence. This ambivalence characterizes not only the texts themselves as an aggregate, but also individual sages who sometimes speak with favor of a gibbor and other times with disapproval.[35] On the one hand, the texts present the mighty heroes of Israel as men in whom to take pride and pleasure. Their strength had value in defending Israel. But on the other hand, the same texts convey a sense of concern about gibborim, because their strength was liable to make them presumptuous. Refusing to acknowledge its transcendent source, or losing control, they could use it in a sinful manner. The gibbor was a dangerous hero.

Messiah as Gibbor

A further danger was that the gibbor might be mistaken for the Messiah. In Midrash Genesis the tradition is recorded that Jacob mistook Samson for the Messiah: "Our father Jacob foresaw him [Samson] and thought that he was the King Messiah. But when he saw him die, he said, 'He too is dead: *I wait for your salvation, O God*'" (Gen. 49:18).[36] This mistake resembles R. Akiba's with Ben Koziva, in which he proclaimed Ben Koziva the Messiah because of his feats of strength in battle, the powers that distinguish a gibbor.

We meet in these legends about Jacob and Ben Koziva the image of the messianic king conceived as a great gibbor, found especially in the Targumim, and related to the ideal king portrayed as gibbor in Psalms 45 and 89. These psalms explicitly call the king a gibbor, and they describe him wielding his sword to fight for righteousness (Ps. 45) and conquering all his enemies (Ps. 89). We have already seen that the Targum renderings of Num. 24:17–24 portray the Messiah as a fierce, bloody warrior, fighting the great final war against Rome. Other passages in the Targumim, notably Gen. 48:10, portray him similarly.

The extraordinary martial power displayed by gibborim and this warrior-Messiah points to God. A tradition about Samson states that his strength

---

35. R. Isaac on Samson, b. Sanh. 9b; and R. Yoḥanan in b. Sotah 10a, where he speaks disapprovingly of Samson's sins but then praises him for judging Israel "in the same manner as their father in heaven." If we were able to analyze these opinions historically, we might discover that the positive and negative opinions reflect different periods of time or opposing political factions among the sages. My present purpose, however, is only to examine the final edited texts, which record both positive and negative opinions together (and also from the same sages).

36. Gen. Rab. 98, 17–18; 99, 16.

was created in the likeness of God's: *me'eyn dugma shel ma'lah;* another tradition views Samson's astounding powers and terrifying appearance as manifestations of the Shekhinah, the divine presence.[37] R. Akiba considers Ben Koziva's feats in battle a sign that he was the man who would fulfill God's messianic promises.

Legendary Greek heroes also exhibit superhuman powers. Achilles is nearly invulnerable to weapons, and Heracles performs extraordinary feats of strength, daring, and military prowess. Such power was explained in legend by the hero's birth from the seed of Zeus and by the constant intervention of the gods. Hesiod conceived of the heroes as "half-gods" (*hemitheoi*); Pindar called Heracles *heros theos* (hero and god).[38] The strength of Greek heroes in early legend thus resembles that of Samson in rabbinic legend, who was endowed with a sacred transcendent quality. What does this similarity between gibborim and Greek heroes mean? We may simply be seeing separate internal developments of typical hero-myths found in many different cultures, or perhaps Jews of the Hellenistic and Roman periods were magnifying the powers of their indigenous military heroes under the stimulus of Greek and Roman myths.

I have argued that Ben Koziva is portrayed in the Jerusalem Talmud and Midrash Lamentations as a gibbor, a charismatic warrior who shared certain features in common with Greek legendary heroes. Since the rabbinic legends view Ben Koziva as an instance of this general character-type, the gibbor, we shall discover that the attitudes we saw expressed toward other gibborim will resemble the attitudes we find expressed toward Ben Koziva.

Literary Elements in the Story

The Opposing Armies

The legends tell the story of the last days of Betar, beginning when Ben Koziva's power is at its height, just before the critical turn of events. He has withstood the Roman siege for three and a half years, and Hadrian is ready to yield and return home. Hence, as these legends tell it, the war was not futile from the outset and Ben Koziva might actually have defeated Hadrian. Why he did not is the subject of the story.

---

37. B. Sotah 10a; b. Sotah 9b; Lev. Rab. 8, 2 (168–69).
38. Hesiod, Works and Days, 160; Pindar, Nemean Odes 3.22.

The first scene pictures the two opposing armies, both of equal strength, facing each other over the siege walls that surround Betar: "Eighty thousand pairs of trumpeters surrounded Betar, and each of them was set over many soldiers. And Ben Kozba was there, and he had two hundred thousand [soldiers]. . . ."

All the numbers in this story are immense; the legends suggest a total sum of at least two million soldiers, and Betar itself is later ascribed an enormous population. These tremendous sums, far greater than the modern historian would permit,[39] express the extraordinary significance attached to the event in the memory of the people: the fates of nations were at stake, the outcome was momentous, every move affected multitudes. The huge size attributed to the Roman forces shows, in addition, the strength Ben Koziva possessed—holding them back for so long and nearly defeating them.

The story goes on to describe Ben Koziva's army. It was composed entirely of men who had passed formidable tests of courage and strength. The point of the story is to show how exceptional Ben Koziva's army had been and to proclaim that Israel in those days had men brave enough to chop off a finger and strong enough to uproot a cedar of Lebanon.[40] This expression of pride in Israelite warriors accords with the pride expressed elsewhere in rabbinic literature over other gibborim.

The second theme to notice in this section—and it is a major theme of the Ben Koziva legends—is that of the conflict between Ben Koziva and the sages. On just what grounds the sages object to Ben Koziva's test is unclear. Their concern could have been a matter of halakhah (rabbinic law), since maimed priests and Levites would be disqualified from serving in the Temple, or a matter of practical advice (as Samuel Kraus suggested), since the loss of a finger reduces a soldier's effectiveness.[41] In either case, the sages

---

39. Based on the conclusions of Vermes and Millar, eds., in Schürer, *History of The Jewish People*, 547–48, that six legions and seven cohorts were involved in the war in Judea (not all of whom would be deployed at Betar), the number of Roman soldiers at Betar could not have been more than 40,000.

40. A cedar of Lebanon can reach forty feet in girth and ninety in height—an enormous size. Rabbinic comments (Num. Rab. 3, 1 and 19, 3) refer to it as the tallest and largest of trees. There are no models in Scripture or rabbinic literature for such tests. Gideon's test of his soldiers (Judges 7:1–8) does not evaluate their endurance or strength; in rabbinic literature, it was interpreted as a test for piety. See Louis Ginzburg, *Legends of the Jews* (Philadelphia, 1962), 4:40, and his sources. The prototype for Ben Koziva's tests must therefore have derived from elsewhere, and after all, trials for admission into an elite army and tests of valor are common folklore motifs.

41. The phrase *ba'al mum*, applied here to Ben Koziva's soldiers, has also a technical meaning referring to a sacrificial animal that has a blemish disqualifying its use at the altar, as in m. Bekh. 5.5. But the phrase can also be applied to men, as in m. Bekh. 7.1: "These same blemishes [*mumim*]

are not objecting to the war itself but only to the way Ben Koziva is conducting it. Their demand for a new form of trial gives the storyteller the opportunity to show that Israel's warriors could excel in any test given them. The story's ending may have been told ironically, with a pleased chuckle: undisturbed by the arduousness of the sages' new test, Ben Koziva's men proceed easily to master that one, too.

The Battle Prayer

The prayer uttered by Ben Koziva before going forth to battle reveals a significant feature of his character. "Master of the World," he says in the legend, "neither help us nor shame us [as it is written], *Do not, O God, cast us down, and do not, O God, go forth against our enemies*" (Ps. 60:12).[42] This same prayer is also placed in the mouths of the other Judean gibborim, Bar Daroma and the two brothers of Haruva (whose stories are, in the main, elaborations upon this motif in the Ben Koziva legends). In the case of Bar Daroma, we learn that uttering these words constitutes a grave sin, for the legend states that "the mouth of Bar Daroma caused his downfall," and immediately thereafter a snake (considered an agent of divine punishment in rabbinic legends) kills him.

Ben Koziva's prayer, then, implies a sin—that of refusing to trust in God. It shows him to be a warrior who took so much pride in his own strength and the might of his army that he thought he needed no help from God. He wanted to win the battle unaided and unhindered by divine intervention. As we saw with Samson and Abner, this is an attitude associated with gibborim as a character-type. The gibbor had such extraordinary strength that he tended to become boastful and overconfident, forgetting that his strength depended upon the will of God. Sennacherib is ascribed a similar fault in 2 Kings 19:21–28 and Isaiah 10:12–15. Isaiah rebukes the Assyrian king for the insolence and blasphemy of thinking that he had conquered foreign

---

disqualify a man" (from serving in the Temple). Samuel Kraus, in "Hayyalot Bar Kokhba," *Sefer Ha-Yuval Likvod Alexander Marx* (New York, 1950), imagines the sages saying to Bar Kokhba, "You are weakening the strength of your warriors!"

42. This is not the usual translation of the verse, but Ben Koziva's prayer assumes this midrashic reading. There is also some question as to how the prayer itself should be translated. Whom does Ben Koziva ask God not to aid and not to shame, Israel or Rome? Abramsky, *Bar Kokhva*, 66, offers two possible translations: "Do not help us and do not shame us [for good or for evil]," and "Do not help our enemies and do not shame us." But the general intent is clear in any case—from the context, from Ps. 60:12, and by comparison with the stories of Bar Daroma and the two brothers of Haruva.

nations through his own might—when in truth he had merely served as an instrument of God. The victories were God's.

Ben Koziva's prayer is reminiscent of these passages, and it is also reminiscent of that rabbinic concept of *gassut ha-ruaḥ* (arrogance), which conceives of a person magnifying himself to such an extent that he leaves no room for the presence of God.[43] Our text portrays Ben Koziva in just this way—as a gibbor so confident of his strength that he left no room for providence in the conduct of the war.

Rabbi Elʿazar of Modiʿim

In total contrast is the prayer of R. Elʿazar, revealing a character and mode of action that are the opposite of Ben Koziva's. R. Elʿazar's prayer and the Cuthean's statement about its efficacy reflect the viewpoint of the storytellers and show us how they understood the historical events. In their view, Betar had only precariously and provisionally held out against the Roman forces, a single day at a time. This presents a far different impression of Ben Koziva's power than had appeared earlier, for now we discover that God's judgment had in fact been looming over Betar the whole while, ready to give Hadrian the victory, and that only the prayers and fasting of R. Elʿazar had enabled Betar to hang on this long. Therefore, as the Cuthean states plainly and the voice from Heaven will later declare, the true defender of Betar was not Ben Koziva with his mighty army, but R. Elʿazar, who "wallows in ashes."

These ashes and the sackcloth and fasting are clearly related to R. Elʿazar's prayer. They are meant to add force to his plea that God not judge Betar or that God judge Betar mercifully. This is one of the main functions of fasting in Scripture, where it is often accompanied by sackcloth and ashes.[44] Abaye, in the Babylonian Talmud, reaffirms this meaning when he assumes that the Ninevites fasted, wore sackcloth, and sat in ashes (Jonah 3:5–6) as a means of seeking God's forgiveness so as to avert the destruction of their city.[45] Likewise, Midrash Esther Rabbah (based on Esther 4:1 and 4:16) pictures Esther putting on sackcloth, filling her hair with ashes,

---

43. God and the arrogant man cannot exist together; pride amounts to a denial of God (b. Sotah 4b-5a). A proud man treads upon the feet of the Shekhinah, the presence of God (b. Ber. 43b). There is no room for self-magnification before God (Num. Rab. 4, 20 and 5, 8).

44. See 2 Sam. 12:15–23, 1 Kings 21:27, Ps. 35:13, Isa. 58:5, Neh. 9:1, Joel 2:13, Jonah 3:5–6, Dan. 9:3.

45. B. Taʿan. 16a. One role ascribed to fasting by the Mishnah is that of supporting prayers for rain: God is asked to "listen to the voice of your [Israel's] crying" and "answer in time of trouble" (m. Taʿan. 2.4).

and afflicting her body with hunger in time of danger;[46] she throws herself upon the mercy of God, calling herself homeless and destitute, which is what these actions make her. For fasting in all these cases is a kind of self-negation, giving up everything of value in the world so that one becomes utterly helpless and passive before God, displaying one's total dependence upon God's mercy. R. El'azar's fasting must be understood similarly, as an appeal for divine mercy through dramatic demonstration of humility and dependence.

Thus, prayer and fasting, as a defense against Rome, proceed in a way opposite to Ben Koziva's. The story sets Ben Koziva's approach against that of R. El'azar. They represent two opposing modes of action, two opposing views of history, power, and national policy. The way of Ben Koziva, as indicated by his prayer, is to rely solely on human strength and military might, and is characterized by arrogance and a refusal to trust in God. This is the danger of gibborim. But the way of the sage, insofar as R. El'azar represents it, is to rely totally upon God for help, and is characterized by humility and an acknowledgment of the nation's absolute dependence on God's will. R. El'azar's fasting signifies his surrender of all power and advantage within the world, and a casting of his entire existence upon the power and compassion of God. The story clearly takes the side of R. El'azar. In showing that Betar's true power derived far more from R. El'azar than from Ben Koziva, it clearly accentuates Ben Koziva's blindness and arrogance in thinking he could win the war by his own strength. Yet the story leaves open the possibility that a humble gibbor, acknowledging his dependence on God and the power of prayer and fasting, could have succeeded where Ben Koziva failed.

Rabbinic legends about the two conquests of Jerusalem teach similar lessons and do so using a plot structure and character-types similar to those of the Ben Koziva legends. Jerusalem is defended by extraordinary warriors (such as Abiqa, who catches catapulted stones like Ben Koziva),[47] and its downfall is attributed to the will of God rather than its conquerors' strength or defenders' weakness.[48] Just as Betar has its R. El'azar, so Jerusalem had

---

46. Esther Rab. 8, 7. Elsewhere in Esther Rabbah, the cries of fasting children, threatened by Haman, rise to heaven "like the bleating of kids and lambs," and God is moved to sit upon the Throne of Mercy instead of the Throne of Judgment (Esther Rab. 9, 5).

47. Pesiq. R. 29; Ginzburg, *Legends* 3:301–2. The feats of Abiqa may have been modeled after those of Ben Koziva, since Pesiq. R. is a later compilation than Lam. Rab.

48. For example, Lev. Rab. 5, 3 and 28, 4 on Hezekiah's victory over Sennacherib; Ginzburg, *Legends* 6:392, in which God has angels destroy the Temple; Lam. Rab. 4, 15 on God's lowering the city walls for Nebuzarradan to enter.

its R. Ṣaddoq and earlier, its Jeremiah. R. Ṣaddoq observed fasts for forty years, reports a legend, "in order that Jerusalem not be destroyed"; nor would it have been, a sage comments, had there been one more man there like R. Ṣaddoq.[49] The prayers of Jeremiah, too, were "a strong wall" protecting the city. Jeremiah's role is even closer to R. El'azar's, for when God decides to destroy Jerusalem, he must first command Jeremiah (or trick him) to leave the city so that it may be conquered.[50] Likewise, before Betar can be conquered, R. El'azar must be removed; and a new character, the sly Cuthean, is introduced to carry out this role.

The Cuthean

In rabbinic legends, Cutheans (a name usually synonymous with Samaritans) are generally portrayed as hypocrites, idol worshippers, and cunning tricksters who try repeatedly to harm the people of Israel.[51] For example, a legend in Midrash Genesis has Cutheans collaborating with Rome to prevent Israel from rebuilding the Temple. They succeed by slandering Israel to the Romans and by using "inside information" about halakhah to Israel's disadvantage.[52]

The Cuthean of the Ben Koziva legends is portrayed similarly—as a malicious and guileful enemy of Israel. Only such a one as he could have overcome Ben Koziva because, first, he perceives from his knowledge of Israelite life the importance of R. El'azar in the defense of Betar. Second, appearing to be an ally or perhaps an Israelite, he can enter Betar and attack from within. This role in the story accords with the anomalous position that Cutheans occupy in rabbinic thought, neither a part of nor apart from Israel, difficult to define as to halakhah and doctrine.[53] Furthermore, the Cuthean

---

49. B. Git. 56a; Lam. Rab. 1, 32.

50. *Apocalypse of Baruch*, chap. 2; Pesiq. Rav Kah. 13.13. Ginzburg (*Legends* 4:393) points to another parallel: the story told in *Pseudo Philo* that God tricked Samuel into leaving the battle so that the Philistines could capture the ark.

51. The Simon of Acts 8:9–24 (known in ecclesiastical tradition as Simon Magus) has a distant resemblance to this image of Samaritans, although Acts never states that he was a Samaritan. As a magician, Simon distorts reality and deceives people; before his conversion, he is a heretic. According to ecclesiastical tradition, Simon reverts to sorcery and becomes an ideological opponent of the apostle Peter, like the Cutheans portrayed in rabbinic legends as ideological opponents of the sages. See Eusebius, *Eccl. Hist.* 2:8, on Simon Magus, and 3:26, on Menander the Samaritan.

52. Gen. Rab. 44, 10.

53. In halakhic matters such as circumcision, marriage, wine, and the sabbath, the sages had repeatedly to decide on the status of Cutheans (Samaritans) because they were an anomaly—like uncircumcised, unobservant, or apostate Jews, and minors. Samaritans shared much of the same

possesses the character traits necessary to overcome Ben Koziva, succeeding by deceit and flattery where physical strength has failed.

The Cuthean succeeds by playing upon the flaws in Ben Koziva's character—revealed thereby as credulity, suspicion, and a quick temper. In particular, the episode shows up Ben Koziva's credulity, his lack of astute intelligence. This is another trait characteristic of several gibborim in rabbinic legends and Scripture, which portray them as rough, simpleminded folk who cannot quite comprehend the intricacies of Torah and human affairs. For example, sages criticize Abner for starting a war because of his erroneous exegesis of Scripture, and rebuke Jephthah and Gideon for committing bloodshed and idolatry through their ignorance of the law.[54] In the Book of Judges, Samson resorts more to his strength than his brains and is conquered by a cunning woman. Heracles, too, is overcome by means of a clever stratagem, this one set up by a devious centaur and carried out unknowingly by Heracles's own wife. In these stories of Heracles, Samson, and Ben Koziva, cunning is the final victor over brute strength, an idea found in the legends of many cultures.

But when cunning meets cunning, as in the contests between Cutheans and sages recounted in rabbinic legend, it is always the sages who come out ahead. They are shown outwitting the Cutheans at their own game, as when, for example, Shimʿon Ha-Ṣaddiq foils a Cuthean plot to trick Alexander the Great into destroying the Temple and then induces him to destroy the Cuthean temple instead.[55] In the light of these legends, it is significant that Ben Koziva fails in his contest with a Cuthean. One implication is that gibborim like Ben Koziva lack the requisite intelligence for effective leadership and that the sages, possessing this intelligence and a deeper understanding of reality, are better suited to lead the nation.

A large portion of the Ben Koziva story is devoted to the Cuthean (although later writers show no interest in him), and all this attention suggests a certain fascination with what the Cuthean represents. Interpreted phenomenologically, as a perception of reality, the Cuthean manifests a dangerous and deceptive world where the unwary are easily tripped up. Both this episode and R. Elʿazar's prayers show the reader that reality is more complex than gibborim think it is: prayers reach beyond the realm of the gibbor's

---

Scripture and laws with Jews, but they also diverged significantly in several points of doctrine and practice.

54. Abner: Gen. Rab. 82, 5, Ruth Rab. 4, 6; Gideon: Gen. Rab. 44, 20, Lev. Rab. 22, 9; Jephthah: Gen. Rab. 60, 3, Lev. Rab. 37, 4.

55. B. Yoma 69a; Gen. Rab. 94, 7; Eccl. Rab. 5, 10.

physical strength, and Cutheans confound any simple perception of human affairs.

Ben Koziva's Downfall

In the encounter with the Cuthean, Ben Koziva exhibits a lack of discernment, an inability to see. Likewise with his execution of R. El'azar: Ben Koziva judges the sage impetuously, uncritically, and without the due process prescribed by rabbinic jurisprudence. This reflects the same character flaw revealed already by his battle prayer, an overweening pride in his own power—which is also an attitude characteristic of gibborim.

The fatal flaw, then, in Ben Koziva's character is his blind reliance on his strength to the exclusion of all else, which makes him vulnerable to the Cuthean and unjust to R. El'azar, and ultimately brings his downfall.

God acts now to punish Ben Koziva. What Ben Koziva had wanted to prevent and tried to deny—God's involvement in the war, God's presence in human affairs—now reveals itself clearly. Divine judgment is pronounced by a voice from heaven, and its words reflect the storytellers' understanding of what Ben Koziva's death signified: the judgment of God upon a sinner.

> A Bat Qol went forth, saying, "*Woe to the worthless shepherd who abandons the flock; the sword shall be upon his arm and upon his right eye; his arm shall be wholly withered and his right eye utterly blinded*" (Zech. 11:17): you slew R. El'azar of Modi'im, the arm of all Israel and their right eye. Therefore, your own arm *shall be wholly withered* and your own right eye *utterly blinded.* Immediately, Betar was captured and Ben Koziva was killed. (Jerusalem Talmud)

The verse from Zechariah is particularly appropriate. In its scriptural context it refers to wicked rulers who neglect their duty to protect and guide the people. By applying the verse to Ben Koziva, the Bat Qol (Heavenly voice) calls him a worthless leader who "abandons the flock" by killing R. El'azar, its true shepherd, and so leaving Israel defenseless before the Roman slaughterers. The verse is apt also because it speaks of a warrior dying in battle. His punishment is to lose his strength (his arm) and accuracy (his right eye), the two chief virtues of a gibbor, and then to die powerless before the enemy. Ben Koziva's punishment, as phrased in the following exegesis of the verse, is conceived according to the traditional logic of *middah ke-*

neged middah, "measure for measure," the idea that the reward or punishment of an action corresponds to it in kind: because Ben Koziva has destroyed Israel's strength, which is R. El'azar, Ben Koziva must forfeit his own strength.

By calling R. El'azar "the arm of all Israel," the Heavenly voice states clearly an idea that has been merely implied before—that Ben Koziva's military successes had depended on R. El'azar's prayers and ultimately on God's mercy. Moreover, addressed to Ben Koziva directly, this revelation resembles in function what Aristotle calls *anagnorisis*, the tragic hero's recognition of the truth about himself, as occurs, for example, with the Oedipus of *Oedipus Rex*. In the rabbinic story, Ben Koziva discovers that his glorious strength had in truth been nothing without R. El'azar's prayers and in the end had served only to destroy the very cause for which he had fought. The irony is intense.

Such tragic irony is another point of similarity with Greek tragedy, particularly the drama of Sophocles. There are other similarities. Like tragic heroes, Ben Koziva is a man of superior abilities whose actions display a fatal hubris. Aristotle's term, *hamartia* (flaw, mistake), aptly describes the weakness in Ben Koziva's character that brings about the downfall. In addition, Ben Koziva's recognition of the hidden truth (*anagnorisis*) occurs exactly at the dramatic moment that Aristotle calls *peripateia*, the sudden reversal of the hero's fortunes.[56]

Nevertheless, Ben Koziva differs in one significant way from Greek tragic heroes: he is not involved in an irresolvable conflict so much as in a rebellion that could have ceased and been forgiven.[57] Moreover, the tragic effects of the Ben Koziva story can be explained fully from earlier Israelite concepts of the divine-human relationship. Isaiah's oracle, mentioned earlier, for example, accuses Sennacherib of presuming to have conquered the nations by his own power (2 Kings 19:21–28; cf. Isa. 10:12–15): the same hubris, recognition, and irony are implied. Such similarities as exist between the Ben Koziva story and Greek tragedies therefore derive mainly from the similarity of dramatic situation—a heroic individual setting himself up against a higher order or will that, unknown to him, controls his life.

---

56. Aristotle, *The Poetics*, Loeb Classical Library, 1927, chaps. 13 and 16. Albin Lesky, *Greek Tragedy*, trans. H. A. Frankfort (New York, 1964), chaps. 1, 4–7.

57. See Lesky, *Greek Tragedy*, chap. 1, for his argument that tragedy always involves an insoluble conflict. He distinguishes between a "totally tragic worldview," a "total tragic situation," and a "tragic situation." The story of Ben Koziva fits none of these types of "tragedy" because he is always free to trust and obey God.

Hadrian's Eulogy

Ben Koziva dies in battle, and the last scene offers one final picture of the man, a final judgment passed by those who told his story.

A snake is found coiled around his body, an especially fitting form of punishment for a gibbor, since it completely nullifies his strength. The snake is an agent of divine retribution, as we learn from numerous legends and comments elsewhere in rabbinic literature. For example, "R. Abba b. Kahana said: Never does a snake bite unless it has been incited from above," and R. Shim'on b. Yoḥai reportedly taught that the snake, for its trespass in the Garden of Eden, was made executioner of all other trespassers.[58] Death caused by snakes, then, represented retribution from heaven, and in Ben Koziva's case, it meant that he was brought down not by Rome but by God.

This is the conclusion that Hadrian draws; and it gains in authority coming from Ben Koziva's foremost enemy, ruler of the mighty Roman empire. The Scriptural verse quoted by Hadrian ("not unless their rock had handed them over") adds a tone of authority, dignity, and finality to this last verdict upon Ben Koziva.[59] As the foregoing analysis suggests, that verdict judges him both hero and sinner, praising him as it condemns him. It expresses the contradictory feelings—pride and disapproval—that later generations felt toward the man. Hadrian's eulogy casts Ben Koziva, on the one hand, as a great and splendid hero, the magnificent opponent of Rome whom Rome had never conquered; and it casts him, on the other hand, as a reprehensible sinner who, for misusing his strength, had it taken away by God. To Ben Koziva's glory, he was never conquered by men, and to his shame, God had directly intervened to strike him down. This understanding of Ben Koziva's defeat both comforts and warns later generations: it leaves his glory and heroism intact while proclaiming his sins, and it affirms the power and justice of God in history while nullifying the accomplishments of Rome.

Explaining the nation's defeat as divine punishment derives directly from the prophets and Deuteronomic writers. Since, in this view, God had used

---

58. Eccl. Rab. 10, 1. See also Gen. Rab. 10, 7; Lev. Rab. 22, 4; Pesiq. R. 30.3; b. Shab. 156a.

59. Pesiq. R. 30.3 translates the verse in this way: "Had not the Holy One, Blessed Be He, brought us into your hands, you nations of the world could not have prevailed against us." In the predominant understanding of this verse, found also in Gen. Rab. 44, 21, Exod. Rab. 51, 7, Pesiq. Rav Kah. 5.2, and Pesiq. R. 15.2, it is read as a reference to Israel's subjugation by the nations, showing that Israel had been defeated not by them but by God as punishment for its sins.

foreign nations as "the rod of my anger" (Isa. 10:5), Jerusalem had not really been conquered by Babylonia but by the "anger and wrath" of the Lord (Jer. 32:31). Yet the prophets never drew the further conclusion that Nebuchadnezzar needed God's help because Jerusalem was otherwise unconquerable. So when the tellers of Ben Koziva's story use Hadrian's eulogy to praise Ben Koziva for never having been conquered by Rome, they reinterpret the prophetic idea.

Betar's End

Following immediately upon Hadrian's eulogy in both the Jerusalem Talmud and Midrash Lamentations, a series of traditions recalls the Roman massacre of Betar's population:

> And they [the Romans] went on killing them, until horses waded through blood up to their nostrils. And the blood rolled rocks weighing forty *seah*, until the blood reached the sea forty *mils* away. You might say that it [Betar] is closer to the sea, but is it not indeed forty *mils* from the sea?

> They say that on just one rock they found the brains of three hundred children. They also found three baskets of phylactery capsules, of nine *seah* each, and some say: nine baskets of three *seah* each.

> It teaches: R. Shim'on b. Gamliel says: there were five hundred schools in Betar, and the smallest of them had not less than five hundred children, who said, "If the enemy comes upon us, then we shall go out against them with these styluses and pierce their eyes." But when sins brought it to pass, they [the enemy] wrapped each and every child in its scroll and burned them [to death], and none remained of them all except I, and he applied to himself the verse, *My eye torments me because of all the daughters of my city* (Lam. 3:51).

> Hadrian the wicked had a vineyard, eighteen *mils* by eighteen *mils*, as far as from Tiberias to Sepphoris. They surrounded it with a wall of the slain inhabitants of Betar, a whole body's length [in height] and an arm's reach [in width]. And he did not decree that they should be buried until another king arose and decreed that they could be buried.

> R. Huna said: when the slain of Betar were allowed burial, [the benediction] "Who is kind and deals kindly" was instituted: "Who is kind," because they did not putrefy, "and deals kindly," because they were allowed to be buried.[60]

These legends do not constitute a necessary or inherent part of the story of Ben Koziva, for they also appear in the Babylonian Talmud (b. Git. 57a–58a) without mentioning him.[61] Nevertheless, the location of the destruction tales in Midrash Lamentations and the Jerusalem Talmud immediately after the Ben Koziva legends implies a connection—one which the Heavenly voice reinforces in calling Ben Koziva a "worthless shepherd who abandons the flock" (to the Roman butchers). The tales of the destruction thereby tell the consequences of Ben Koziva's sins and so constitute the denouement of his story.

Yet it is not clear that the storytellers hold Ben Koziva exclusively responsible for the destruction of Betar. R. El'azar's prayer that God not "sit in judgment today" suggests a generality of sin, of the whole city or whole generation, not just one man's; and the stock phrase, 'avonot garmu, "sins brought it to pass" (in both versions of the story), could likewise refer to the many sins of the multitude. In fact, other legends entirely ignore Ben Koziva in explaining the destruction of Betar. One tradition begins with the statement, "Over the axle of a carriage, Betar was destroyed," and goes on to show how a trivial misunderstanding between a few Romans and the inhabitants of Betar led to a catastrophic war out of all proportion to the incident that precipitated it.[62] Another tradition, attributed to R. Yosi, explains that Betar was destroyed "because they lit lamps after the destruction of the Temple," rejoicing in the fall of Jerusalem, whose crooked politicians had been robbing Betar's inhabitants of their land.[63]

Whomever the destruction tales fault for the fall of Betar, they clearly accuse Hadrian and his soldiers of inordinate cruelty after the city had fallen: *Vehayu horgin bahem veholkin*, the text says, "And they went on killing

---

60. Y. Ta'an. 4.8 (24a–b). See parallels, with some variations, at Lam. Rab. 2, 5, on Lam. 2:2, and b. Git. 58a.

61. Peter Schäfer argues in *Der Bar Kokhba-Aufstand*, chap. 6, esp. 190–93, that most of the legends constituting what he terms "the Betar complex" have no historical connection with either Bar Kokhba or Betar but derive from various legendary motifs about warriors and war or about the first war against Rome (66–70 C.E.). Schäfer concludes that redactors used these motifs to transform the later historical figure of Bar Kokhba and the city of Betar into a dramatic homily.

62. B. Git. 57a.

63. Y. Ta'an. 4.8 (24a); Lam. Rab. 2, 5.

them." This relentless savagery of the Romans is one of the main themes of the destruction tales. Another, shown by the number of schools and phylactery capsules, is the piety of the inhabitants; the version in B. Gittin has the capsules still "on the heads of the slain," implying that they died as martyrs to the truth written inside the capsules. The mounds of children's brains and the story of the schoolchildren convey a third theme, that of the innocence and helplessness of the victims. What makes the greatest impression, however, is the overwhelming number of people killed—depicted vividly by the torrents of blood, the brains piled in mounds, and the walls of corpses.

The destruction of Betar was remembered principally for this, the annihilation of its entire population.[64] Nothing else in rabbinic literature equals these legends for the horror and revulsion they elicit. Told orally, they must have shocked and dismayed those who heard them, stirring up pain and terror. Listeners would have felt pity for the helpless victims, anger at the Romans, and grief over the disastrous outcome of this last great war against the Roman empire.

Because the story of Ben Koziva precedes these scenes, his image became irrevocably linked with the carnage and bloodshed that marked the end of Betar.

Implications of the Story

I have argued that the legends about Bar Kokhba in the Jerusalem Talmud and Midrash Lamentations portray him in the character of a charismatic warrior displaying the same extraordinary physical strength as the biblical gibborim of rabbinic legend, as well as their characteristic virtues and vices, the danger and glory of their strength. At the same time, this image of Bar Kokhba bears some resemblance to Greek legendary heroes and to Isaiah's image of Sennacherib (2 Kings 19:21–28); and as a narrative protagonist, Ben Koziva undergoes the sudden recognition and plot reversal suffered by heroes of Greek tragedy.

We must now ask about the political and religious implications of the

---

64. In contrast to the legends about the Babylonian and Roman conquests of Jerusalem (Lam. Rab. 1, 39 and 45–48; 2, 4 and 23; 4, 4 and 11–12; and b. Git. 56b) and the Roman destruction of Judean towns (2, 4)—only the conquest of Betar was remembered for the ruthless extermination of an entire population. The other tales speak of different kinds of suffering, such as famine, deportation, enslavement, and the desecration of the Temple.

story. Before doing so, however, let us return to the legends and review them with an eye to their rhetorical and dramatic effects upon the people hearing or reading them. For they are clearly intended to teach a lesson, and they do so not only through their thematic content (their *logos*, in Greek rhetorical terminology), but also through the emotional effects of the narrative on the character of the audience (*pathos* and *ethos*).[65] Aristotle attempted in *Poetics* and *Rhetoric* to describe the effect of tragedy and oratory on an audience, and this way of understanding the story will help us discern its function in fostering political attitudes and affecting religious perceptions.

Audience Response

According to Aristotle's theories, the audience's response to the unfolding story of Ben Koziva would follow a pattern corresponding to the changing ethos of Ben Koziva—that is, the way in which he is presented, whether in an admirable or blameworthy light.

At the beginning of the story, he appears wholly admirable: his strength and courage in battle and his goal of freeing Israel all seem praiseworthy, so that listeners begin by admiring him. He is doing in a superior way what they themselves want to do. But as the story progresses listeners gradually discover faults in Ben Koziva's character. Hearing the battle prayer voiced in its arrogant tone, they discover the overweening pride he takes in his own strength, presumptuously refusing to trust in God. His ignorance of the crucial role of R. El'azar's prayers while being himself dependent on them reveals a blind disregard for the truth, particularly the truth of God's involvement in the outcome of the war. This gradual discovery of faults in a man who had at first appeared admirable might raise questions in the minds of the listeners, since they had begun by identifying with his goals and valuing his strength. How would they themselves have acted in his place? Did they really trust God to provide for Israel? What is it that brings victory? And what is the role of the gibbor in promoting the nation's welfare? They might also recall legends about biblical gibborim who used their strength in sinful ways.

Then the Cuthean enters the story. When he succeeds easily in outwitting Ben Koziva, listeners perceive the limitations of Ben Koziva's strength. His overconfidence, quick anger, and simplicity have tripped him up in the deceptive world represented by the figure of the Cuthean. With Ben

---

65. See John H. Mackin, *Classical Rhetoric for Modern Discourse* (New York, 1969).

Koziva's execution of R. El'azar, listeners discern the dark, destructive potential in Ben Koziva's strength. They see that this apparently glorious strength has destroyed the cause it tried to serve, has brought the opposite of its intended outcome. Finally, when the Heavenly voice intervenes to judge Ben Koziva for his sins, listeners assent readily to the verdict of guilt.

Yet listeners are not allowed to repudiate him entirely, for they would apprehend in the manner of his death the magnitude not only of his shame but also of his glory. As suggested earlier, it was to Ben Koziva's shame that God had intervened to strike him down, but it was to his glory that he had never been defeated by Rome. The story thus upholds an image of Ben Koziva in which listeners could take pride, as a splendid hero of Israel's past, and invites them to remember him with both pride and disapproval together. Such an ethos resolves the conflicting aspects of Ben Koziva's character by saving the glory of his strength while warning of its danger. In addition, by nullifying Rome's conquest of Ben Koziva, the story turns Betar's defeat into victory—not the kind that the audience would have preferred, but a victory for the justice of God, which the story encourages the audience to comprehend and to accept.

Now the storyteller recounts the horrible scenes of Betar's end. Connecting them with the story of Ben Koziva implies that Betar's destruction was an act of divine judgment, and hence necessary, issuing out of the justice and righteousness of God. This perspective opens up a redeeming dimension to the catastrophe, allowing listeners to make peace with the event and its consequences for themselves. These scenes also constitute a warning about the danger of men like Ben Koziva and show how grave the consequences are of one's conduct and attitude toward God. Listeners might therefore be moved to examine themselves and to ask whether they did not still deserve their present sufferings.

Political Implications of the Story

The Ben Koziva legends convey a political teaching in that they speak about national power. The Heavenly voice's speech states that R. El'azar is "the arm of all Israel," the source of Israel's power in the war, and that Ben Koziva is a "worthless shepherd," an irresponsible leader of the nation. Moreover, the very subject of the story, the war with Rome, is a political event, and the legends take a definite interest in the exercise of authority at Betar, as in the controversy between the sages and Ben Koziva over the testing of his soldiers. (In contrast, rabbinic legends about other gibborim generally lack such a political dimension.) Therefore, when the story moves listeners to react to Ben Koziva in a certain way, it encourages them to react in the same way to the political approach that he embodies.

The legends present Ben Koziva and R. El'azar as the embodiments of two different political responses to Roman rule. R. El'azar represents the way of prayer and piety, whereas Ben Koziva seeks to free Israel through aggressive military action. These two approaches are not mutually exclusive, since military action could conceivably be pursued in a spirit of piety and trust. But in our story, it is R. El'azar, not Ben Koziva, who is called "the arm of all Israel"—which implies that R. El'azar's prayers come prior to Ben Koziva's military efforts, and that the latter depend on the former. Moreover, because Ben Koziva is portrayed through motifs belonging to a general class of heroes, the gibborim, who are the exemplary soldiers of society, his approach to freeing Israel would represent the approach of gibborim as a class. His approach also represents the particular sins typical of gibborim, which through the Ben Koziva legends acquire a political dimension that they lack in other legends.

The political function of the Ben Koziva legends is to show what is wrong with the military approach to saving Israel. First, the story implies that the way of the gibbor is apt to manifest or engender the sins characteristic of gibborim—blindness and insolence, a presumptuous use of power, and a refusal to trust in God. Second, the story teaches that because military action is likely to manifest these sins, it cannot succeed. The tales of Ben Koziva's strength become, in this context, an argument for the political inefficacy of military force. Just because Ben Koziva was so strong and acted with such fierce resolve, this itself proves that strength and fervor, no matter how great, are insufficient in themselves to save the nation. Expressed as an inference a fortiori: if Ben Koziva, for all his enormous might and fervor, could not achieve freedom for Israel, then no man can do so by military means alone. The inefficacy of military means is explained not only by theological causes, the tendency of gibborim to rebel against God, but also by immanent causes: gibborim make poor leaders, use force in a heavy-handed manner, and lack the wit and cunning to deal with men like the Cuthean. The story teaches, third, that military efforts, being ineffectual, are dangerous and bound to lead to disaster. The final result of Ben Koziva's fighting is that he "abandons the flock" to its slaughter. The destruction tales constitute a warning of what the policy of gibborim could bring upon the nation.

The Ben Koziva legends come close to suggesting that a military attempt to free Israel shows a lack of faith in God. The freeing of Israel means its redemption, its restoration to the political power of old, an event that would occur "at the end of days"; therefore, people who take it into their own hands to effect this redemption could be said to be, in the rabbinic phrase, "forcing the end," *dohim al ha-qes,* which is what the Midrash on the Song of Songs says of Ben Koziva's generation.⁶⁶ They "forced the end" in that they arrogated to themselves a role which belonged to God alone.

> *I adjure you, O daughters of Israel, by the gazelles and by the hinds of the field, do not awaken or stir up love until it is ready* (Cant. 2:7). . . . R. Onya said: He [God] addressed to them [Israel] four adjurations corresponding to the four generations who tried to force the end and came to grief. These are: one generation in the days of Amram, one in the days of Dinai, one in the days of Koziva, and one in the days of Shutelah b. Ephraim.⁶⁷

In a following statement, R. Onya attributes forcing the end to a lack of faith in God: he explains that the generation of Shutelah b. Ephraim "transgressed upon the end" because of the reason given in Ps. 78:22—"Because they did not believe in God and did not trust in God's salvation." Applied to Ben Koziva's generation, this means that they forced the end because they did not trust God to intervene and effect redemption when they wanted it.⁶⁸

Such an interpretation of the messianic movement led by Bar Kokhba accords well with the image of the man in the Jerusalem Talmud and Midrash Lamentations, even though these legends hardly mention the Messiah. For whether they portray a false messiah or a presumptuous *gibbor,* both R. Onya and the Ben Koziva legends concur that Ben Koziva refused to trust in God to save the nation but tried to force history by his own powers. This is what a military approach such as Ben Koziva's implied to those who told his story.

---

66. See Gershom Scholem's explanation of the phrase in "Toward an Understanding of the Messianic Idea in Judaism," in *The Messianic Idea in Judaism* (New York, 1971), 14; and also Lev. Rab. 19, 5 for an example of the term's application.

67. Cant. Rab. 2, 18 on Cant. 2:7.

68. See ibid. for the midrash of R. Helbo also warning Jews not to take radical political and military action: "There are four adjurations here. God adjured Israel that they not rebel against the kingdoms, that they not try to force the end, that they not reveal their mysteries, and that they not go up from exile like a wall [in mass, by force]. But if so, why does the King Messiah come? To gather in the exiled of Israel." Cf. also b. Ketub. 111a, R. Zera's interpretation of Cant. 2:7.

The final effect of the Ben Koziva legends in fashioning political attitudes would therefore be to raise grave doubts as to the value of any large-scale military endeavor to achieve national freedom. By showing what was wrong with Ben Koziva and thereby moving the audience to reject his conduct, the story works to discredit military action in general. If another charismatic hero were to ask people to join a new war against the ruling government, they would have to pause and consider whether to risk again the disastrous consequences of Ben Koziva's war and whether, in taking such action, they would not be in effect doubting the salvation promised by God.

Indeed, while the story works to disparage military action, it tries also to turn the hopes of its audience toward heaven, asking them to wait patiently for redemption to begin from there. The figure of R. El'azar in the story exemplifies this mode of action. The storytellers assert that his prayers, faith, and utter abandonment of worldly power, his casting himself wholly upon the mercy of God, have more effect upon events than all of Ben Koziva's reliance on the might of his army. This idea alters the frame of reference from the military and political sphere to that of the individual's relationship with heaven, which becomes the crucial realm for influencing history. From a purely military perspective, such an orientation appears useless and inward-turning, but the story asserts that it constitutes the nation's only effective way of changing history.

These teachings express the military and political quietism that many historians have identified as the dominant political position of the early rabbis. After the failures of the Zealots and Bar Kokhba, and the disastrous outcomes of their wars, the majority of sages came to reject military force as a means of gaining national freedom. For the time being, they abandoned the way of the gibbor and espoused instead their own solution, a turning toward God in hope of moving God, through prayer, righteous conduct, and Torah, to save the nation; at the same time, they worked actively to build the public institutions and political relationships needed to ensure the community's survival until the Messiah arrived.

Salo Baron, for example, called this attitude a "mood of quiet resignation" that was expressed in the determination never to rebel again but to concentrate instead on reconstructing the community while waiting confidently for the eventual redemption promised by God.[69] Nahum Glatzer, in an article on the attitudes of third-century sages toward Rome, similarly

---

69. Salo W. Baron, *A Social and Religious History of the Jews*, 2nd ed. (Philadelphia, 1952), 2: 126–28, 312–13.

found that rabbinic eschatology had changed "from activist and militant into passivist and peaceful; from an urgent expectation of change into a distant, quiet hope; from a history-centered doctrine into a meta-historical one."[70] Jacob Neusner, too, in many of his studies of early rabbinic thought, has written of a rabbinic "program of political passivity and inwardness." "Prayer, study, fulfillment of the Torah, therefore, represented a very vigorous response to the cataclysmic events of the age, and from the rabbis' perspective, embodied more powerful instruments than any other for the achievement of the better age for which Jews longed."[71] In the Ben Koziva legends, of course, R. El'azar does not seek redemption itself through his prayers; he tries only to prevent Betar's destruction. But in teaching that prayer is more effective than military action, the story espouses the cautious and quietistic approach to political power typical of the dominant national policy of the rabbis after the second century.

This study of the Ben Koziva legends, then, has shown one way in which the political quietism of the sages came to be expressed in rabbinic literature.

These ideas about national policy imply corresponding ideas about political authority within the nation. The story teaches that the sages provide the best leadership for the nation, not only because its salvation lies in prayer and Torah, but also because gibborim tend to use power in dangerous ways and (as the episode with the Cuthean suggests) lack the wit and insight to deal effectively with the complexities of human affairs. The story of Ben Koziva thus warns readers to follow the wiser and more effective leadership of the sages.

We can perhaps define the political standpoint of the legends more precisely. In *The Jews of Palestine*, Michael Avi-Yonah identifies among the sages living after the Bar Kokhba war a range of opinions on the question of

---

70. Nahum Glatzer, "The Attitudes toward Rome in Third-Century Judaism," in *Essays in Jewish Thought* (University, Alabama, 1978), 3, 11–12. Since Glatzer does not substantiate the dates he gives for his rabbinic sources, we must broaden the period he assigns them.

71. Jacob Neusner, *There We Sat Down* (Nashville, 1972), 39, Neusner, "Religious Uses of History," *History and Theory* 5 (1966): 170. See also Neusner's recent studies of the idea of the Messiah in rabbinic literature. He discovers in the Mishnah an intentional omission of messianic themes in response to the failure of the Bar Kokhba Revolt and then in later Jewish literature a reconstruction of the messianic idea in a new form that makes the coming of the Messiah dependent on the non-apocalyptic tasks of prayer and obedience to halakhah: *Judaism: The Evidence of the Mishnah* (Chicago, 1981), and *Messiah in Context: Israel's History and Destiny in Formative Judaism* (Philadelphia, 1984). Cf., however, the corrective insights by David Biale in *Power and Powerlessness in Jewish History* (New York, 1986), reminding us that Jews never lost interest in practical political affairs and nearly always engaged in moderate political actions to improve the position of Jewish communities.

Roman rule—a pro-Roman position, a moderate stance, and a militant anti-Roman stance.[72] Where do the Ben Koziva legends fit within this spectrum? First, the destruction tales express a distinctly anti-Roman attitude: they depict the Romans as savage slaughterers and call the emperor "Hadrian the Wicked." But the Ben Koziva legends proper take a more moderate position. While they never reject the goal of gaining freedom from Rome, they do disparage military action in general, commending nonmilitant means instead. Furthermore, they depict Hadrian as an honorable foe, especially at the end of the story when he delivers his eulogy over Ben Koziva. They never blame Hadrian for starting the war but do blame Ben Koziva for bringing down divine punishment upon Betar. The political stance of the Ben Koziva legends therefore accords basically with the position of those sages whom Avi-Yonah calls "the moderates," who deplored Roman rule but chose to wait and watch, meantime working out a *modus vivendi* with the Roman government. This was the policy that Judah Ha-Nasi pursued and the attitude toward Rome that Glatzer identified among the majority of third-century sages.

We see this moderate viewpoint expressed also in the talmudic legends that begin, "Over a Qamṣa and a Bar Qamṣa was Jerusalem destroyed; ... over the shaft of a carriage was Betar destroyed."[73] The first legend tells how a petty quarrel between two residents of Jerusalem, named Qamṣa and Bar Qamṣa, drew the Roman emperor against his will into a devastating war with Judea. The second legend, mentioned earlier, tells how a minor misunderstanding between a few Judeans and Romans precipitated a major war ending in Betar's destruction. Both legends absolve Rome of responsibility. In the first, Rome is drawn into a quarrel against its will, and in the second, there was misunderstanding on both sides. These legends thus evince a tolerant attitude toward Rome and, for this reason, probably derive from a period of good relations such as the late second or third centuries. The Ben Koziva legends may derive from the same period.

Our consideration of the story's political teachings has so far dealt only with its criticisms of Ben Koziva. But we must not forget that the story elicits conflicting feelings toward the man—disapproval together with pride and admiration. The story's final message could not therefore be any simple

---

72. Michael Avi-Yonah, *The Jews of Palestine* (New York, 1976), 64–71, 83, 127–33. The political divisions and their viewpoints are not nearly so evident as Avi-Yonah assumes, but in this particular case, the texts speak explicitly of attitudes toward Roman rule.

73. B. Git. 55b.

repudiation of the political policy he represents. What do these opposing attitudes toward Ben Koziva mean as attitudes toward the use of military power? A comparison with the legends of other gibborim suggests an answer, for in these legends gibborim are admired as great national warriors, but they are warriors belonging to a past era. Their strength continued to evoke pride but had no practical relevance to present-day problems. Likewise with Ben Koziva. His story seems to relegate him to the past as a glorious (if also painful) memory of Israel's lost splendor, and to the future as a bright anticipation of Israel's eventual messianic triumph. Military force is shown to be impractical, dangerous, and even sinful as a political policy for the present, but not to be an inherent evil. It had its proper role in the past (before Ben Koziva) and in the indeterminate future, subordinated to the will of God. Its role in the present, however, was only to remind and symbolize as the nation worked to rebuild, adjust to political realities, and seek its final freedom through prayer and a life of Torah.

Religious Implications

There are a number of reasons to think that the Ben Koziva legends were told in connection with the national fast day held annually on the ninth day of the month of Av. This was the date, according to the Mishnah, on which Betar was conquered: "On the ninth of Av, it was decreed against our fathers that they should not enter the Land, and the Temple was destroyed the first and second times, and Betar was captured, and the city was destroyed. When Av comes in, gladness must be diminished."[74]

The contexts in which the Ben Koziva legends appear in the Jerusalem Talmud and in Midrash Lamentations imply that they were associated with this fast day. In the Jerusalem Talmud, they work to explain the phrase from the mishnaic passage above, "And Betar was captured," showing just how this occurred; and they appear in the fourth chapter of Tractate Ta'anit ("Fasting"), along with other stories and reflections elaborating upon the disasters that were thought to have occurred on the Ninth of Av. In Midrash Lamentations, the Ben Koziva legends are introduced as part of an exposition of a verse from the Book of Lamentations: "The Lord has swallowed unsparingly all the dwellings of Jacob" (Lam. 2:2). The story of Ben Koziva recounted one of those acts of divine wrath to which Lam. 2:2 was thought to allude. Since

74. M. Ta'an. 4.6.

the Book of Lamentations was the scriptural text read in synagogues on the Ninth of Av, scholars have suggested that the material collected in Midrash Lamentations is based on studies of this book carried out by the sages in schools and synagogues during the weeks preceding the Ninth of Av—a conclusion supported by statements in Midrash Lamentations itself.[75] The Ben Koziva legends, collected together with that material, would have been part of those annual reflections upon the Book of Lamentations.

Not only the textual setting of the Ben Koziva legends, but also their subject matter connect them with the Ninth of Av. For this fast day was a sacred time devoted to remembering all the national disasters that had become linked to that date, and it was, therefore, the proper time to reflect upon the downfall of Betar. The other legends explaining Betar's destruction—the tale of the "axle of a carriage," the account of Betar's rejoicing at the downfall of Jerusalem—may indicate specific ways in which the event was remembered, since these legends, too, are found in literary contexts related to the Ninth of Av. But one way the event would surely have been remembered would have been by telling the story of Ben Koziva, whose name was inextricably associated with Betar. For these reasons, we may surmise that the Ben Koziva legends, or something resembling them, were told and reflected upon during the period of national mourning that led up to and culminated in the fast of the Ninth of Av.

Let us further examine this fast day of the Ninth of Av. On this day each year, congregations recalled the national calamities that had occurred on the same date in the past—the destruction of the Temples and Betar, and the nation's subjugation and exile that resulted. The Ninth of Av echoed with wars, flames, and outcries of the past, with human sins and divine wrath, and with the congregation's grief and lamentations. A tradition found in the Talmud and Midrash just before the Ben Koziva legends, for example, reports that when R. Judah Ha-Nasi gave sermons on Lam. 2:2 (probably around the time of the Ninth of Av), old men in the congregations who lived before the Temple was destroyed would remember its destruction and begin to weep and be so overcome that they had to leave the synagogue. "When Av comes in," the Mishnah says, "gladness must be diminished."[76]

One of the major purposes of the scriptural texts and homilies connected with this day was to bring about repentance. The stories and midrashim

---

75. Lam. Rab. 4, 23 about Rabbi and R. Ishmael; 3, 5; 3, 6.
76. Other texts related to the Ninth of Av echo this same mood, e.g., b. Git. 57–58, y. Ta'an. 4.6 (25b), Pesiq. Rav Kah. 15.

collected in Midrash Lamentations explain the calamities of the past as divine judgments visited upon the nation in punishment for its sins. The congregants belonged to this same nation, were descendants of the victims of the past, identified with them, and still suffered the consequences of their sins. As they heard these stories and lessons, therefore, they would be expected to take thought and examine their own lives, asking whether they, too, did not deserve the subjugation and exile they were suffering. That is the rhetorical effect at which much of this literature implicitly aims. By teaching that the nation's condition depended upon its relationship with heaven, the literature of the Ninth of Av implied that the congregation could be saved only by turning to God in faithfulness and repentance.

Thus the Book of Lamentations, the scriptural reading for this day, laments Israel's iniquities—"Our fathers have sinned" (5:7)—and concludes with a plea for repentance: "Turn us unto You, O Lord, and we shall be turned" (5:21). The readings from the Prophets for the fast day and for the preceding three sabbaths (the "Three Weeks of Retribution") consist of impassioned denunciations from Isaiah and Jeremiah, rebuking the nation for its sins and threatening it with the wrath of God.[77] Many of the individual midrashim and legends in Midrash Lamentations also speak of the nation's sins, as do the three *pesiqta* (sections) of Pesiqta d'Rav Kahana designated for the Three Weeks of Retribution.

A brief study of the last of these three *pesiqta* will illustrate some of the religious themes and functions of the literature of the Ninth of Av, especially since many passages in this *pisqa* (section) are found also in Midrash Lamentations. The *pisqa* is entitled "Ekhah" (the Hebrew name for Lamentations) and is designated for *Shabbat Ḥazon*, the sabbath preceding the Ninth of Av. Lewis Barth surmises that "Ekhah" was composed for a select audience of rabbis and their disciples trained in the academies, who would read and study the composition.[78] It is thus a "literary sermon," but like other literary sermons, it "undoubtedly drew upon material that had been used in public sermons," an editor having reassembled the material in a new structure.[79]

---

77. The readings for the three sabbaths of Retribution are, respectively, (1) Jeremiah 1, 2:1–3, (2) Jeremiah 2:4–28, 3:4, and 4:1–2, and (3) Isaiah 1:1–27. For the Ninth of Av, the reading is Jeremiah 8:13–23 and 9:1–23. See b. Meg. 31b.

78. Lewis M. Barth, "Literary Imagination and the Rabbinic Sermon: Some Observations," *Proceedings of the Seventh World Congress of Jewish Studies: Studies in Talmud, Halakhah, and Midrash* (Jerusalem, 1981), 29–35.

79. Joseph Heinemann, *Literature of the Synagogue* (New York, 1975), 107–12. Cf. his article, "Preaching in the Talmudic Period," EJ 13:994–98.

"Ekhah" is therefore not an actual sermon delivered to the wider community on *Shabbat Ḥazon*, but it does represent what a rabbinic editor considered appropriate for scholars to read in connection with that sabbath and thereby indicates at least the general themes and ritual functions of the day and perhaps also the role that sermons served in the day's ritual.

The proems (opening homilies) of the sermon begin in a tone of lamentation, comparing God's grief over Israel's disobedience to the grief of a father who must punish his own children. Theme and mood having been set, the (literary) preacher then turns his eye upon Israel and the sins that necessitated the punishment. He speaks of Israel's faithlessness and neglect of Torah, which he blames for the nation's subjugation and exile. He then recalls the glorious golden age of Jerusalem, when the city had been righteous and faithful, and then the crimes of its later inhabitants—the murder of Zechariah, the crooked practices of its merchants, and the corruption of its leaders and judges. These are the crimes for which God punished the city. The sermon concludes with an eschatological peroration, promising that God would ultimately redeem Israel and that their suffering would cease. The ethos of the preacher (or sermon) has progressed from a position of sympathetic grief to one of rebuke and then to a final position of hope. In rebuking Israel for its sins, the sermon seems to be alluding to the sins of the present, and by blaming the nation's present circumstances on those sins, it is implicitly urging the congregation (or readers of the sermon) to repent and turn again to God so that God might forgive them and redeem the nation. The congregation's response to the sermon is expected to correspond to the changing ethos of the preacher: its response would begin in grief and progress to repentance and eschatological hope.

The religious function of this sermon is therefore to bring about repentance, which also appears to be the function of the Ninth of Av as a whole—recalling the calamities of the past as a means of transforming the community in its relationship with God. The literature of the Ninth of Av suggests that the ritual experiences of these weeks were structured according to a process that began in grief and mourning and moved through self-examination and repentance to arrive finally at a position of eschatological hope. The "Seven Weeks of Consolation" following the Ninth of Av in the annual liturgical cycle indicate the mood of hope and comfort into which the darkness of the Ninth of Av emerged.

We may now ask how the Ben Koziva legends contributed to the ritual experiences of this fast day and its preceding weeks. They contributed first by telling the story of the destruction of Betar and allowing the congregation to grieve over the event. The legends contributed also by promoting the self-examination and repentance that were the essence of the day's ritual process. We have seen how the legends taught ideas about sin and punishment that explain why the congregation should repent on the Ninth of Av. I have also discussed the dramatic effects of the story. I argued that it allows listeners at first to identify with Ben Koziva, but then, upon showing them the consequences of his actions, it impels them to examine their own attitudes and conduct. The story asks listeners to reject Ben Koziva's arrogant self-reliance, his presumptuous attempt to force history to obey his will, and asks them instead to turn to God with humility and patient faith. For salvation comes not by human hands but by the will of God. (The story's message of political quietism is thus reinforced by being told in association with the Ninth of Av.) In this way, by turning the calamity of Betar into a call for repentance, and repentance into a means to national redemption, the story of Ben Koziva tries to transform the congregation not only in its relationship with heaven but also with history.

In this context of the Ninth of Av, the figures of Ben Koziva and R. El'azar acquire additional connotations related to the day's themes and ritual experiences. The actions of Ben Koziva would represent those of a sinner who refused to turn to God on the Ninth of Av and as a result, continued to bring down upon the nation the calamities belonging to that day. In contrast, the figure of R. El'azar would exemplify the proper response to the day: confessing one's sins and those of the nation, casting one's whole existence upon the mercies of God, praying to God to save Israel from its misfortunes.

The Ben Koziva legends serve two additional functions appropriate to the Ninth of Av. First, they work to reconcile the congregation to the fallen state of Israel. They do this by explaining the fall of Betar as an act of divine judgment rendered against Ben Koziva and the nation in punishment for their sins. Recognizing the justice of what had occurred at Betar, and God's involvement, the congregation could begin to make peace with the event and with its consequences for themselves. Second, the Ben Koziva legends offer comfort to the grieving congregation by recalling the glorious feats of Ben Koziva and his army. These feats would console by reminding the congregation that Israel, though now a fallen nation, had once boasted magnificent gibborim, and that its last great hero, Ben Koziva, had been a warrior whom not even mighty Rome had been able to conquer. The lesson implied is that since God had struck down Ben Koziva, God could also have given him victory, and hence, if the congregation wants to be saved from its oppressors, it is to God that they must turn.

As with the political message of the Ben Koziva legends, so their religious function on the Ninth of Av also preserves Ben Koziva as a glorious memory and hope. His memory offers comfort in the present, while it exemplifies what is possible in the future if only Israel turns to God.

The Two Traditions

We have discovered in the rabbinic legends about Bar Kokhba two distinct images of the man, two traditions in the way that later generations perceived him and responded to him. The first image, that of a messianic impostor, is associated with eschatological expectation; the second image, that of a flawed gibbor, is associated with the downfall of Betar as it was retold each Ninth of Av. Judging simply by the length of the texts, the image of Bar Kokhba as a flawed gibbor was far and away the more important image of the man as he was remembered during the Talmudic period.[80]

However, the two images of Bar Kokhba share several features in common. In both traditions, Bar Kokhba acts with arrogance and self-aggrandizement, forcing things that should not be forced. In the first tradition, he tries to take the place of the real Messiah, and in the second, he tries to replace God's assistance with his own strength. Both traditions express an anxiety, therefore, about self-determined quests for redemption and warn readers to beware of any man, whether messianic claimant or charismatic hero, who bids them follow him in his attempt to achieve redemption, that is, national freedom. Instead, readers are advised by both traditions to heed the guidance of the sages who, in the first case, expose the impostor's lies, and in the second, provide more effective leadership than gibborim.

In this way both traditions about Bar Kokhba ask people to look beyond him, beyond his falsehood or his failings, and turn their eyes to heaven, from which alone would come redemption and the power to attain it.

---

80. See Joshua Efron, "Milḥemet Bar Kokhva Le'or Ha-Mesurat Ha-Talmudit Ha-'Ereṣ Yisra'elit keneged Ha-Bavlit," in *The Bar Kokhba Revolt: New Studies*, ed. A. Oppenheimer and U. Rappaport (Jerusalem, 1984), for an attempt to identify the historical bases for the differences between the two rabbinic images of Bar Kokhba.

2

Bar Kokhba in the Writings of Ibn Daud and Maimonides

In this chapter we shall examine how two Jewish writers living in Muslim societies, Abraham ben David (Ibn Daud) and Moses ben Maimon (Maimonides), portrayed Bar Kokhba in books appearing between 1160 and 1180. I shall argue that these writers' images of Bar Kokhba had both positive and negative sides. As a "false messiah," he represented for them the failure and danger of messianic movements, but they also grant him the limited validity of approximating the true Messiah closely enough to have justified rabbinic support.

For purposes of comparison, however, let us first consider the references to Bar Kokhba that appear in the writings of two Ashkenazi Jews living in Christian Western Europe. Less than a century before Ibn Daud and Maimonides wrote, Rabbi Solomon bar Isaac (known as Rashi by later Jews) had made brief mention of Bar Kokhba while explaining two passages in the Babylonian Talmud. Although written for eleventh-century Ashkenazi Jews, his commentaries have now had a long and influential history among European Jews. But readers learned little from him about Bar Kokhba—only that he was "one of the Herodian kings" ruling before the destruction of the Second Temple and that "the kingdom (*malkhut*) of Ben Koziva lasted two and a half years."[1] This last sentence merely repeats the statement in the Talmud that Rashi is explaining. Ben Koziva appears in these few words, and through their context, to be a king similar to Herod and the Hasmoneans; like them he ruled only briefly over Israel before it again lost its sovereignty. Referring to these kingdoms, Rashi remarks (or quotes a source), "Their chief glory and their crown was that no foreign nation ruled over them." Ben Koziva's messianic claim of b. Sanhedrin 93b and his military exploits of Midrash Lamentations and the Jerusalem Talmud receive no comment. For Rashi and the many readers whose education was limited to his commentaries on the Babylonian Talmud, Bar Kokhba's reign was a brief and insignificant flash of "glory" during the sorrowful years before the Second Temple was destroyed and the Jews were exiled.[2]

The second Ashkenazi writing is a chronicle composed by Jacob ben Abraham in northern France about a century later.[3] It closely follows one of the many versions of *Seder Olam* ("Order of the World"), an early rabbinic chronology. In the section of his Seder Olam that assigns a date to "the war of Ben Koziva," Ben Abraham adds the following description of him: "Ben

1. Comment to b. Sanh. 93b and 97b.
2. Rashi comments on a talmudic tradition attributed to R. Nathan warning against messianic speculation (b. Sanh. 97b). In this passage, R. Nathan points to three rabbis whose speculations were mistaken. One of them was R. Akiba, who thought that a verse from Haggai hinted at the date of the coming of the final redemption: "Once again in a little while I will shake the heavens and the earth" (Haggai 2:6). The relevant part of Rashi's explication follows:
    Again a little: a little glory will I give to Israel, and again I will not give them all the days of the last Temple. And so it was, for the first kingdom, that of the Hasmonean dynasty, continued in existence seventy years, even though we say in *Seder Olam* that the kingdom of the Hasmonean House lasted one hundred and three years and the kingdom of Herod, one hundred and three. Their chief glory and their crown was that no foreign nation ruled over them. [But actually] it [the first kingdom] did not continue in existence that long. And the second kingdom, that of Herod, lasted fifty-two years. And the kingdom [*malkhut*] of Ben Koziva lasted two and a half years. And again they did not have a king. . . . Another interpretation: *Again a little:* a little sovereignty will I give to Israel after the destruction [of the first Temple], and after that, *Behold I will shake the heavens and the earth* and the Messiah will come. But this interpretation is worthless, for see, we have observed how many kingdoms Israel had after the destruction [of the first Temple] while still the Messiah did not come. For the first kingdom [the Hasmonean] that Israel had after the destruction lasted seventy years, Herod [ruled] fifty-two years, Ben Koziva [ruled] two and a half years (Ben Koziva reigned in Betar).
3. Adolph Neubauer, *Medieval Jewish Chronicles* (London, 1887), 2:198.

Koziva was there and he had two hundred thousand mighty men of war skilled in battle, who had cut off a finger. What was the strength of Ben Koziva? When he went out to war, he would catch catapult stones on one of his knees and crush part of it and would kill many souls. At the end of three and a half years, they killed them great and small, eighty thousand myriads of human beings."

This passage is a summary of the legends in Midrash Lamentations and the Jerusalem Talmud, but in comparison, it accentuates the military exploits of Ben Koziva and his army, omitting mention of Bar Kokhba's messianic claims or R. Akiba's mistaken proclamation. The result is an image of a glorious warrior, perhaps a folk hero defeated when he tried to free his people. No explicit responsibility is assigned him for the aftermath.

These two Ashkenazi images of Bar Kokhba are basically reverent repetitions or abstractions of certain rabbinic stories and chronology. Rashi considers Bar Kokhba only as a king, Ben Abraham only as a warrior, but the two images fit together. Neither shows interest in the "messianic side" of Bar Kokhba, and neither presents him as a particularly important historical figure.

Ibn Daud's Image of Bar Kokhba

In contrast to the Ashkenazi writings, Ibn Daud's image of Bar Kokhba represents one of the most startling changes that will occur in the long history of those images. The rabbinic descriptions undergo dramatic modification and reinterpretation at the hands of Ibn Daud or his sources, and these modifications were adopted by numerous subsequent Jewish authors.

Ibrahim ibn Daud (c. 1110–1180) tells his story of Bar Kokhba in two historical works composed around 1161—in the brief *History of Rome* (*Zikhron Divrei Romi*) and in *The Book of Tradition* (*Sefer Ha-Qabbalah*), his much longer history of the transmission of revelation from Moses to the rabbinate of twelfth-century Andalusia, where Ibn Daud lived and wrote.

The Book of Tradition

In their days a certain man arose whose name was Koziva, and he claimed that he was the Messiah, son of David. He stretched forth his hand against King Domitian, king of Rome, and killed his viceroy who was in the Land of Israel. But Domitian, king of Rome, was still a boy and could not act strongly against him. So this Koziva ruled in Betar in the fifty-second year after the destruction of the Temple, and died while still being king. And his son ruled, whose name was Rufus (the meaning of Rufus is "red"), and he, too, died, and his son ruled, whose name was Romulus. And there were gathered to Koziva and to his sons a very great multitude from Israel, who returned from all their dwelling places. In the days of Romulus ben Rufus ben Koziva, Hadrian mobilized his forces and went up to the Land of Israel, and captured Betar on the ninth day of Av in the seventy-third year after the destruction of the Temple, and killed Romulus. And he smote Israel a great blow such as had never been seen or heard of before, not even in the days of Nebuzarradan or in the days of Titus.[4]

History of Rome
In the days of Domitian, Koziva arose, and he ruled in the days of Nerva and the days of Hadrian. Koziva and his son and grandson fought great wars with all the nations, and conquered the Land of Egypt. But Hadrian mobilized his forces and went up to the Land of Judea, and slew Ben Koziva and killed him. And a great many people from Israel died, and they suffered more from Hadrian than they had from Nebuchadnezzar and Titus.[5]

The Book of Tradition
All of this [martyrdom] came upon them [the sages] in the war of Hadrian because of the provocation of Ben Koziva. And there was fulfilled for them what was written by Daniel: *And the learned ones of the people will cause many to know, and they shall stumble by the sword and by flame and by captivity and by plunder for many days* (Dan. 11:33).[6]

As a composite from both books, the story tells how a man named Koziva, claiming to be the Davidic Messiah, rebelled against Rome and established

---

4. Gerson D. Cohen, *The Book of Tradition by Abraham Ibn Daud*, A Critical Edition with a translation and notes (Philadelphia, 1967), 3:28–36. Cohen's translation (28, English section) was consulted.

5. Abraham ben David Ha-Levi (Ibn Daud), *Zikhron Divrei Romi*, in *Ḥibburei ha-Qronografiyah shel Ha-Rabad Ha-Rishon*, Mantua edition, ed. H. H. Ben-Sasson (Jerusalem, 1964), 22.

6. Cohen, *Book of Tradition*, 3:44–46.

a Jewish monarchy. This monarchy lasted for three generations, as the reign passed from father to son in natural succession. During this time, Koziva and his heirs, named "Rufus" and "Romulus," fought great wars in Egypt and elsewhere, and Israelites from all over the Diaspora returned to the Land of Israel. But finally Hadrian defeated the grandson of Koziva at Betar and then the Jews, including the sages, suffered unparalleled destruction.

New Features in the Story

This account contains several entirely new features: the presence of three Kozivas instead of one, their names, the linking of the first Koziva with the reign of Domitian (81–96 C.E.), their wars against many nations and their conquest of Egypt. What is the source of these new elements, and what are we to make of them? Moreover, the character of Bar Kokhba and the explanation of the events take a much different form from that of the rabbinic legends. Gone is the arrogant, hot-blooded gibbor who can be stopped only by miraculous intervention from Heaven. We observe instead, as from a distance, three essentially featureless kings lacking in apparent motive and emotion, yet kings who achieve far greater political success, and for a longer period, than the gibbor of the legends. God is not mentioned even once to explain the events. How are we to understand this transformation of the story of Bar Kokhba? Can we discern any lesson that this transformed story conveys?

Gerson D. Cohen has written the most important recent study of *The Book of Tradition*, and my understanding of its account of the Kozivas owes much to his perceptive and erudite scholarship. He explains most of the new elements as eschatological motifs that Ibn Daud added to the rabbinic legends to convey a message about messianic speculation. According to Cohen, these new elements had a basis in biblical prophecy, rabbinic traditions, and reports from Christian chronicles, but their major source was medieval apocalyptic symbolism. Cohen suggests, for example, that the names "Rufus" and "Romulus" are connected with Islamic traditions about *al-Masiḥu 'd-Dajjal*, "the Lying Messiah"—a demonic figure who, like the Antichrist, arises at the end of days to lead people astray through his resemblance to the true Messiah or Mahdi. Cohen thinks that Ibn Daud intended the name "Rufus" as an allusion both to *al-Dajjal*, who had red hair, and to David, who had a ruddy complexion (1 Sam. 16:12); and the name "Romulus" (in reference to Rome) led people to believe that this Koziva was destined to conquer Rome in a great final war.[7] Through revisions such as these, Ibn Daud had fashioned, in Cohen's words, "a highly original tapestry," "a highly doctored version" of the rabbinic story. Its purpose was to show how closely the Kozivas (as Antichrist) resembled the Messiah and thus how easily people can be misled by false messiahs. At the same time, Ibn Daud was rebuking the sages of Koziva's time for having publicized their messianic speculations, because in doing so, they had stirred up expectations that culminated in the disastrous messianic movement focused on the Kozivas. Cohen argues that Ibn Daud used the story of those sages' misjudgment to warn the rabbinic leaders of Spain against repeating the same mistake.[8]

There will probably always remain a considerable degree of uncertainty in our understanding of Ibn Daud's account of the Kozivas, but several elements of Cohen's analysis seem especially open to question. Nowhere else in *The Book of Tradition* can we find an example of so extensive a "doctoring" of events and names as Cohen claims for the story of the Kozivas. Ibn Daud may very well have adjusted the dates of historical events in order to discover repetitions of time periods (what Cohen calls "the symmetry of history"),[9] but such an overt rewriting of the events themselves is uncharacteristic of the book. Moreover, the names "Rufus" and "Romulus" are open to a variety of interpretations unrelated to the Antichrist. Indeed, the book in no way attributes to the Kozivas the sinister motives, the attempt to deceive people, that characterize *al-Dajjal* and Armilus (the Jewish version of the Antichrist). Claiming to be the Messiah and provoking Rome may be foolish or dangerous actions but need not be malevolent. Furthermore, the Armilus of Jewish apocalyptic legends is usually pictured as a monster with two heads and golden hair.[10]

An alternative approach to the story might seek the origin of some of the

7. Ibid., 248–49.
8. Ibid., 28, 120, 240–50.
9. See ibid., 189–200, for Cohen's argument that Ibn Daud interpreted historical dates as a meaningful symmetry, that is, equal repetitions of time periods in history as evidence of the workings of Providence. Ibn Daud did not freely change accepted dates in order to demonstrate this symmetry, but when he found varying dates for the same event, he tended to reconcile them in line with his search for historical symmetry. His role was one of reconciling diverse testimony with a view to the meaning it held for his own day.
10. On Armilus, see J. Even-Shmuel, ed., *Midreshei Ge'ulah* (Jerusalem, 1954): "Sefer Eliyahu," 42; "Yemot Ha-Mashiaḥ," 96–97; "Nistarot shel R. Shim'on b. Yoḥai," 195; "Pirqei Ha-Mashiaḥ," 320; and esp. "Sefer Zerubbavel," 80ff. A summary appears in Jacob Plotzkin, "Armilus," EJ 3:476–77.

new elements in earlier literature from which Ibn Daud might have drawn. This method encounters serious difficulties, too, because our knowledge of the sources available to Ibn Daud is fragmentary and because there is no exact match between what any of these sources say about Bar Kokhba and what we find in Ibn Daud's story. No wonder that Cohen, after failing to find clear parallels to the new elements in either rabbinic or Latin literature, concluded that the story was a "historical fantasy"![11] A further possibility, although Cohen considers it a remote one, is that Ibn Daud copied his account from an earlier writer unknown to us—in which case we are at even more of a loss to explain the new features.[12] I shall nevertheless argue that a new consideration of earlier documents, specifically the Latin chronicles circulating at that time, reveals a sufficient degree of similarity with several of the new elements in the story to suggest that Ibn Daud meant his entire account as historical reconstruction rather than fantasy. If so, the new elements derive from Ibn Daud's use of documents that reported conflicting evidence which he had to correlate and synthesize.

An examination of the Latin chronicles is called for particularly because two later Jewish writers, Isaac Abravanel and Abraham Zacuto at the beginning of the sixteenth century, included in their own account of Bar Kokhba several of the new elements found in Ibn Daud's story, yet introduced these elements in such a way that their versions could not have depended upon Ibn Daud's (because their versions are more detailed and reflect the chronicles more accurately). Abravanel named his source as "Roman history books," and Zacuto stated his as Eusebius, author of the world chronicle upon which, through Jerome's Latin rendition, the chronicles of Orosius and Isidore were based.[13]

Ibn Daud's Sources

Modern scholars, Cohen among them, have long recognized that Ibn Daud's historical writings contain segments of material that derive from no known Jewish source but show varying degrees of similarity with accounts found in the Latin chronicles of Paulus Orosius, Isidore of Seville, and

---

11. Cohen, *Book of Tradition*, 250.
12. Ibid., 176 and 120, notes to lines 40–52, on the "remote possibility that Ibn Daud drew on some Saadyanic source."
13. See Chapters 3 and 4 of this book for further discussion of Abravanel's and Zacuto's reliance on Latin chronicles.

other Christian writers. As early as 1915, I. Elbogen suggested that Ibn Daud had relied upon Spanish and Arabic translations of Isidore's works or "other chronicles in circulation which employed the chronicle-style created by Eusebius and Jerome," and in 1924 Mordechai Klein and Elhanan Molnar demonstrated numerous points of correspondence between Ibn Daud's *History of Rome* and the writings of Orosius and Isidore.[14] The form by which Ibn Daud appropriated this material, however, whether from actual copies of the chronicles, through intermediate writings such as Mozarabic renditions, or by oral report, as well as the accuracy of their transmission, is far from certain.

The information that Abravanel and Zacuto attribute to the chronicles deals with wars fought by Bar Kokhba in Egypt and Mesopotamia, a theme found also in Ibn Daud's story (limited to Egypt) but entirely absent from the rabbinic legends. This suggests a starting point in our search for the sources of its new elements. Can we find in the chronicles any description of Jews fighting in Egypt and Mesopotamia? (See Appendix for excerpts from Orosius's *History Against the Pagans* and Eusebius's world chronicle).

If we examine what these chronicles say about the Jewish leader of a revolt whose name is Cochebas (the Greek version of Bar Kokhba), we discover nothing about Jews fighting outside of Judea. And indeed, Ibn Daud clearly did not identify the Cochebas of the chronicles with the Ben Koziva of the rabbinic legends (nor did any other Jewish writer up until Azariah de' Rossi in the sixteenth century). How could Ibn Daud have missed this connection between Cochebas and Ben Koziva? An odd statement in Ibn Daud's *History of Rome* provides a clue. There Ibn Daud writes, "In the days of Domitian Koziva arose, and he ruled in the days of Nerva and the days of Hadrian." Notice that Ibn Daud omits "the days of Trajan," the emperor whom we today recognize as having reigned between Nerva and Hadrian. In fact, Ibn Daud omits Trajan altogether from his account of the Roman emperors in *History of Rome*—even though Eusebius, Orosius, and Isidore all include Trajan. In Trajan's place, Ibn Daud inserts a Hadrian who in all but name resembles the Trajan of the chronicles, and then adds "another Hadrian" (*'Adriyanos 'Aḥer*) who wages a later war against the

---

14. Elbogen, "Abraham ibn Daud als Geschichtsschreiber," in *Festschrift zum siebzigsten Geburtstage Jakob Guttmans* (Leipzig, 1915), 199. Cohen (1967:162) argues that Ibn Daud had no direct access to the *History* of Orosius and the *Chronicon* of Isidore of Seville because there is no exact match between their reports and what we find in Ibn Daud's books. Nevertheless, Cohen continues, "there can be little doubt that his knowledge of Gentile history derived from these men by way of intermediate channels."

Jews (no leader is named) and who survived the war waged by the first Hadrian. This first Hadrian is the one whom Ibn Daud portrays conquering the last of the Kozivas at Betar. It is therefore clear that the emperor whom Ibn Daud calls the first Hadrian, whom he connects with the reign of the Kozivas, is identical with the man known in the chronicles (and by modern historians) as Trajan.[15]

If we then turn to the chronicles and search their accounts of the reign of Trajan, we discover events that suggest a clear basis for several of the new elements in Ibn Daud's story. Orosius reports in his *History Against the Pagans* that once during Trajan's reign (around 116–117 C.E.), after natural disasters had struck a number of cities in the Roman empire, a series of rebellions broke out among the Jews of Egypt and Mesopotamia. It would not be difficult for Ibn Daud to interpret these rebellions as manifestations of a widespread messianic movement. Orosius tells the events in this way:

> At the same time [the beginning of the reign of Trajan], an earthquake laid low four cities in Asia, Elaea, Myrina, Pitane, and Cyme, and in Greece, the two cities of the Opuntii and the Oriti.... Lightning struck and burned the Pantheon at Rome, while at Antioch an earthquake laid almost the entire city in ruins. Then violent rebellions among the Jews broke out simultaneously in various parts of the world.... They disturbed all Egypt, Cyrene, and the Thebaid by sedition and bloodshed. In Alexandria, however, the Jews were defeated and crushed in a pitched battle. When they also rebelled in Mesopotamia, the emperor ordered war to be declared against them; many thousands of them were exterminated in a vast carnage.[16]

Several elements in Ibn Daud's account bear a distinct resemblance to the incidents described by Orosius. Ibn Daud's statement that the Kozivas "fought great wars with all the nations and conquered the Land of Egypt" could be an interpretation of the widespread rebellions reported by the chronicles. These rebellions could suggest to Ibn Daud a massive messianic effort by Diaspora Jews to return to the Land of Israel: "There were gathered to Koziva and his sons a very great multitude from Israel who returned

---

15. Cohen (ibid., 28) recognized that Ibn Daud had confused Trajan and Hadrian, but he did not pursue the question of how this affected Ibn Daud's view of Bar Kokhba.
16. Orosius, *Historiarum Adversum Paganos*, 7:12. See Appendix for complete text and documentation.

from all their dwelling places." The earthquakes reported in the chronicles could serve as the basis for Ibn Daud's description of the natural calamities that inspired messianic expectations during the reign of "Hadrian I." Let us compare Ibn Daud's description in his *History of Rome:*

> In the days of Hadrian, wonders occurred on the earth, for the Land of Asia was split open, and four great kingdoms and all their inhabitants sank down into the abyss and perished from the world; and likewise, in Greece, two great kingdoms and their inhabitants. And the Land of Galicia shook, and three kingdoms and all their inhabitants sank into the abyss. And the fire of God descended from heaven upon a kingdom named Bananiah, and it and all its inhabitants were burned up, like Sodom and Gemorrah. All the inhabitants of the world trembled and lost their strength and were dumb, for the Lord was of a mind to overturn the world.[17]

Ibn Daud is here elaborating on the idea implied by Orosius that the Jews had viewed the natural calamities as signs of the end of days and that this expectation had stirred up their rebellions. Ibn Daud probably drew the further conclusion that it was specifically to Koziva that the Jews believed these portents were pointing.

It thus seems evident that Ibn Daud interpreted the Jewish rebellions and natural calamities described by the chronicles as one protracted messianic movement stirred up by those calamities, and that he connected this mass movement with the Ben Koziva of the rabbinic legends.

Yet if Ibn Daud read the chronicles accurately enough to reproduce these motifs, why could he not also have reproduced the name of Trajan correctly? Why, furthermore, would he have inserted additional generations of "Kozivas" not found in the chronicles? Cohen remarks on the frequent confusion of names typical "in ancient times."[18] Possibly, too, an error occurred in the act of transmission from the chronicle to Ibn Daud: an intermediate text or oral report may be responsible. But the discrepancies may have greater significance. No one before Ibn Daud had tried to correlate Roman history with Jewish history in such a detailed fashion, and Ibn Daud was drawing upon diverse and sometimes contradictory sets of testimony. The omission of Trajan, for example, may be explained by a

---

17. Ibn Daud, *History of Rome*, 22.
18. Cohen, *Book of Tradition*, 28.

Talmudic report that Hadrian massacred a large number of Jews in Alexandria: "*The voice is the voice of Jacob and the hands are the hands of Esau* [Gen. 27:22]: the voice refers to [the cry caused by] Hadrian Caesar who killed in Alexandria of Egypt sixty myriads, twice as many as went forth from Egypt."[19] Ibn Daud may have thought that the Talmud was referring to the Jewish rebellion and defeat which the chronicles reported as occurring in Alexandria during the reign of Trajan (see excerpts from Eusebius's *Chronicon* and Orosius's history in the Appendix). If so, he may have decided that the Talmudic tradition was more accurate, reasoning that the chronicles (or his reporter) had confused the names of Hadrian and Trajan. Certain details in Ibn Daud's account, perhaps all the new elements not yet explained, may derive from such an attempt to reconcile contradictory information from diverse sources.

Those remaining additions in Ibn Daud's story—the presence of three Kozivas, their names, and the dates—bear no direct relationship to anything in the Latin chronicles. Nor do comparisons with Jewish sources yield persuasive results. The evidence remains too ambiguous to carry us very far beyond conjecture. If, however, as I have argued, Ibn Daud drew upon historical testimony in composing significant portions of his story, trying to reconstruct a plausible account of the events on the basis of actual reports he read or heard; and if, as Cohen as well as Molnar and Klein have argued, most of Ibn Daud's historical writings have an identifiable basis in earlier documents, then the rest of the additions to the story of Bar Kokhba are likely also to represent efforts of historical reconstruction rather than "fantasy."

To demonstrate the plausibility of such an interpretation, I shall outline a number of directions for explaining these narrative elements as documentary reasoning. Cohen suggests several of these explanations himself. They all assume an attempt by Ibn Daud to reconcile conflicting historical data in Christian and Jewish texts. Beginning with the presence of three Kozivas, we might pursue Ibn Daud's interest in chronology, especially his interest in correlating dates from a variety of sources. From this viewpoint, the existence of more than one Koziva can be seen as a solution to the problem of how a man who arose at the beginning of Domitian's reign ("Domitian, king of Rome, was still a boy") could live long enough to fight Hadrian (Trajan) at the end of that emperor's reign—a span calculated by Ibn Daud as lasting at least twenty-one years, the period of the Kozivan kingdom, and possibly much longer if Koziva "arose" many years before he "ruled in Betar."

---

19. B. Git. 57b.

It is also possible that the idea of three Kozivas issued out of an interpretation of a rabbinic tradition that speaks of a war occurring between the war of Vespasian against Jerusalem and the war of Ben Koziva. Mishnah Sotah 9.14 mentions a "war of Vespasian," a "war of Titus" (or "Quietus" in the Cambridge manuscript), and "the last war," namely, that of Ben Koziva. In connection with this mishnaic tradition, *Seder Olam Rabbah* ("Greater Order of the World"), an early rabbinic chronology, attempts to assign dates to these wars. The relevant sentences from Seder Olam follow, together with major manuscript variations: "From the war of Vespasian to the war of Titus [or Quietus]: twenty-four years [or fifty-two]. From the war of Titus [or Quietus] to the war of Ben Koziva [or the House of Koziva, or the Kingdom of Koziva]: sixteen years. The war of Ben Koziva lasted two and a half years [or fifty and a half, or three], which was fifty-two [or twenty-two] years after the destruction of the Temple."[20] These variations show a great fluidity among the various manuscripts in regard to the time periods and names assigned to these wars, and we cannot ascertain which form of this tradition of the three wars reached Ibn Daud, or whether any form of Seder Olam reached him at all.[21] But the fluidity of the traditions also shows us the range of interpretation possible at this time. Ibn Daud's account of the three Kozivas may have been influenced by the mishnah's tradition of the three wars, and his understanding of those wars may derive from interpretations of the kind found in Seder Olam.

Ibn Daud may easily have identified the second war listed in this tradition, "the war of Titus" or of "Quietus," with the "great wars with all the nations" fought by the first Koziva. Especially if Ibn Daud's version of the tradition associated Titus with that war, Ibn Daud may have decided to correct his source in line with the history he had learned from the *Yosippon* (a Hebrew history of the fall of Jerusalem based loosely on the writings of Josephus) and the Christian chronicles, which portrayed the Jerusalem campaign of Titus (ending in 69/70 C.E.) as merely a continuation of the campaign begun by Vespasian only a few years earlier—which is indeed the view

---

20. B. Ratner, ed., *Seder 'Olam Rabbah*, (New York, 1966), chap. 30, 146; M. Weinstock, ed., *Seder Olam Rabbah Hashalem* (Jerusalem, 1962), 474–75. In the opinion of A. Neubauer, *Medieval Jewish Chronicles*, vii, the Amsterdam version of Seder Olam, which reports the name Quietus instead of Titus, was the version of the book that circulated in the Spanish Jewish communities.

21. Cohen (1967: 165–67) argues that the many discrepancies between the dates found in Seder Olam and *The Book of Tradition* rule out the possibility of Ibn Daud's having had a copy of Seder Olam at hand. We must note, however, the many areas of agreement between the two books, as well as the possibility that Ibn Daud chose to ignore Seder Olam in favor of his own calculations based on other sources or interpretations.

followed by *The Book of Tradition* itself. But as we saw, the chronicles speak of major Jewish rebellions occurring in 116–117, which Ibn Daud distinguished from the war that culminated at Betar.[22] If Ibn Daud identified the second war mentioned in the mishnaic tradition of Sotah 9.14 with these Jewish rebellions, which he thought were led by a messianic claimant, then he had to account for a war many years later led by a man called "Ben Koziva" in the same passage. (Where might the third Koziva have come from? A literalistic reading of Seder Olam mentions two "Ben Kozivas," two "sons of Koziva": one whose war, or simply "kingdom," occurred sixteen years after the war of Titus/Quietus, and a second Ben Koziva whose war lasted two and a half years, who would be the Ben Koziva conquered by Hadrian according to Midrash Lamentations. This reading produces, then, a Koziva who fought "great wars with all the nations," a Ben Koziva who fought a war many years later, and another Ben Koziva who was conquered by Hadrian after a war lasting two and a half years.)[23]

The name "Rufus" may represent an interpretation of the Turnus Rufus of rabbinic legends,[24] or an attempt by Ibn Daud to combine this Turnus Rufus with the Tinieus Rufus of the chronicles. Today we know this man as the Roman governor of Judea during the Bar Kokhba rebellion, but rabbinic literature nowhere identifies him explicitly as a Roman. It usually portrays him debating with R. Akiba about theological matters, and sometimes calls him "wicked"—which could mean merely that he was a heretical Jew.[25] As for the chronicles, Orosius and Isidore never mention him, but Ibn Daud may have received a garbled report of what Jerome wrote about Tinieus Rufus (translating Eusebius's chronicle), which even in the original Latin is ambiguous: "The Jews, taking up arms, devastated Palestine, the province being held by Tinieus Rufus [*tenente provinciam Tinio Rufo*], to whom [*cui*] Hadrian sent an army to crush the rebels" (entry for 133 C.E.). Was this Rufus a Roman or a rebel? The sentence could be read as saying that Rufus

---

22. The Latin rendition of Eusebius's world chronicle even identifies Quietus as the Roman general who fought the Jews rebelling in Mesopotamia. Had this report reached Ibn Daud, he would have considered Quietus the opponent of Koziva in those "great wars with all the nations."

23. Ibn Daud may also have been thinking of the *baraita* (an early rabbinic tradition) in the Babylonian Talmud (b. Sanh. 97b) that reports R. Nathan speaking of a "first kingdom," a "second kingdom," and "the kingdom of Ben Koziva," and associating all three with R. Akiba's messianic speculations.

24. This is Cohen's (1967) suggestion, 249.

25. Turnus Rufus is mentioned in Midr. Gen. 9, 5; b. Sanh. 65b; b. Ta'an. 29a, 50b; b. Avod. Zar. 20a; b. B. Bat. 10a; and elsewhere. B. Ta'an. 29a says that Turnus Rufus destroyed the Temple, but this could mean simply that his actions as a Jewish rebel led to that result.

was the leader of the rebels holding Judea and that Hadrian sent troops against him to crush the rebellion. From such readings of the rabbinic legends and this chronicle report emerges a picture of a rebel leader who seemed to be a different man from the Koziva who fought in Egypt. This Rufus had to be Ben Koziva, the "son of Koziva" of the rabbinic legends.

Why did Ibn Daud give the third Koziva the name of "Romulus"? In this case, the name is not found in any known source. But the name may nevertheless have resulted from a process of historical reasoning. Ibn Daud, wanting to give a name to the grandson of Koziva (perhaps to indicate his character), may have selected a name that the evidence suggested would be most likely. First, if Rufus had a Latin name, then his son would surely have one, too. Moreover, Ibn Daud's study of the Hasmonean kings had shown him that the second- and third-generation kings had adopted foreign names. In *The History of the Kings of the Second Temple*, Ibn Daud draws his readers' attention to the name "Hyrcanus": "and his name was Horqanos in the Greek language"—and he recounts how all of Hyrcanus's sons bore typical Greek names: Aristobulus, Antigonos, and Alexander.[26] Calling the third Koziva "Romulus" was an application of the Hasmonean pattern. "Romulus" was merely the most common, or characteristic, Latin name, like calling an American Jew "John Smith" (or pointedly calling an American Jew "Mr. Smith" or "Mr. Jones").

There are documentary explanations possible for the dates, also. Ibn Daud tells us that Koziva began to reign in Betar fifty-two years after the destruction of the temple and that Romulus was defeated on the Ninth of Av, twenty-one years later. The number fifty-two can be explained easily. Midrash Lamentations states that Betar lingered (*'astah*, an unusual word that later commentators had to explain) fifty-two years after the destruction of the Temple.[27] The number is also found in the tradition of Seder Olam about the three wars, several manuscripts stating that the second war, that of Titus/Quietus, took place fifty-two years after the destruction (which solves our puzzle perfectly), other manuscripts introducing the fifty-two years only after mentioning Ben Koziva. We may therefore conclude that the date of fifty-two years derives from rabbinic passages where this number is found.

The number twenty-one presents a more difficult problem, and we must follow Cohen in recognizing it as a number that bore special significance to

---

26. Ibn Daud, "Divrei Malkhei Yisra'el Be-Bayit Sheni," in *Ḥibburei*, 62–63. One might also note Midr. Lev. 32, 5, which lists both "Rufus" and "Alexander" as typical choices among Jews who take foreign names.

27. Lam. Rab. 2, 5.

Ibn Daud because of his search for repetitive patterns in Jewish chronology.[28] Such a search had shown him that "twenty-one years passed from the beginning of their exile [in Babylonia] until the destruction of the Temple [by Nebuchadnezzar] and the cessation of the monarchy," a period balanced exactly by the twenty-one years during which the Temple was rebuilt.[29] Ibn Daud saw such correspondence of time periods as a sign of God's involvement in Jewish history and hence concern for the Jewish people.[30] In discovering a twenty-one year period in the history of the Kozivas, Ibn Daud had uncovered yet another sign of Providence, in this case a sign connecting the destruction of Betar with the destruction of the first Temple, both occurring over a twenty-one year period that culminated on the ninth day of Av. But as we might also expect in the case of the Kozivas, the basis for Ibn Daud's calculation of these twenty-one years is difficult to identify. One possibility is that the number comes from adding together the years between the war of Titus/Quietus and the downfall of Ben Koziva in accord with the dates found in Seder Olam. Thus, to the sixteen years between the war of Titus/Quietus and that of Ben Koziva, we add the two and a half years during which the war of Romulus ben Koziva lasted, with the remaining two and a half years accounted for by assuming that the war of Rufus lasted the same duration as the war of Romulus. These twenty-one years fit quite reasonably with the dates of the Roman emperors during whose reigns Ibn Daud thought the Kozivas had lived, since, according to Ibn Daud's *History of Rome*, Domitian had ruled for sixteen years, Nerva one year, and Hadrian (i.e., Trajan) nineteen.[31]

These explanations of the three Kozivas, their names, and the dates in their story remain, however, only conjectures, and in the end, we must recognize

28. See Note 9.
29. Cohen, *Book of Tradition*, 1:56–57 (p. 6). Cohen's translation is from p. 10 of the English text.
30. Remarking on this correspondence, Ibn Daud wrote, "Behold how trustworthy are the consolations of our God, blessed be His name, for [the period of] their exile equaled [the period of] their redemption." Cohen, *Book of Tradition*, 1:55–56 (p. 6), p. 10 of English text (Cohen's translation). The number twenty-one also appears in the number of generations between Moses and Solomon and between Solomon and Hezekiah, and in the number of princes between Jehoiachim and R. Judah the Prince I.
31. Another possible source for Ibn Daud's idea of the twenty-one years of Kozivan rule, a suggestion from Cohen (1967: 120 n. 44), is that Ibn Daud derived the number from the Talmudic tradition stating, "Bar Koziva ruled for [usual reading: "two"] and a half years" (b. Sanh. 93b). Ibn Daud may have misread ב (=2) as כ (=20), or כ may have appeared in his manuscript through scribal error—thus producing the number of 20 ½.

the great ambiguity of the evidence available to us. I am arguing only that the evidence is sufficient to suggest a documentary basis for the new motifs in Ibn Daud's account of Bar Kokhba. It does so because three of his additions to the rabbinic story—the Egyptian war, the return of the multitudes, and the earthquakes—bear a clear relationship to reports found in the Christian chronicles circulating in Ibn Daud's time, and because reasonable possibilities can be formulated for documentary sources of the remaining and more puzzling features. A documentary basis for the first three motifs suggests a similar basis for the others. Textual sources have, moreover, been identified for most of the rest of Ibn Daud's historical writings. The weight of the evidence points, therefore, to an attempt on Ibn Daud's part to make sense out of received information, out of reports often derived from confused and conflicting sources. His idea, for example, that the Jewish rebellions occurring between 116 and 135 in Egypt, Mesopotamia, and Judea constituted one protracted messianic movement is an intelligent and plausible theory to explain the events described in rabbinic legends and Christian chronicles. Indeed, Ibn Daud's is the first attempt by a Jewish historian to synthesize Jewish with non-Jewish accounts of Bar Kokhba and is ultimately the foundation of our own modern understanding of the man.

Ibn Daud's Image of Bar Kokhba

If, as I have argued, important elements of Ibn Daud's account of Bar Kokhba derive from reports in the Christian chronicles, then those chronicles constitute a third tradition in the portrayal of Bar Kokhba, subsidiary to the two rabbinic traditions portraying him as a false messiah and as a flawed gibbor. But this new viewpoint does not alter the two earlier images so much as give them realistic political and geographical features. The older images have been refashioned into a messianic dynasty of successful military leaders that Ibn Daud inferred from the chronicle reports of protracted Jewish rebellions.

Ibn Daud may have considered the rabbinic folktales a metaphorical version of the political events depicted in the chronicles. In his philosophical work, *The Sublime Faith* (*Ha-Emunah Ha-Ramah*), he treats certain biblical phrases as metaphors intended for the common people (*ra'ui lehamon*) and explains their true meaning on the basis of Aristotelian physics and ontology. In the case of Bar Kokhba, Ibn Daud has substituted immanent political and military processes for the transcendently determined events of the rabbinic legends. Instead of explaining history through the concepts of human sin and divine punishment, as do the rabbinic legends, Ibn Daud explains it through human causes: Koziva succeeded at first because Domitian was weak; Romulus was defeated later because Hadrian mobilized his forces. This explanation accords with the three lower orders of causality that Ibn Daud sets forth in *The Sublime Faith*: causation by nature, by chance, or by human volition, as opposed to causation by divine will, the first order.[32] (As I shall suggest below, however, Ibn Daud apparently did see transcendent forces at work in the history of the Kozivas, but these forces affected them through intermediate causes.)

Ibn Daud's image of Bar Kokhba thus reflects the mergence of Jewish with non-Jewish traditions which was typical of Ibn Daud's Andalusian culture. His image of Bar Kokhba combines sacred sources (the rabbinic legends) with secular sources (the chronicles, albeit unnamed), and exhibits a conceptualization deriving from neo-Aristotelian thought, particularly in the story's attention to political and institutional consequences.

Implications of the Story

We come now to the question of what Ibn Daud meant to convey to his readers through his account of the Kozivas. His intentions are exhibited most clearly not from what he repeats from the rabbinic legends but from what he adds to them. We may therefore begin with the names, Rufus and Romulus. The only explicit comment Ibn Daud makes is to translate Rufus into Hebrew. This may have no significance, since he often translates foreign names in the course of telling history—"May" and "June," "Novillah," "Julius Caesar," "Bahram"—without any obvious comment being intended.[33] But in the case of Rufus, Ibn Daud may have had a reason to remind his readers that the name was foreign. Romulus is likewise a foreign name, the quintessentially Roman name, so that not the meaning of the names but the fact of their foreignness may be what struck Ibn Daud. In telling the history of the Hasmonean monarchy, Ibn Daud, unlike his source, the *Yosippon*, draws attention to the fact that Hyrcanus is a Greek name. Also unlike the *Yosippon*, he makes a point of explaining Simeon's death by poisoning and Hyrcanus's imprisonment as punishments for dis-

---

32. See Ibn Daud, *Ha-Emunah Ha-Ramah*, ed. S. Weil (Berlin, 1919), 93–98, and *The Exalted Faith*, ed. Gershon Weiss, trans. Norbert Samuelson (Rutherford, N.J., 1986), 303 in Hebrew text, 249 in translation, on what Ibn Daud or an editor in Weil's ms. calls *siddur ha-sibbot*, the order of causes.

33. Ibn Daud, *History of Rome*, 23, and Cohen, *Book of Tradition*, 83 and 114.

obeying the commandment not to marry foreign women.³⁴ For Ibn Daud, the great sin of the Hasmonean kings Hyrcanus and Alexander Yannai was that they "led Israel astray from the traditions of the prophets to the lies of the Sadducees."³⁵ "The lies of the Sadducees" are related to the lies of the Cutheans (Samaritans), a foreign nation, and both heresies are the origin of the Karaite heresy, a refusal to accept the authority of the rabbis and rabbinic law.³⁶ Ibn Daud, observing the pattern he found in the fall of the Hasmonean monarchy, the later generations of which bore foreign names, may have interpreted the foreign names of the Kozivan kings as a sign of the same process of decay.

This does not mean, of course, that Ibn Daud rejected foreign thought and culture as such. Like many other Andalusian Jews of his time, he had acquired an education in the Greek sciences and philosophy and saw no inherent conflict between them and his rabbinic inheritance; he applied Aristotle's thought to the Bible and used the Latin chronicles to understand Jewish history. Yet Ibn Daud did distinguish between mere correlation and actual heresy, which was the corruption of those inherited doctrines and laws. One of the main purposes of *The Book of Tradition* was to demonstrate, against the claims of the Karaites, that the truths and precepts in possession of the rabbis had never been altered or corrupted.³⁷ Moreover, Ibn Daud shows that in the long history of Israel, those Jews who had corrupted this inheritance had never prospered: the Karaites had remained an insignificant minority, and the Hasmonean kings had come to ruin when they rejected "the traditions of the prophets." Foreign culture was therefore permissible, even useful, but only so long as the rabbinate remained the final arbiter of Jewish life; the Hasmoneans had ignored the sages and "led Israel astray," crossing that boundary from synthesis to conflict and corruption.³⁸ In addition, since the Rufus of rabbinic literature is an ideological opponent of R. Akiba, Ibn Daud may have understood this as evidence of Ben Koziva's fall into heresy. What I am suggesting, therefore, is that Ibn Daud explained the

---

34. Ibn Daud, *History of the Kings*, 29. Cf. *Yosippon*, Venice and Mantua eds., ed. A. Wertheimer (Jerusalem, 1956), 102–3.

35. Ibn Daud, *History of the Kings*, 33–34.

36. On Karaism and its relevance to Ibn Daud, see Cohen, *Book of Tradition*, xliii–l. For fuller treatments of Karaism, see Leon Nemoy, *Karaite Anthology* (New Haven, 1952), and Salo W. Baron, *A Social and Religious History of the Jews*, vol. 5.

37. Cohen, *Book of Tradition*, prologue and epilogue, 3–4, 91–103.

38. Foreign names in *The Book of Tradition* often seem to accompany such corruption. Few rabbinic heroes in the work bear foreign names, in contrast to the Karaite villains Al Qirqisani, Abu 'l-Taras, and Abu 'l Farag.

rise and fall of the Kozivan kings along the lines of the pattern he found in the history of the Hasmonean kings. The names Rufus and Romulus meant to him that the Kozivan monarchy, like the Hasmonean, had fallen into corrupt ways and false beliefs, and had come to its ruin for this reason.

The history of the Kozivan monarchy would then have a practical import for Ibn Daud's own day. Like the story of the Hasmoneans, that of the Kozivas supported Ibn Daud's polemic against the Karaites, whom he considered the greatest internal Jewish threat of his time, and stood as a warning against intellectual heresy, against rejection of rabbinic doctrine and authority by the growing number of philosophical skeptics in the Jewish community of Spain.[39]

Another lesson Ibn Daud found in the story of the Kozivas, identified already by Cohen, is revealed by his statement that the death of the sages and the calamity of Betar were caused by "the provocation [ka'aso] of Ben Koziva." Ibn Daud uses the same word in describing the rebellion of the Zealots: they "provoked" (hik'isuhu) Rome into an angry reprisal. In *The History of the Kings of the Second Temple*, Ibn Daud declares that the Zealot El'azar b. Ananias "brought all the woes by his insurrection against the Roman procurator and by seducing the Jews to rebellion." Had the Zealots tolerated Nero's oppression until his death, "Vespasian and Titus would have ruled them with kindness . . . and would have set up Jewish kings over them." In the end, Jerusalem was destroyed "not by its enemies but by its lawless ones [periṣim]. Come and see how much more harmful the periṣim of Israel were for them than the periṣim of foreign nations."[40]

Of course, Ibn Daud does not portray the Kozivas as outlaws killing wantonly or attacking the Pharisees as did the Zealots. The Kozivas do nothing that is inherently evil unless it be in the form of an ideological downfall indicated by their names. The primary sin of the Kozivas, however, was causing the harm that resulted from the very act of rebelling against Rome.[41] As the Zealots had provoked Rome into destroying the Temple, so the Kozivas had provoked Rome into devastating the population of Judea after conquering Betar—"a greater affliction than had ever been seen or heard before, even in the times of Nebuchadnezzar and Titus."

---

39. See Cohen, *Book of Tradition*, 300, and Yitzhak Baer, *A History of the Jews in Christian Spain*, trans. Louis Schoffman (Philadelphia, 1966), chaps. 5, 6, 9, and 12.

40. Ibn Daud, *History of the Kings*, 54; Cohen, *Book of Tradition*, 9.

41. The name Romulus may have implied the same message. As a typical Roman name, it may have suggested an emulation of the Roman ideals of empire and military might, of political power rather than trustful waiting.

Ibn Daud is thus asking his readers to wait patiently for God to act. Rebellion, taking matters into one's own hands, only made conditions worse. Koziva should have tolerated Rome, just as contemporary Jews should tolerate the present Muslim and Christian powers until the Messiah actually comes. In teaching this lesson from the history of the Kozivas, Ibn Daud is repeating the message of the rabbinic legends, which also taught political quietism and warned against forcing the end. But Ibn Daud speaks of the anger of the nations instead of the anger of God: he has changed the primary realm of historical action from Israel's relationship with heaven to Israel's relationship with the nations.

This message implies that Ibn Daud sensed an impatience among the Jews of his time, an impatience that he feared might break out into active messianic revolt. Indeed, he had probably received reports of a number of messianic claimants who had appeared in Europe, northern Africa, and the Middle East during the eleventh and twelfth centuries. One of these men, Ibn Aryeh, was recognized as the Messiah by a group of Jews in Cordova around 1117; a decade later, a certain Moses al Dar'i traveled around Andalusia proclaiming the arrival of the Messiah and urging Jews to prepare for their journey to the Land of Israel.[42] But we have no record of an actual armed rebellion breaking out among the Jews of those centuries. Apparently, then, Ibn Daud was thinking more of the intense messianic expectations that seem to have been prevalent among the scholar-courtiers of his own class and perhaps also among the Jewish masses. The first and second crusades had been waged in Palestine, and Muslims and Christians were battling over control of Spain itself. The Almohades, a militant sect of pious Muslims from North Africa, had recently invaded Spain, forcing large numbers of Jews, Ibn Daud among them, to flee to the Christian-dominated north. Jews such as Abraham bar Ḥiyya viewed these events as the final showdown between the two great world powers, Islam and Christendom, before the advent of redemption.[43] Cohen writes, "At no other time in the history of the Jews after the second century was there such a concentration of messianic speculation and of vigorous reaffirmation of the messianic

---

42. Baer, *History of the Jews* 1:65–66. Abba Hillel Silver, *A History of Messianic Speculation in Israel* (New York, 1927), 76–80; Baron, *Social and Religious History* 5:197–205; Gerson D. Cohen, *Messianic Postures of Ashkenazim and Sephardim* (New York, 1967), 19–21; Stephen Sharot, "Jewish Millenarianism: A Comparison of Medieval Communities," *Comparative Studies in Society and History* 22 (1980): 394–415, esp. 396 n. 10.

43. See Joel Kraemer, "On Maimonides' Messianic Posture," in *Studies in Medieval Jewish History and Literature*, ed. Isadore Twersky (Cambridge, 1984), 2:117.

hope." In evidence Cohen points to the writings of the Jewish courtier-scholar class, of men such as Solomon ibn Gabirol, Abraham ibn Ezra, Abraham bar Ḥiyya, Moses ibn Ezra, and Abraham ibn Daud himself, all of whom expressed great interest in the coming of the Messiah and many of whom tried to calculate the date of his arrival.[44] Yitzhak Baer similarly identifies an "awakening of messianic hopes" that affected "the souls of the simple masses and the communal leaders alike."[45]

Ibn Daud seems himself to have engaged in messianic speculation and, as we shall see, he intended his writings to sustain messianic hope among the Jews of his day. But his comments about the results of Koziva's "provocation" show that he also recognized the dangers of actual armed rebellion. The lesson he discovered from the sufferings of Betar was that although one may, indeed one must, continue hoping for the Messiah, one must never take military action to achieve the messianic goals. (In fact, most of the few messianic movements of Ibn Daud's time seem to have followed this policy: groups of Jews would acclaim a man the Messiah but never actually rebel against the government.)

Yet Ibn Daud interpreted the wars of the Kozivas as more than acts of rebellion of the Zealot type. Not only did he discover in the chronicles a widespread messianic movement, but he seems also to have discovered good reasons for people to have believed Koziva to be the Messiah. His account of the events shows the Kozivas fulfilling most of the major messianic expectations. (1) Koziva claimed to be a descendent of David. (2) He freed Israel from the yoke of Rome and reestablished a Jewish monarchy, ruling Israel as its king—this being the core of all messianic expectations. (3) Koziva "fought great wars with all the nations"—another role assigned the Messiah by most eschatological literature, as, for example, we saw in the Targum's renditions of Num. 24:17. Ibn Daud elsewhere speaks of a great final war to be waged against Gog and Magog, eschatological figures typically envisioned as leading the assembled nations of the world against the Messiah.[46] Koziva's "great wars with all the nations" suggests such a battle. (4) "There were gathered [neqabeṣ] to Koziva and his sons a very great number of Israelites who returned from all their dwelling places." This refers to the final ingathering of the exiles (qibbuṣ galuyot). The Amidah prayer of the traditional prayerbook uses the same verb (qabeṣ) in praying for

---

44. Cohen, *Book of Tradition*, 288.
45. Baer, *History of the Jews* 2:65.
46. Ibn Daud, *History of the Kings*, 62–63.

the return of the exiles. (5) Finally, in his *History of Rome*, Ibn Daud describes violent earthquakes and heavenly portents occurring "in the days of Hadrian," so that "all the inhabitants of the world trembled and lost their strength and were dumb, for the Lord was of a mind to overturn the world." People perceived these phenomena as signs of the end of days and the messianic travails—another familiar eschatological motif.[47]

If, then, as it appears, Ibn Daud explained these events as a messianic movement and describes its leader as a man exhibiting all the attributes of the Messiah, what did Ibn Daud want his readers to learn from the story? On the one hand, as Cohen suggests, the story shows how easily one may be mistaken by appearances. Koziva's early successes were merely accidental, occurring because of the immaturity of Domitian; only when Hadrian later overpowered Romulus could people know that Koziva was not the Messiah. This perspective on the events, along with Ibn Daud's forceful statement on the final consequences of "provocation," warns readers to act cautiously in deciding whether to believe a messianic claimant.

But on the other hand, I think that Ibn Daud's account acts to defend the mistake of those who believed Koziva, rather than, as Cohen argues, to condemn them. Cohen's only evidence for his theory is Ibn Daud's citation of Dan. 11:13, and the verse is open to several meanings. Abraham bar Ḥiyya, as Cohen notes, does interpret it as a condemnation, but Abraham ibn Ezra and Samuel bar Hofni, from the same period, do not.[48] The verse from Daniel may represent simply a continuation of the main line of interest in *The Book of Tradition*, the history of the rabbis, showing how they, too, suffered with everyone else at the fall of Betar.

The story makes more sense as a defense of the rabbis than as a condemnation, and for two reasons. First, a condemnation would contradict the central intention of *The Book of Tradition*, which was to reply to Karaite

---

47. On the eschatological signs, see the medieval apocalyptic texts in Even-Shmuel, ed., *Midreshei Ge'ulah*. Raphael Patai's *The Messiah Texts* (New York, 1979) contains useful translations, esp. 145–88 on the messianic signs. The preceding analysis of the ways Koziva and his sons fulfilled messianic expectations derives in outline from Cohen's interpretation, *Book of Tradition*, 240–50.

48. Cohen (1967:242) asserts that Ibn Daud read Dan. 11:33 as a statement of cause-and-effect: *because* the sages caused the many to know (i.e., publicized their messianic speculations), they stumbled by the sword (were punished for this sin). Although this is indeed the way Abraham bar Ḥiyya read the verse (*Megillat Ha-Megalleh*, ed. A. Poznanski [Berlin, 1924], 100), at least two other medieval exegeses of the same verse refer to the martyrdom of the sages of R. Akiba's generation without any suggestion that their death was a divine punishment or that any sin was involved: H. J. Matthews, ed., "Abraham Ibn Ezra's Shorter Commentary on Daniel," in *Miscellany of Hebrew Literature* (1877), vol. 2, 13; and Samuel bar Hofni's letter in A. E. Cowley, ed., "Bodleian Geniza Fragments," JQR 18 (1906), 405.

polemics. The principal Karaite contention was that the body of rabbinic laws and doctrines not found in Scripture had been fabricated by the sages. In reply, *The Book of Tradition* argues that the entire tradition in possession of the rabbinate had been transmitted to the ancient sages through an unbroken chain originating with Moses at Sinai and, furthermore, that it had then been transmitted without distortion to the present generation of rabbis. The reason Ibn Daud asks his readers to believe that the sages had never lied about or distorted this tradition was that they were men of high character who had brought great benefit to the nation. He tries to demonstrate this through history while also showing that the Karaites were mean characters who had never benefitted anyone.[49] The incident of Ben Koziva, however, could undermine this argument, since opponents of the rabbinate could point to R. Akiba's support for Koziva as proof of the rabbis' irresponsible and unreliable leadership. Rather than agreeing with the Karaites (even implicitly, as Cohen suggests), we would expect Ibn Daud to be defending R. Akiba, and this defense seems to consist of showing that, in light of Koziva's military successes and reestablishment of the monarchy, and with the return of the exiles and appearance of supernatural portents, R. Akiba's mistake was justified: Koziva had exhibited all the markings of the Messiah.

We learn from Ibn Daud's portrayal of the Kozivas that he conceived of the Messiah in a fairly naturalistic (i.e., Aristotelian) manner. The Messiah's advent may be heralded by heavenly portents and the date may be calculable from biblical prophecy, but he himself is basically a human king who performs tasks of a political and military nature, without recourse to miracles and superhuman powers. This makes Ibn Daud's concept of the Messiah similar to that of Maimonides, as we shall see; and one problem with a naturalistic messiah is that he is harder to identify than a messiah who works miracles. Maimonides explicitly discusses this problem, how one can determine whether a man who appears to be performing the essential roles of the Messiah while exhibiting no miraculous powers is in fact the true Messiah.

This is the second reason I disagree with Cohen. Ibn Daud was fully aware of the disaster that resulted from the sages' support of Koziva, but he could not hold the sages responsible because the Messiah, in Ibn Daud's concept, cannot be immediately distinguished from a temporarily successful rebel.

The history of the Kozivan rebellion had thus a further relevance for the Andalusian Jews of the twelfth century, a community agitated by religious

---

49. Cohen, *Book of Tradition*, prologue and epilogue; and Cohen's exposition, lviii-lxii.

schism, messianic excitement, and impatience with the continuing powerlessness of Jewish life. Karaite polemicists could point to the sages' involvement in the Kozivan rebellion as evidence for the disastrous misguidance of the rabbinate; and the event itself, showing how messianic hopes had been disappointed in the past, questioned the validity of those very hopes. But these were not the final meanings that Ibn Daud discovered in the event. His story of the rebellion stood, first, as a warning against the dangers of armed "provocation," urging patience and political restraint upon his readers, and it earnestly cautioned them about messianic claimants. At the same time, it indirectly defended the role played by the rabbinic leadership in the rebellion, avoiding overt mention of R. Akiba while implicitly exonerating him and his generation for their misjudgment.

The Midrash on the Ten Exiles, appended by Ibn Daud at the end of his *History of the Kings of the Second Temple*, suggests two final meanings Ibn Daud found in the story of the Kozivas. This work, of obscure origin, recounts the "ten exiles by which Israel was exiled: four by the hand of Sennacherib, four by the hand of Nebuchadnezzar, one by Vespasian, and one by Hadrian, blasted be his bones." Regarding the tenth exile, the author says that Hadrian destroyed Betar and exiled Israel to "Aspamya," which is Spain, and then quotes Obadiah 20: "And the exile of Jerusalem that is in Sefarad"—with "Sefarad" being understood here as Spain. We may infer, then, that one reason Ibn Daud wrote such a long account of the Kozivas is that the story had special meaning to him as a Spanish Jew. It explained the origin of the Spanish Jewish community and spoke specifically to Spanish Jews about the particular sins that had led to the exile of their foreparents.

But in addition to this message of warning, there are reasons to think that Ibn Daud also found in the story of Betar a message of hope and comfort.[50] For the Midrash on the Ten Exiles concludes with the statement, "Just as God decreed upon us this exile, so in the future he will surely bring us back." Ibn Daud follows up this statement with his own personal declaration of eschatological hope, arguing that because the House of David had not appeared in the time of the Second Temple, nor had the war of Gog and Magog, or the other events of redemption, they were for this very reason "sure to come in the future."[51] Applied to Koziva, who claimed to be of the House of David, this means that precisely because Koziva was not the Messiah, precisely because

---

50. He speaks often of the duty of giving comfort, *neḥamot*, to Israel: Cohen, *Book of Tradition*, 20, 100, 103; Ibn Daud, *History of the Kings*, 62.
51. Ibn Daud, *History of the Kings*, 60–63.

he failed in the messianic tasks—just for this reason were there real grounds for messianic hope. Moreover, an idea occurring frequently in medieval Jewish apocalyptic writings was that Israel would be redeemed only after it had endured ten calamities;[52] and if Ibn Daud interpreted the Midrash in this way, Betar would represent the cause of Israel's last exile, the event that made redemption possible in Ibn Daud's time.

Bar Kokhba in the *Mishneh Torah* of Maimonides

Bar Kokhba enters the writings of Moses b. Maimon (1135–1204) as a proof of messianic doctrine and as an event remembered on the Ninth of Av. Both references to Bar Kokhba appear in the *Mishneh Torah*, Maimonides' codification of Jewish law completed around 1180 in Fostat. Unlike most earlier codes, the *Mishneh Torah* included extensive discussions of laws of correct belief.[53] Indeed, the first two precepts listed are those of knowing that there is a God and of not thinking that there is any God except the Lord. Likewise, among the laws concerning kings at the end of the last book of the *Mishneh Torah*, there appear laws of correct belief about the messianic king. Believing in the Messiah and awaiting his coming are said to be fundamental teachings of the Torah and the Prophets.[54] Here, in the course of defining these messianic doctrines, Maimonides refers to R. Akiba's proclamation of Bar Kokhba, adducing it as evidence for what to believe about the Messiah:

> Let it not enter your mind that the King Messiah needs to work signs and wonders and to bring novel things into the world and to revive the dead and similar such things. The matter is not so, for look at the case of R. Akiba, who was one of the great sages of the Mishnah and yet was an armor-bearer (*no-se kelav*) of Ben Koziva the king. He would say about him that he was the King Messiah, and he and all the sages of his generation held the opinion that he was the King Messiah, until he was killed in his iniquities. When he was

---

52. Noted by Cohen. See Even-Shmuel, ed., *Midreshei Ge'ulah*, 311–23.
53. For a detailed discussion of Maimonides' goals in writing the *Mishneh Torah*, see Isadore Twersky, *Introduction to the Code of Maimonides (Mishneh Torah)* (New Haven, 1980), 61–81.
54. Moses ben Maimon (Maimonides), *Mishneh Torah*, "Laws Concerning Kings" 11.1.

killed, it was known to them that he was not [the King Messiah]. Yet the sages had not asked from him either sign or wonder.[55]

Bar Kokhba as Evidence for Messianic Doctrine

Maimonides has introduced the example of Ben Koziva in order to refute the belief that the Messiah must perform miracles. As pointed out by Gershom Scholem and Isadore Twersky, Maimonides was surely thinking of the popular images of the Messiah that we find reflected in medieval apocalyptic literature and in the claims made by contemporary messianic pretenders.[56] These apocalyptic books, whose popularity is attested by the large number of extant manuscripts, generally envisioned the Messiah as a warrior and holyman exhibiting supernatural powers. He is pictured, for example, riding on clouds, arrayed in brilliance; waging war against the wicked and killing great multitudes at once; resurrecting the Messiah ben Joseph, the Patriarchs, and even Adam; and transforming the world's landscape.[57] The messianic claimants of the time behaved in ways that presupposed similar images of the Messiah, for they usually sought to prove their authenticity through miracles; and it was primarily miracles that convinced people to believe them. Maimonides mentions a number of such incidents in his *Epistle to Yemen*. Jews in Isphahan acclaimed a certain man the Messiah because his leprosy was cured overnight; Moses al-Dar'i tried to prove his messianic prophecies through miraculous predictions, such as the one that blood would fall from the sky like rain; and a claimant in Linon convinced people by gliding from tree to tree on moonlit nights.[58] The specific ideas to which Maimonides objects—"that the King Messiah needs to work signs and wonders and to bring novel changes into the world and revive the dead"— are to be found, therefore, in the apocalyptic literature and popular messianic movements of the time.

Maimonides replies with a syllogism based on the assumption that R. Akiba's concept of the Messiah is valid evidence for correct messianic

---

55. Ibid. 11.3.
56. Scholem, "Toward an Understanding of the Messianic Idea in Judaism," in *The Messianic Idea in Judaism* (New York, 1971), 29–32; Twersky, *Introduction*, 450–51, esp. n. 231.
57. Even-Shmuel, ed., *Midreshei Ge'ulah:* "Midrash Va-Yosha," 97; "Pirqei Ha-Mashiah," 388; "Alphabet of R. Akiba," [Heb.] 331; "Sefer Zerubbavel," 83, 88; "Midrash Zuta" to Song of Songs, 326–27; "Story of Daniel," 226. Cf. Patai, *Messiah Texts*, 153–55, 174–78, 202–3.
58. Maimonides, *Epistle to Yemen*, ed. Abraham S. Halkin (New York, 1952), 98–103.

doctrine. Maimonides argues that (1) because R. Akiba and the sages thought Ben Koziva was the Messiah, (2) even though he had performed no miracles, (3) it is therefore unnecessary for the Messiah to perform miracles. Ben Koziva had exhibited all that was essential in the Messiah, and this did not include supernatural powers.

Bar Kokhba thus served Maimonides as evidence for a naturalistic concept of the Messiah. In the *Mishneh Torah*, in the *Treatise on Resurrection* (written in 1191), and in the general tendency of the *Commentary on the Mishnah* (1168), Maimonides conceives of the Messiah as a king who fulfills his role through immanent human abilities, however highly developed these may be. Even the Messiah's power of prophecy, "approaching [the rank of] Moses our teacher,"[59] and his ability to perceive a person's ancestry by means of the Holy Spirit,[60] which is one form of prophecy, are not conceived as miraculous powers but as naturally developed human capacities to apprehend "the wisdom of God as displayed in His creatures"[61]—or, as formulated in *The Guide of the Perplexed*, the capacity to apprehend the divine emanation mediated through the natural functioning of the active intelligence.[62] In Maimonides' concept, the Messiah differs from other people only in excelling in virtues that they too can attain—wisdom, righteousness, piety, and prophecy. His essential tasks are basically political and pastoral: leading Israel in the observance of the Torah, restoring the monarchy, rebuilding the Temple, fighting the wars of the Lord, and gathering the exiles, all of which are accomplished without recourse to miraculous powers.[63] The principal change that redemption will bring for the life of Israel, moreover, will be simply the freedom from foreign rule, and "the accus-

---

59. *Mishneh Torah*, "Laws of Repentance" 9.2.
60. Ibid., "Laws of Kings" 12.3.
61. Ibid., "Principles of Torah" 7.1.
62. Maimonides, *Guide of the Perplexed*, trans. Shlomo Pines (Chicago, 1963), 2: 36–43. See Menachem M. Kellner, "Maimonides and Gersonides on Mosaic Prophecy," *Speculum* 52 (1977): 62–79, with studies listed in n. 7.
63. See the extensive discussion of Maimonides' concept of the Messiah in Kraemer, "On Maimonides' Messianic Posture," esp. 128–42. Kraemer concludes that Maimonides conceived of the Messiah as "king, sage and prophet" having endowments that were natural but "transcended the disposition of the ordinary run of mankind." Kraemer's most interesting contribution is his argument that Maimonides saw the Messiah as restoring the *milla fadila*, "virtuous community," an Arabic term echoing Alfarabi. That is, Maimonides' Messiah is to restore the glory and wisdom of the Jewish polity and the primordial intellectual perfection of humankind. See also David Novak, "Maimonides' Concept of the Messiah," *Journal of Religious Studies* 9 (1982), 42–50, which argues that Maimonides "de-apocalypticizes" the traditional rabbinic doctrines of the Messiah.

tomed order of the world will not be abrogated nor creation renewed, but the world will follow its normal course."[64]

In the *Treatise on Resurrection*, written eleven years after the *Mishneh Torah*, Maimonides distinguished between two types of miracles: (1) those that violate the order of nature, such as the parting of the Red Sea or the earth swallowing up Koraḥ, and (2) miracles deriving from possibilities inhering in nature (*moftim . . . b'inyanim ha'efsharim beteva*), such as the hail and locusts that afflicted Egypt.[65] Miracles are thus defined as exceptional events brought about by God either as an interruption of the normal course of nature or indirectly, through intermediate causes within nature. In *The Guide of the Perplexed* (1190), Maimonides spoke of just one kind of miracle, that which changes the nature of matter only temporarily and in a particular form, so that the world retains the essential nature given to it by God at the time of creation.[66] (This concept of miracles thus corresponds to the second type of miracle defined in the *Treatise*.) An example in the *Guide* of God working his will in such a way is the manner by which God abolished idolatry among the Jews—not through a radical transformation of human nature but through a gradual transition by way of Temple sacrifices.[67]

Thus, when Maimonides says in the *Mishneh Torah* that the Messiah need not work miracles, he is defining "miracles" in accordance with what he would later, in the *Treatise*, distinguish as the type of miracle that violates nature, the first of the two types. It may be, as Amos Funkenstein suggests, that Maimonides conceives of redemption as a miraculous event in the second sense of the term, a transformation deriving out of contingencies present in history and brought about indirectly by God—since redemption does involve radical changes. The nations will all acknowledge God, war and famine will cease, and people will live longer and in greater comfort.[68]

---

64. *Mishneh Torah*, "Laws of Kings" 12.1. See "Laws of Repentance" 9.11 and *Ma'amar Teḥiyat Ha-Metim* (*Treatise on the Resurrection of the Dead*), ed. Joshua Finkel (New York, 1939), par. 30, pp. 20–21. See also the extensive discussion in Aviezer Ravitsky, " 'Kefi Koaḥ Ha-'Adam—Yemot Ha-Mashiaḥ Be-Mishnat Ha-Rambam," in *Messianism and Eschatology*, ed. Zvi Baras (Jerusalem, 1983), 191–220.

65. Maimonides, *Ma'amar Teḥiyat Ha-Metim*, par. 48, p. 34. For a discussion of Maimonides' theory of miracles, see Ralph Lerner, "Maimonides' Treatise on Resurrection," *History of Religions* 23 (1983), 140–55, esp. 153 on the above passage.

66. Maimonides, *Guide* II:47, 48. Also II:25, 29.

67. Ibid., III:32.

68. Amos Funkenstein, "Maimonides: Political Theory and Realistic Messianism," *Miscellanea Mediaevalia* 9: 81–103. Funkenstein proposes that Maimonides conceived of redemption as a case of "divine accommodation." On the changes brought by redemption, see "Laws of Kings" 12.5 and Commentary on *Ḥelek*, trans. in *Maimonides Reader*, ed. Isadore Twersky (New York, 1972), 414.

But Maimonides does not conceive of these changes, extraordinary as they are, as miracles that interrupt the basic order of nature, and these changes do not require a Messiah who achieves them through supernatural means. This explains why Ben Koziva, whom Maimonides pictures as a man possessing natural human powers, could have been thought to be the Messiah. The Messiah develops out of the "raw material" of history, and Ben Koziva was an example of such potential messianic material.

In one of Maimonides' writings, however, the *Epistle to Yemen* written eight years before the *Mishneh Torah*, there appears a concept of a Messiah who performs miracles like the Messiah of apocalyptic literature. The *Epistle* explicitly describes the Messiah performing signs and wonders (*'otot umoftim*): he proves his authenticity through them and they have the effect of frightening the nations into submission. Maimonides also envisions great tribulations and the cataclysmic war of Gog and Magog occurring in those days, and generally pictures redemption as a radical interruption of history.[69] We might explain the differences between the *Epistle* and the *Mishneh Torah* as a progression in Maimonides' ideas or from differences in the audiences and purposes of the two writings. In either case, Maimonides could not have likened Ben Koziva to the Messiah of the *Epistle to Yemen*. His image of Ben Koziva is compatible only with the *Mishneh Torah*'s concept of a Messiah who works within history to effect change through immanent political processes.

The "Great King" of Betar

Bar Kokhba enters the *Mishneh Torah* also in connection with the Ninth of Av. He appears in a chapter devoted to historical fast days, that is, fasts commemorating national calamities (*ṣarot*) of the past. These are the fasts of the Third of Tishri, the Tenth of Tevet, the Seventeenth of Tammuz, and the Ninth of Av, and, on a less important level, the Thirteenth of Adar. Maimonides explains that the purpose of these fasts is to "awaken the heart and open paths of repentance" by recalling to mind "the evil deeds of our fathers, which resemble our deeds now," that caused the tribulations of the past as well as the present. Thus, "through the memory of these things," and an awareness of "our evil deeds," "we shall repent and do good."[70]

---

69. Maimonides, *Epistle to Yemen*, 90–93. Kraemer (1984: 130) notes these differences without attempting to explain them. See also Twersky, *Introduction*, 450–51 and n. 233, and Ravitsky, 206–7.
70. *Mishneh Torah*, "Laws of Fast Days" 5.1.

Maimonides then explains the significance of the various fast days, giving the most attention to the Ninth of Av and then, of the events commemorated on the Ninth of Av, to the story of Betar.

> And the Ninth of Av: five things happened to [Israel]. The decree was issued upon Israel in the wilderness that it should not enter the Land. The Temple was destroyed the first and second times. A great city named Betar was captured, and in it were thousands and myriads of Israelites, and they had a great king (*melekh gadol*) whom all Israel and the greatest sages thought was the King Messiah, but he fell into the hands of the Romans and all of them were slain, and it was a calamity as great as the destruction of the Temple. And on that day destined for misfortune, Turnus Rufus the Wicked plowed up the Temple and its surroundings, in fulfillment of what was said: *Zion shall be plowed as a field* (Micah 3:12, Jer. 26:18).[71]

Although Maimonides does not name the "great king" of Betar, the reference to Ben Koziva is obvious. Two themes stand out in this account of Betar—first, the glory and power of the "great city," with its "great king" and multitude of inhabitants, and then, in contrast, its fall and the slaughter of all its people, a calamity comparable in magnitude to the destruction of the Temple itself. This story of the lost glory of a kingdom and the slaughter of myriads is Maimonides' principal example of the tribulations remembered on the Ninth of Av.

A fairly clear image of Bar Kokhba emerges from these two references in the *Mishneh Torah*. First of all, he is described as a "great king," "Ben Koziva the king." Like Rashi and Ibn Daud earlier, Maimonides imagined Bar Kokhba as a king, indeed as a powerful and impressive one, a *melekh gadol*. Maimonides' term *melekh* implied the dignity and duties of legitimate kingship set forth in the "Laws of Kings" of his *Mishneh Torah*. Maimonides further states that R. Akiba, "all the sages of his generation," and "all Israel" "held the opinion that he [Ben Koziva] was the King Messiah." And since Maimonides' argument about the nature of the Messiah depends on the assumption that R. Akiba and the sages held the correct concept of him, we must infer that Maimonides thought that Ben Koziva really had exhibited the character and actions of the Messiah (or to be precise, of a tentative messiah, as I shall explain). One of these actions was to have established the

---

71. Ibid. 5.3.

Davidic monarchy, which is what Maimonides would have meant in calling Ben Koziva a "king."

Maimonides states in "Laws of Kings," that Ben Koziva "was killed in [his] iniquities" (*ba'avonot*). Maimonides is surely referring to iniquities reported in the rabbinic legends, but in which legends? Ben Koziva's sin in the Babylonian Talmud differs from his sin in Midrash Lamentations and the Jerusalem Talmud. Rabbi Abraham ben David of Posquieres (known as the Rabad) thought that Maimonides was alluding to the story in the Babylonian Talmud in which Bar Koziva claims to be the Messiah and is killed by the sages when they discover that he is not. His sin, in Rabad's opinion, was that of being a false claimant. But there is reason to question this explanation. Maimonides would not have considered Ben Koziva sinful for having thought he was the Messiah after R. Akiba had proclaimed him as such and all the sages had agreed. Moreover, the legends in Midrash Lamentations support better Maimonides' statement that Ben Koziva "was killed in his iniquities," because they use the same word, *'avonot*, that Maimonides uses, and they expressly say that Ben Koziva was killed because of his sins— *'avonot garmu*: "[his] iniquities caused it . . . and Ben Koziva was killed." It therefore seems likely that Maimonides was referring to Ben Koziva's sin as told in Midrash Lamentations, that of killing R. El'azar. It was to this sin, and not to the sin of being a false messiah, that Maimonides attributed Ben Koziva's downfall.

The sin in the second account of Betar, in "Laws of Fast Days," might also appear to be that of claiming to be the Messiah, especially since Maimonides seems to suggest a causal connection by first telling how people thought their king was the Messiah and then describing the terrible calamity they suffered. Furthermore, the purpose of the fast days by his definition is to remind the congregation of the sins that caused the tribulations of Jewish history, and misjudging Ben Koziva certainly led to Betar's tribulation. Nevertheless, if this were the central sin in the story, the goal of the Ninth of Av would be defeated. For the whole point of Maimonides' explanation of the fast days is that they remind people of sins which they themselves commit, the universal recurring sins of daily life, so that people might "repent and do good"; and misjudging a messianic claimant is not such a sin. Maimonides does not even use the opportunity to attribute a single wrong to the "great king" of "Laws of Fast Days." Rather, the sins that caused Betar's downfall must have been of a category common to all the calamities commemorated by the fasts: "the sins of our fathers, which resemble our sins"—that is, the recurrent individual sins that delay redemption.

Only the recollection of sins like these would bring worshippers on the fast days to "repent and do good." In connection with Betar, the lesson seems to be, therefore, that this great and powerful city, with its king who had every appearance of being the Messiah, was captured and destroyed because of Israel's sins, the same sins that Jews today continue to commit, and further, that Jews can never have a king so long as they persist in their sinful ways.

Maimonides' image of Ben Koziva is derived from those rabbinic sources noted in the first chapter of this book. Seder Olam and the Christian chronicles show up not at all. The idea that Ben Koziva was a king derives from R. Akiba's declaration and from the legend in b. Sanhedrin; the idea of R. Akiba's support for Ben Koziva (being his "armor bearer") and the idea of Ben Koziva's sins derive from Midrash Lamentations; and the idea that all the sages considered him the Messiah is an interpretation of the fact that the only reported objection came from one insignificant rabbi. Maimonides synthesized these various items into an image of Ben Koziva that explained why R. Akiba would believe him to be the Messiah—which means a Messiah who does not work miracles but succeeds through political and moral strength. Maimonides could have interpreted as a supernatural power Ben Koziva's ability to catch catapult stones and hurl them back at the enemy, as described in Midrash Lamentations; but he chose not to, and probably understood the motif as a metaphor for military strength. Later writers, in contrast, sometimes understood it as a literal description of supernatural powers.

The Tentative Messiah

In *Sefer Zerubbavel*, the Messiah makes his identity known instantly by resurrecting the Messiah ben Joseph,[72] but the Messiah as described by Maimonides does not have to perform miracles. How, then, is he to be recognized? In the same chapter of "Laws of Kings" in which Maimonides refers to Ben Koziva, the philosopher sets forth the identifying character traits and actions of the Messiah. They all relate to political and pastoral roles and distinguish him from other men only in the degree of his success. Moreover, since he need not work miracles and so cannot prove himself in a flash of certainty like the messiah of *Sefer Zerubbavel*, recognition requires a period of time. He appears at first like any other human king and only gradually, as he works within history to accomplish his tasks and begins to

---

72. Even-Shmuel, ed., *Midreshei Ge'ulah*, 83.

achieve what no other king could do, does his identity become known. In Maimonides' view, this process of recognizing the Messiah consists of two stages: tentative assumption and certain knowledge.

> If there arise a king from the House of David who meditates on Torah and occupies himself with the commandments as prescribed in the Written and Oral Torah, as did David his father, and compels all Israel to walk in it [the way of Torah] and to repair its breaches, and fights the wars of the Lord—behold, this man **may be assumed** to be the Messiah. If he does these things and succeeds, and builds the Sanctuary on its site, and gathers the dispersed of Israel—behold, this man is **with certainty** the Messiah. But if he does not succeed this far, or is killed, then it is evident that this man is not the one whom the Torah promised, and behold, he is like all the true and worthy kings of the House of David who died. The Holy One, Blessed be He, raised him up only to try the multitude, as it is said: *And some of those who are wise will err, in order to refine them* [the multitude] *and to cleanse and purify them, up until the time of the end, for he* [the Messiah] *is yet for the appointed time* (Dan. 11:35).[73]

A man must fulfill the requirements listed in order to be considered tentatively the Messiah. Now, Maimonides' argument about miracles is based on the assumption that R. Akiba is an authority for correct belief about the Messiah and that he knew how to identify the Messiah. He had identified Ben Koziva. It follows, therefore, that in Maimonides' view, R. Akiba had acted correctly in identifying Ben Koziva as the Messiah—but from what we just read in "Laws of Kings," we must infer that Maimonides interpreted R. Akiba's proclamation as a tentative assumption made about a messianic candidate.

Moreover, since Maimonides thought that R. Akiba had acted properly in identifying Ben Koziva as the Messiah, Maimonides must further have supposed that Ben Koziva had fulfilled all the qualifications required for a tentative assumption. Two of these qualifications are plain to see. First, Maimonides considered Ben Koziva a king; and second, Ben Koziva had fought the Romans, which could be interpreted as "fighting the wars of the Lord." But Maimonides also had to assume that Ben Koziva had fulfilled the rest of the qualifications required for R. Akiba's tentative assumption.

---

73. *Mishneh Torah,* "Laws of Kings" 11.4; emphasis mine.

This means, specifically, that Ben Koziva had to be a descendant of David, that he studied Torah and obeyed the commandments fully, and that he had prevailed on all Israel to do the same.

If Ben Koziva had exhibited such character traits and had accomplished such tasks in Israel's behalf, then it must follow, finally, that Maimonides considered him in the category of "the true and worthy kings of the House of David," mentioned at the end of the same passage, who tried and failed to accomplish the messianic tasks.

All in all, we may conclude that Maimonides considered Ben Koziva a true king of Israel who had merited R. Akiba's initial support by restoring the Davidic kingship and conducting himself in the proper manner, and yet a king who had failed ultimately to complete his messianic tasks because he was not sufficiently worthy of them, his "iniquities" having caused his downfall.

One additional implication follows from Maimonides' concept of "the worthy kings of the House of David" who failed to redeem Israel. Maimonides says that God "raised them up only to try the multitude," and then quotes Dan. 11:35 (translated here according to Maimonides' reading of it)—"And some of those who are wise will err, in order to refine them [the multitude] and to cleanse and purify them, up until the time of the end, for he [the Messiah] is yet for the appointed time." Maimonides interprets this verse in reference to the sages who erred by supporting "worthy kings" who later turned out not to be the Messiah. Their mistake resulted in great suffering for the multitudes. Maimonides' idea about "trying the multitude" appears to be an answer to objections that could be raised not only against his principles for identifying the Messiah but also against the sages who had erred by following these principles. How could Maimonides justify the suffering that had resulted from every messianic movement stirred up by the "worthy kings" who had appeared to be the Messiah and were identified as such by the sages? How could it be permissible to identify a man tentatively as the Messiah before he had achieved lasting success? The example of Betar raised this question more forcefully than did any of the later messianic movements, especially the minor affairs mentioned in Maimonides' *Epistle to Yemen*.

Maimonides replies that the failure of messianic candidates represents in reality a process of refinement and purification. Each failure ultimately advances the will of God by preparing Israel for the king who finally does succeed. Maimonides does not explain how these failures prepare Israel, but we could suppose that this preparation occurs as a natural process, such as the self-examination and new resolve, the winnowing out of those too easily discouraged, or the learning and clarification that could emerge through each failure of a messianic movement. This idea is reminiscent of Maimonides' metaphor of the "divine ruse" mentioned in *The Guide of the Perplexed* and fits his general understanding of the way God works in history: indirectly, without violating the course of nature, using the contingencies of history cunningly to advance God's will.[74] By this viewpoint, Maimonides (like the God he describes) has turned the failure of messianic movements into cause for hope.

Rather than blaming the sages for their mistakes, Maimonides thus ascribes these episodes to the mysterious will of God.[75] It was God who had chosen to "raise up" "true and worthy kings" who genuinely merited the tentative assumption of being the Messiah. It was also God who works in ways that made the Messiah difficult to recognize at first, for God effects redemption only gradually and only by means of the raw material of history, a king with essentially human powers. Therefore, it is this naturalistic process of redemption that allows the sages to err, and yet it is also this process that turns their errors into a means of purification. In relation to R. Akiba, this implies that Maimonides could not condemn him for declaring Ben Koziva tentatively the Messiah, because it is the mysterious will of God that raises up a potential messiah like Ben Koziva who might either succeed or fail in completing his messianic tasks. Whatever the outcome, however, redemption would be advanced.

On the other hand, Maimonides clearly implies that Jesus of Nazareth would not have qualified under the rules of "Laws of Kings" to be considered even tentatively as the Messiah; the mistake his followers made in believing in him could therefore have been avoided:

> Also about Jesus of Nazareth, who held the opinion that he would be the Messiah but was killed in the courthouse—already Daniel had

---

74. Maimonides, *Guide* III:32. On "the Deity's wily graciousness and wisdom" (Pines' translation, 252), see Pines' introduction to *Guide*, lxxi-lxxiv; and Funkenstein, "Maimonides," 92.

75. Likewise, speaking about Jesus of Nazareth, Maimonides asserts that God turned even this mistake, with its dire consequences for correct belief, into a means of furthering "the designs of the Creator" (*maḥshavot ha-bore*): "It is beyond the human mind to fathom the designs of the Creator.... All these matters relating to Jesus of Nazareth and the Ishmaelite who came after him [Muhammad] only served to clear the way for the King Messiah and to prepare the whole world to worship God with one accord"—by making the world familiar with the messianic hope, the Torah, and the commandments, though in a diluted form (*Mishneh Torah*, "Laws of Kings" 11.4, in Yemenite ms. and Rome, Amsterdam, and Soncino editions). See Twersky, *Introduction*, 452–53.

prophesied about him, as it is said: *And men of violence shall raise themselves up over the people in order to establish a vision, but they shall fail* (Dan. 11:14). And is there a greater failing than this, that all the prophets said that the Messiah would redeem Israel and deliver them and gather together their dispersed and strengthen their obedience to the commandments, but this man caused the destruction of Israel by the sword and the scattering and humiliation of their remnant and caused the Law to be changed and the majority of the world to turn aside to worship a god other than the Lord?[76]

As portrayed by Maimonides, Ben Koziva and Jesus were alike in having been thought to be the Messiah and having failed in their attempts. But Maimonides considers Jesus' failing the greater. For whereas Ben Koziva merited R. Akiba's support by actually accomplishing some of what the Messiah was destined to do, Jesus, by contrast, had caused just the opposite to occur. Jesus neither deserved nor received the support of the sages. Seen against Maimonides' condemnation of Jesus, his positive image of Ben Koziva emerges the more clearly.

Political Implications

The Ben Koziva legends in Midrash Lamentations and the Jerusalem Talmud teach political quietism, warning listeners not to take part in military attempts to gain national freedom; and the legend in b. Sanhedrin promotes a skeptical attitude toward messianic claimants. Ibn Daud's account likewise discourages armed rebellion, even though it apparently defends the sages for thinking Koziva was the Messiah.

Maimonides likewise, in his *Epistle to Yemen*, takes a sternly skeptical position toward messianic claimants, demanding that they prove their authenticity by performing true miracles, conquering the nations of the world, and exhibiting charismatic gifts of prophecy, learning, and leadership. No ordinary man could meet such criteria, and certainly not the messianic claimant of Yemen, whom Maimonides describes as a demented lunatic.

But Maimonides' image of the Messiah in the *Mishneh Torah* is less

---

76. *Mishneh Torah*, "Laws of Kings" 11.4 (Yemenite ms. and Rome, Amsterdam, and Soncino eds. only). As with Ibn Daud's citation of another verse form Daniel, there is no indication from Maimonides' citation of Dan. 11:35, either from the context or by comparison with medieval commentaries, that he meant any criticism of the sages.

exalted and his criteria different. He adduces the example of Ben Koziva to illustrate from a historical model what the minimally essential features of the Messiah are, and these do not include performing miracles or the immediate conquest of the world.[77] Ben Koziva earned the support of R. Akiba by being "a true and worthy king" who won initial successes in reestablishing the political sovereignty of Israel. These criteria shift the burden of proof into the political realm by requiring clear evidence of significant changes in military power, government, and the geography of Jewish life.

What would be the practical intention of such criteria? Twersky has shown that one of Maimonides' main goals in writing the *Mishneh Torah* was to make clear the philosophic and moral meaning of the law. Maimonides did this by demonstrating throughout how the laws aimed (in Twersky's words) "to discipline the human faculties, quell evil impulses, subdue inclination to vices, discipline the moral disposition, and advance the individual toward ethical-intellectual perfection." Such an exegesis of the laws accords with the theory of their general purpose that Maimonides sets forth later in *The Guide of the Perplexed*—which was to promote "the welfare of the soul and the welfare of the body" by teaching true beliefs, inculcating moral virtues, and fostering the bodily health and social framework that enable people to pursue intellectual and spiritual perfection.[78] Kraemer has argued, in addition, that Maimonides perceived these goals in an eschatological context, hoping that his books would help the Jewish community prepare itself for the coming of the messianic era. Maimonides apparently believed, on the basis of an old prediction preserved by his family and through observation of the world's turbulent political conditions, that the times were appropriate for the appearance of a true Messianic King.[79] Nevertheless, the *Epistle to Yemen* and the writings we studied from the *Mishneh Torah* show that Maimonides also recognized the physical dangers and false beliefs engendered by the apocalyptic expectations and messianic movements of the period.

Maimonides' laws for recognizing and proclaiming the Messiah express these ideological and social concerns. On the one hand, the laws for the Messiah assume and promote the expectation of a Messiah who will fulfill

---

77. See Scholem, "Messianic Idea," 29–30, on Maimonides' criteria for identification of the Messiah, and Kraemer, "On Maimonides' Messianic Posture," 135–36, on Maimonides' "test of the Messiah's authenticity" and the roles of Jesus and Muhammad in the ultimate process of redemption.

78. Twersky, *Introduction*, 432 and 61–81; Maimonides, *Guide* III:27.

79. Kraemer, 109–24. See also Silver, *Messianic Speculation*, 74–76.

the general goals of the laws as understood in the *Mishneh Torah*. He does this by establishing the orderly society that those laws legislate so that Jews and eventually the whole world will gain the security and leisure necessary to pursue the highest spiritual and intellectual insights of which they are capable. This is the main purpose of the messianic era, according to "Laws of Kings": enabling "Israel to be free to devote itself to the Law and its wisdom, with no one to oppress and disturb it." "The one preoccupation of the whole world will be to know the Lord."[80] On the other hand, Maimonides' laws for proclaiming the Messiah disqualify claimants who ignore those practical goals of the law, who offer miracles in place of the individual effort and meditation that the *Mishneh Torah* affirms. By making political achievement the principal criterion of messianic authenticity, Maimonides neutralizes all apolitical claims, however miraculous the proofs offered.

The *Mishneh Torah* thus allows and even encourages active support for a person who makes material progress in achieving these final, practical goals of the laws—which certainly implies armed rebellion at some stage. Maimonides lays out in plain view the procedure for deciding a claimant's validity, on the assumption that rabbis will voice their decision publicly and the community will obey. If the rabbis accept a man tentatively as the Messiah, the community is expected to provide active support. At the same time, however, Maimonides carefully restricts the possibilities of such public support by placing heavy obstacles in the way of a claimant's qualification for rabbinic endorsement. The man must exercise impressive intellectual and moral leadership while also achieving significant military successes—and must do so, apparently, before the rabbis endorse him and thus without their support. The community must wait passively for such a leader to appear and then cannot act as a whole until events have reached a critical stage, when the rabbis have sufficient evidence to judge him. The final effect of such rules, consequently, is to encourage an attitude that values political activism over a passive waiting for miracles and yet responds to acts of political assertion with cautious, studied judgment.

Thus, the image of Ben Koziva in the *Mishneh Torah*, which is the image of a potential messiah, implies a definite role for human action in the process of redemption. The messianic candidate must take practical action consonant with the social goals of the laws, and the rabbis must judge and

---

80. *Mishneh Torah*, "Laws of Kings" 12.4, 12.5, from Abraham Hershman, trans., *Code of Maimonides: Book Fourteen, The Book of Judges* (New Haven, 1949), 242.

then support or oppose him. But Maimonides ultimately ascribes the advent of potential messiahs to the mysterious will of God; and he limits the role of the community to a slow, circumspect response to events already underway.

Changes in the Image of Bar Kokhba

Rabbinic literature portrayed Bar Kokhba under two distinct aspects—the charismatic hero of Midrash Lamentations and the false messiah of the Babylonian Talmud. The images of Bar Kokhba in *The Book of Tradition* and the *Mishneh Torah* represent a synthesis of these two rabbinic traditions, linked together by the assumption that Bar Kokhba's heroism was what aroused messianic hopes. Ibn Daud adds new elements to the rabbinic traditions by attributing to the leadership of Bar Kokhba the widespread uprisings reported in the chronicles—which has the effect of magnifying Bar Kokhba's heroism even further.

Compared with the proud, hot-tempered warrior of Midrash Lamentations, however, the medieval Bar Kokhba lacks particular personality. He is a sober, competent king seen distantly through the eyes of his rabbinic supporters, whose viewpoint Ibn Daud and Maimonides champion. For unlike the rabbinic legends, which portray the sages primarily as opponents of Bar Kokhba, Maimonides and Ibn Daud assume that the sages all supported him. To Ibn Daud, however, this presents a major problem in that R. Akiba's mistake seems to undermine Ibn Daud's argument for rabbinic authority in *The Book of Tradition;* for this reason, addressing a polemical issue that did not greatly disturb the rabbinic storytellers, Ibn Daud turns the story of Bar Kokhba into a defense of R. Akiba.

This suggests that the most significant changes in the image of Bar Kokhba have to do with changes in the story's purpose and context. In Midrash Lamentations, the story was associated with the Ninth of Av and seems to have served the ritual function of expressing grief and bringing about repentance; and in the Babylonian Talmud, the story was part of a discussion of eschatological doctrine. Ibn Daud, however, thrusts Bar Kokhba into the midst of contemporary controversies with the Karaites, Christians, and Muslims of twelfth-century Spain, and his primary concern is to defend rabbinic authority. Maimonides, on the other hand, continues to associate Bar Kokhba with the Ninth of Av and messianic doctrine, but he reaches conclusions about messianic doctrine that are the opposite of the

Talmud's. In the Talmud, the story of Bar Kokhba functioned as an example that proved, by way of contrast, that the Messiah would have miraculous powers, whereas in the *Mishneh Torah,* the example of Bar Kokhba functions to refute this very idea, and the argument is directed against the images of the Messiah found in medieval apocalyptic literature and popular expectations. It is also worth noting that the Bar Kokhba of the *Mishneh Torah* is thoroughly rationalized: he is a point in an argument, an example in an explanation, and merges totally into the overall abstract system of Maimonides' code of law. The account of Betar appearing in "Laws of Fast Days" constitutes an abstraction from, a rationalized reformulation (in a sense, a codification) of, the sprawling collection of legends found in Midrash Lamentations.

Another difference between the rabbinic and medieval stories lies in the way they speak of God. The legends of Midrash Lamentations and the Jerusalem Talmud take an explicitly theological viewpoint: they explain history in relation to acts of divine intervention (R. El'azar's prayer, the Heavenly voice, the snake), and explain Bar Kokhba's fortunes in relation to his attitude toward God. But neither Ibn Daud nor Maimonides expressly mentions God. In Ibn Daud's story, the overt causes of Bar Kokhba's success and then failure are changes in the balance of military power; and Maimonides explains Bar Kokhba's failure through unspecified "iniquities" (which Maimonides himself probably gives a naturalistic interpretation).

It would nevertheless be wrong to conclude that these writers have completely secularized the story of Bar Kokhba, because, for one thing, they retain the basic categories against which the life of Bar Kokhba was traditionally understood—the categories of rabbinic authority (the transmission of revelation), eschatological doctrine, and the ritual themes of the Ninth of Av; and also because, though they do not conceive of God breaking directly into the events of history, there are definite indications that they thought God had acted upon the life of Bar Kokhba, even if at a distance. Ibn Daud seems to have implied this through his use of the significant number twenty-one, and possibly also in connection with the Midrash of the Ten Exiles; and Maimonides attributes the rise of potential messiahs to the mysterious will of God working within history to redeem Israel. Thus, the reason that our two writers do not mention God explicitly in telling the story of Bar Kokhba is that they conceive of God acting through intermediate causes and immanent forces, without interrupting the order of nature. Ultimately, both writers do take a theological viewpoint, but one influenced by medieval Aristotelian ideas.

The medieval images of Bar Kokhba, then, retain a significant element of continuity with the rabbinic images. The story of Bar Kokhba continues to be told as part of the sacred history of rabbinic tradition and the history of God's involvement with Israel—the central subjects of traditional Jewish historical thought; and his life also continues to be associated with religious doctrine, the belief in the Messiah. Indeed, the medieval accounts rationalize these religious topics in a way that emphasizes them more than the rabbinic legends did.

Finally, let us take note that Ibn Daud and Maimonides express an attitude no less ambivalent toward Bar Kokhba than those we found in the rabbinic legends. For Ibn Daud, Bar Kokhba stood as a warning against support for any messianic claimant. Maimonides likewise spoke of the suffering that results from messianic movements, including the endeavors of Bar Kokhba, and he tried to reduce this danger by discovering laws that made support for even a tentative messiah unlikely. Yet Bar Kokhba had also manifested characteristics of the true Messiah to come. I have argued that Ibn Daud used Bar Kokhba's resemblance to the Messiah as evidence in his defense of rabbinic authority. For Maimonides, this resemblance became evidence for correct messianic doctrine; Bar Kokhba was a potential messiah, raw material that might have become the actual Messiah and almost did so.

The two sides of Bar Kokhba were, therefore, first, his actual resemblance to the Messiah, but at the same time, the disappointment and suffering to which this resemblance led. Yet for Maimonides, even this suffering had its redemptive outcome. Hence, although these images of Bar Kokhba differ in significant ways from the rabbinic, the medieval writers express toward him a similar combination of misgivings about the past, coupled with hope for what he signified for the future.

3
Abravanel's Image of Bar Kokhba

The sixteenth century was a period relatively rich in writings that mention Bar Kokhba, and it will be these writings, pushing older traditions of Jewish thought and scholarship in several new directions, that will occupy our attention in the final three chapters of this study.

We begin with Isaac Abravanel (1437–1508), Jewish communal leader, advisor to royalty, and prolific writer, who lived through the Spanish expulsion of 1492. Abravanel wrote biblical commentaries, philosophical tracts, and books of polemical argument and messianic speculation. Bar Kokhba appears in this last category of writings. I shall argue that Abravanel turned Bar Kokhba's story from a polemical embarrassment into a cause for renewed messianic hope, an example for the dejected Jews of the expulsion. Failure and defeat disappeared from the story, as Bar Kokhba became an avenging knight and herald of the Messiah.

The Polemical Context

One of the main types of argument against which Abravanel worked to defend Judaism developed only after the time of Maimonides. Amos Funkenstein traces its first expression to a French philosopher of the late twelfth century, Allain de Lille, who tried to prove that Jesus of Nazareth was the Messiah on the basis of statements from the Talmud. This type of proof—adducing evidence from within rabbinic tradition, from the Talmud and midrashic collections, in proof of Christian doctrine—came to be one of the principal lines of argument used by Christian polemicists during the following centuries, as their efforts to convert Jews became increasingly systematic, vigorous, and hostile.[1] We find the argument adopted by the Spanish Dominicans associated with Raymond de Penaforte; Pablo Christiani used it in the disputation at Barcelona in 1263, as did Raymond Martini in his comprehensive polemical tract, *Pugio Fidei* (1278), which became the standard manual for proving Christian doctrine from the Talmud. Later Christian polemicists, such as Abner of Burgos in the late thirteenth century, Nicholas of Lyra in the fourteenth, and Joshua Ha-Lorki, who cited rabbinic texts in the disputation of Tortosa in 1413–14, all made use of the argumentation in *Pugio Fidei*.[2]

It was expressly to defend Jewish doctrine against this type of Christian argument that Abravanel wrote the book in which Bar Kokhba appears, *Salvations of His Anointed* (*Yeshu'ot Meshiḥo*), in 1497. In it Abravanel collects all rabbinic passages dealing with eschatological subjects, classifies them according to four issues raised by Christian polemicists—whether the Messiah has already come, whether he has been born, whether he is divine, and whether the Torah will be abrogated—and then systematically refutes the Christian interpretation of these passages. *Salvations of His Anointed* is thus a polemical manual belonging in the same category as the *Sifrei Niṣṣaḥon* and Profiat Duran's *Kelimat Ha-Goyim*, but it focuses upon narrower topics and sets them forth in more comprehensive and systematic form.

---

1. Amos Funkenstein, "Basic Types of Christian Anti-Jewish Polemics in the Late Middle Ages," *Viator* 2 (1971): 373–82.

2. See Jeremy Cohen, *The Friars and the Jews* (Ithaca, N.Y., 1982), 103–69, for a comprehensive treatment of the ideas and writings of what he identifies as "the school of Raymond de Penaforte"—a specific group of friars, most notably Pablo Christiani and Raymond Martini, who developed a particularly hostile form of anti-Jewish polemical argument which saw rabbinic Judaism as a satanic heresy that had to be extirpated from Christian lands. On Abner of Burgos and Ha-Lorki, see Yitzhak Baer, *A History of the Jews in Christian Spain*, trans. Louis Schoffman (Philadelphia, 1961), 1:167–68, 2:181–210.

In the book's introduction, Abravanel explains his reasons for writing *Salvations*. First, he saw "the Christians bringing the sages of Israel before kings, to dispute with them, and speaking wickedly about God and Moses," claiming the Messiah would not redeem the Jews. "And our sages had trouble replying to those outlaws [Jewish converts], who argue unfairly and use heretical books." Abravanel blamed the inadequacy of Jewish polemical manuals for the present difficulties, so that "our sages stumble over the rabbinic sayings, both minor and important ones." But Abravanel also saw the despair of his people, "suffering from their expulsions and exile, crying out, 'Why does not he, the son of Jesse, come to establish his kingdom? Why is he late?' " From such doubts about the Messiah, some concluded that he would never come and that "the sun of justice and healing will never arise." In response to the first problem, of polemics, Abravanel offered *Salvations* as an effective guide for answering Christian arguments. In response to the second, his people's despair, he tried to encourage them by promising the immediate arrival of the Messiah, in evidence of which he revealed and argued a date hidden in rabbinic literature. That date was 5263 (1503 C.E.).[3]

He wrote two other eschatological works in which he presented other evidence for this date. The three books, all written between 1497 and 1499, share the same polemical purpose of defending messianic doctrine and strengthening messianic hope. They each argue that, contrary to Christian claims, the messianic prophecies of Jewish tradition have not yet been fulfilled and were consequently promised for the future, the date of which had definitely been revealed. In *Wells of Salvation (Ma'yenei ha-Yeshu'ah)*, Abravanel demonstrates this argument in connection with the Book of Daniel, and in *Announcer of Salvation (Mashmi'a Yeshu'ah)*, in connection with the rest of Scripture. Considered together, these three books represent an impressive attempt to fashion the many diverse messianic allusions of Jewish tradition into a single comprehensive and self-consistent system of eschatological doctrine, defensible against Christian attack and pointing to the immediate future for its fulfillment.

Abravanel wrote these messianic tracts during a time of widespread millennial expectations among the Christian inhabitants of the Italian states. He was writing in Monopoli, harbor to the Venetian armada in the Italian war against Charles VIII. Wandering prophets preaching imminent destruction had appeared in the 1480s and early 1490s; new apocalyptic texts were

---

3. Isaac Abravanel, *Yeshu'ot Meshiḥo* (Koenigsberg, 1861; reprint, Jerusalem, 1967), 4a–5b, 12b.

composed and classic texts were copied and spread; Savanarola, preaching in Florence, hailed Charles as Last World Emperor, destined to purify the Church and fight the final wars of the Lord. Benzion Netanyahu, in his major study, *Don Isaac Abravanel: Statesman and Philosopher* (1953), speculates that the same events that aroused Christian millennial hopes, namely, Charles VIII's invasion of Italy, the struggle against him involving much of Western Europe, and the ominous rise of Turkish power to the East, confirmed Abravanel's belief in the Messiah's imminent arrival.[4]

In the background of Abravanel's messianic and polemical efforts, Netanyahu also pictures a grave crisis of Jewish faith. He argues that three hundred years of Christian ideological attack had weakened the faith of many Jews, causing some to convert and others to despair of the Messiah's coming. For Jews, Netanyahu remarks, messianic hope had immediate practical implications, because messianic redemption was the only solution they could see for their weakening political status among the European peoples. Especially, after the last three hundred years of physical and economic suffering, with various Jewish communities of Europe destroyed or expelled or forcibly converted—most notably the large Spanish and Portuguese communities—Jews were increasingly vulnerable to thoughts that God had deserted them, that Christian claims were true, or even that faith was irrelevant to their situation.[5] Netanyahu judges Abravanel's messianic writings essential to the sustaining of Jewish hope during the sixteenth century:

> The historic task accomplished by Abravanel in reviving Jewish self-confidence and national hopes can be correctly estimated only if we visualize this state of affairs. It was Abravanel who, with powers of imaginative thought perhaps incomparable in the entire messianic literature, restored Jewish faith in salvation, and thus not only demonstrated the worth-whileness of the Jewish struggle for survival in his own time, but also gave meaning and purpose to the entire historic course of the Jewish people.[6]

---

4. Bernard McGinn, *Visions of the End: Apocalyptic Traditions in the Middle Ages* (New York, 1979), 277–79; McGinn, trans., introduction to *Apocalyptic Spirituality* (New York, 1979), 183–91; Stephen Sharot, *Messianism, Mysticism, and Magic: A Sociological Analysis of Jewish Religious Movements* (Chapel Hill, 1982), 66–68; Benzion Netanyahu, *Don Isaac Abravanel: Statesman and Philosopher* (Philadelphia, 1953), 74–76.

5. Netanyahu, *Abravanel*, 199–202.

6. Ibid., 202. But notice Netanyahu's tendency toward nationalistic interpretation—"national hopes," "Jewish struggle for survival," and "historic course of the Jewish people," categories translatable only with qualification to this period of Jewish thought. Further evidence is needed for

The Problem of Bar Kokhba's Story

Bar Kokhba's story, however, containing R. Akiba's proclamation, threatened to topple Abravanel's elaborate structure of eschatological doctrine. The proclamation seemed to undermine, first, the authority of the sages, and second, one of the central theories on which that structure was built.

It undermined rabbinic authority because, being a serious misjudgment of the truth, it brought into question the reliability of rabbinic teachings and leadership in general and particularly in regard to the Messiah. Although the records of the great disputations provide no evidence that Christian debaters had cited R. Akiba's proclamation in their attacks on Judaism, *Pugio Fidei* did clearly declare R. Akiba "a martyr for the devil" for having followed "Bar Cosba" in a satanically inspired act of madness. In Raymond Martini's view, the Jews' rejection of Jesus and subsequent acceptance of not one but two false messiahs named Bar Cosba constituted a clear demonstration that the rabbinic leaders had abandoned both God and reason. R. Akiba's support for Bar Kokhba thus became in *Pugio Fidei* a primary example of the spiritual blindness of the rabbis, the fundamental falsehood of their teachings, and hence the heresy of rabbinic (and thus, contemporary) Jewish doctrine as a whole.[7] This text was well-known in the sixteenth century and Abravanel was likely familiar with its arguments.

Moreover, the specific way in which Abravanel himself conceived of the authority of the sages, treating all rabbinic opinions as expressions of a unified and self-consistent system of doctrine, meant that a challenge to any one element of that system threw the entire system into question. Abravanel takes pains to demonstrate in *Salvations* that all the eschatological statements of the Talmud and midrashic collections are mutually consistent teachings. In particular, he tried to prove that the problematic statements from the sages adduced by Christian polemicists, far from contradicting traditional Jewish hopes for the Messiah, in fact fully confirmed those hopes. One example of such a statement is the so-called *vaticium Elliae* of the Talmud, the *locus classicus* for the Christian argument trying to prove Christian doctrine from Talmudic traditions. This particular tradition, an apocalyptic periodization of history attributed to Elijah, declares that the

---

Netanyahu's thesis of the effectiveness of Christian polemics among the Jews of this period as well as his claim for the influence Abravanel's writings wielded on the Jewish communities.

7. Cohen, *Friars and Jews*, 143, 146–47, 151. On Martini's notion of two false messiahs named Bar Cosba, the second appearing forty-eight and a half years after the first, see 143.

world would last 6,000 years, of which 2,000 would be a period of chaos, 2,000 the period of the Torah, and the final 2,000 years the period of the Messiah, unless sins delayed it.[8] From the account of the Tortosa debate recorded in *Shevet Yehudah*, we learn how Christian polemicists turned this tradition into a proof that Jesus was the Messiah. They argued that if the period beginning with the fifth millennium (240 C.E.) represents the days of the Messiah, then the Messiah must already have come and could be none other than Jesus of Nazareth, whose followers began to succeed in spreading his faith only in the third century.[9] The problem posed for Jewish debaters was therefore as follows: if the *vaticium Elliae* were true, it would seem to validate Christianity or at least confuse Jewish messianic hopes, but if it were false, how could it be logically differentiated from valid rabbinic traditions?

Abravanel's position regarding problematic statements such as these (and he included R. Akiba's proclamation in this group) is set forth in its clearest form in his introduction to the second part of *Salvations*. Here he writes that earlier Jewish debaters had dealt with these problematic statements in three different ways: (1) some had tried to prove that the statements at least did not refer to Jesus of Nazareth, even if their full meanings could not be explained; (2) others had altogether denied their validity, on the grounds that a faithful Jew need not accept the *aggadic* (non-legal) portions of the Talmud; and (3) still others had tried to solve the difficulty by allegorizing the statements into Greek philosophical ideas irrelevant to eschatology. But Abravanel objects to all three approaches—the first, because it leaves the saying unexplained, and the third, because allegorization is wrong. He disagrees with the second position (that taken by Yeḥiel of Paris and Naḥmanides) because in his view, everything the rabbinic sages said contains "superior wisdom" and manifests the spirit of God. "The great sages of Israel commanded all the treasures of knowledge and had correct judgment that never failed." To discount anything they said would therefore desecrate Heaven, and then "what honor and what respect would be left to us for the Fathers of Testimony?" Concluding that "one must accept the words of the sages" absolutely and throughout the Talmud, Abravanel proceeds to demonstrate in *Salvations* that despite any

---

8. B. Sanh. 97a.
9. Solomon Ibn Verga, *Sefer Shevet Yehudah*, ed. M. Wiener (Hanover, 1924), 70, 72. See Baer's summary of the Tortosa disputation, *A History of the Jews in Christian Spain* 2:170–243, esp. 177 on the rabbinic legend in question.

apparent contradictions or errors, every single rabbinic statement was true, binding, and in full accord with the rest of Jewish messianic tradition.[10]

It was from this statement of position that Abravanel had to explain R. Akiba's messianic proclamation of Bar Kokhba. Where was the "correct judgment that never fails"? Could he admit error in R. Akiba's actions without thereby undermining the authority of all the sages?

The second problem posed by Bar Kokhba's story, and the specific one that occupied Abravanel's explicit discussion of Bar Kokhba, was that R. Akiba's messianic proclamation appeared to discredit what Abravanel called the "Three Time Periods," one of the central theories upon which his messianic exegesis and defense of Jewish doctrine were built. To understand how important this concept was for Abravanel, let us examine one additional rabbinic tradition that was often the subject of Christian-Jewish debate. This legend also quotes Elijah, who reveals yet another messianic date. It declares that the world will last no less than eighty-five jubilees (until 490 C.E.) and that the Messiah will come during the last jubilee, that is, during the last fifty years (b. Sanh. 97b). Christian polemicists asserted that the eighty-fifth jubilee corresponded precisely to the time when Christianity had established its dominion, thereby proving Jesus to be the Messiah.

To counter such interpretations and to reconcile such traditions with Jewish messianic doctrine as he understood it, Abravanel proposed his concept of the Three Time Periods (*sheloshah gevulei zemanim*), to which he refers repeatedly in *Salvations*. This idea can be traced back to a line of argument employed by R. Joseph Albo during the disputation in Tortosa.[11] Abravanel's version postulates that God decreed three periods of time governing the Messiah's arrival. During the first period, the Messiah could not possibly come; during the second, his coming was possible but only if Israel repented fully of its sins; and during the last period, his arrival was inevitable and necessary.[12] Compared with the Mishneh Torah's concept of an imminent redemption developing (with God's help) out of the political and military achievements of a messianic candidate, Abravanel's concept, like many of the apocalyptic books of an earlier time, pictures redemption as a transcendently ordained event conforming to a predetermined scheme of history.

---

10. Isaac Abravanel, *Yeshu'ot Meshiḥo* 4a, 16b–17b.
11. Solomon Ibn Verga, *Shevet Yehudah*, 71.
12. See Abravanel, *Yeshu'ot Meshiḥo* 11b–12a, 18b–19a, for the most detailed explanations of the theory.

Abravanel argues that the first of the three periods, being a punishment analogous to the Egyptian bondage, lasted 400 years, counting from the destruction of the Temple in 3829 (69 C.E.). Hence, the period of impossibility lasted until 4229 (469 C.E.). Applying these calculations to the Elijah legends, with certain numerical adjustments, Abravanel concludes that it was to the year 4229, the beginning of the period of messianic possibility, that the two legends referred. They were not saying that the Messiah would actually arrive in the fifth millennium or the eighty-fifth jubilee, but merely that after this date it was possible for him to arrive. (It was therefore impossible for Jesus, born so many years earlier, to be the Messiah.) The concept of the Three Time Periods appealed to Abravanel as the only reasonable explanation for the Elijah traditions, and he found support in other rabbinic sayings, Genesis 15, and Pirqei d'R. Eliezer, which he connected to the concept through a form of analogical reasoning typical of messianic calculations.[13]

Abravanel used the same method to explain the whole series of rabbinic sayings that date the Messiah's arrival within the Talmudic period. Christian polemicists had interpreted these dates as references to the time of Christianity's triumph, but in each case, Abravanel counters with his concept of the Three Time Periods, arguing on its basis that all these sayings spoke only of the second messianic period, the time of mere possibility, beginning in 4229 (469 C.E.), so that contrary to Christian belief, the Messiah could not have come earlier than this date. Abravanel's theory of the messianic periods thus functioned as a cornerstone for his messianic exegesis and his primary means of defending Judaism against a major type of polemical attack.

We now understand the significance that R. Akiba's proclamation held for Abravanel. It implied that R. Akiba thought the Messiah could have arrived during the time that Abravanel claimed it to be impossible. Were R. Akiba's assumption to be accepted, Abravanel's entire scheme of messianic periods would be discredited, thereby allowing anew the possibility that Jesus was the Messiah. Here is what Abravanel says about R. Akiba's proclamation and the story in the Babylonian Talmud (b. Sanh. 93b) of the sages testing Bar Koziva to learn whether he could "judge by smelling":

> Now, this matter is very surprising, because it occurred in Betar before the completion of the eighty-five jubilees, still within the period that precluded [the coming of the Messiah]. So how, then,

13. Ibid. 11b–12a, 18a–21b.

could the sages of Israel think that Ben Koziva might be the King Messiah? And R. Akiba—"a counselor and master of esoteric knowledge, expert in secret lore" [Isa. 3:3]—how could he err in this, that he was his armor-bearer (*no-se kelav*), and how could he think that, when the time precluded the coming of the Messiah, it nevertheless was the time for him to come?[14]

Abravanel had somehow to explain R. Akiba's proclamation in such a way as to save the time periods without thereby undermining rabbinic authority or opposing what Abravanel believed to be R. Akiba's superior knowledge of the hidden ways of God, as expressed in this passage.

Abravanel's Solution: The Yearning for Redemption

Abravanel's solution takes the form of a theoretical reconstruction of R. Akiba's thinking, showing both what was valid and what was faulty in it. Abravanel was not the first writer to analyze R. Akiba in this way: a legend in Midrash Lamentations had tried to reconstruct his thought when it stated, "On account of this [Ben Koziva catching catapult stones], R. Akiba said what he said"; and Ibn Daud may have shaped his story in a way that explained why R. Akiba had supported Koziva. Abravanel's analysis carries on this approach but does so in a manner typical of medieval scholastic argument and even, to a degree, of modern academic research. He analyzes R. Akiba's statement through a systematic exegesis, raising and resolving questions. He tries to separate his own views and feelings from those of R. Akiba, and uses both Jewish and Latin literary sources in an unconcealed manner to illuminate R. Akiba's motivation. Without claiming beforehand to know the answer, Abravanel constructs two hypotheses and then tests their validity. He tries to imagine what R. Akiba was thinking at a historical moment of time, lacking the later hindsight that Abravanel possesses. This is the same manner in which Abravanel interprets the historical books of the Bible, reading them as official documents written to serve the immediate needs of the court at a specific time in history.

In interpreting R. Akiba's proclamation, Abravanel shows that R. Akiba had good reasons for thinking that Bar Kokhba was the Messiah, whether

14. Ibid. 30b.

Davidic or Josephite. But Abravanel goes on to demonstrate that however valid these reasons, and even without historical hindsight, R. Akiba could nevertheless have known, as the other sages of his generation surely did, that Bar Kokhba was not the Messiah.

> It appears to me that in the matter of Ben Koziva, R. Akiba had one of the two [following] ideas about him.
>
> The first, that when he saw Ben Koziva's military success, he thought that the Holy One, Blessed Be He, had hastened the end of the exile determined and decided and decreed by him, and had regretted his decree, because before they entered exile it was easier to rescind the decree, as he had wanted to do with Hezekiah his Anointed.[15] Similarly, Chapter 29 of Pirqei R. Eliezer says that even though the decree for the Egyptian exile was [originally] for 400 years, they stayed there only 210 years, in accordance with the numerical value of the word *redu* in *go down there* [Gen. 42:2], because the Holy One, Blessed Be He, for the sake of the holy patriarchs and holy matriarchs, hastened the end, as it is said, *leaping over the hills* [Cant. 2:8].[16] Therefore, R. Akiba thought that Ben Koziva was the Messiah, despite it being the time precluding him, because [he thought that] the Holy One, Blessed Be He, in his mercy and in his zeal for his Torah against his enemies, had hastened and "leaped over" that time.
>
> But the rest of the sages of Israel did not accept this from him, and said to him, "Akiba, Akiba, grass will grow from your jaws and the son of David will not yet have come." For they continued to accept that the time precluding the Messiah would pass in its proper time. I have already mentioned above what is written in the Zohar about R. Akiba and R. Eliezer his teacher.[17] As they were walking together on the road, R. Akiba asked, "Why was Adam made only on

---

15. According to b. Sanh. 94a, "The Holy One, Blessed Be He, wanted to appoint Hezekiah the Messiah," but the Attribute of Justice objected.

16. This idea derives from chapter 48 of most editions of *Pirqei d'R. Eliezer*. The "hills" of Song of Songs 2:8 signify the patriarchs and matriarchs; Exod. Rab. 15, 4 cites Micah 6:2 as proof. *Pirqei d'R. Eliezer* reads "leaping over the hills" (*medaleg al he-harim*) in this way: *medaleg* = skipping (the time), *al* = for the sake of, on account of, *he-harim* = the patriarchs and matriarchs. The numerical value of the word *redu* is 210, according to the common system of alphabetical enumeration (*gematriah*). See the English translation of *Pirqei d'R. Eliezer* by Gerald Friedlander (New York, 1965), 374–77.

17. Abravanel, *Yeshu'ot Meshiḥo* 13a, citing Chap. Genesis of the Zohar.

the sixth day?" R. Eliezer replied, "Because in this there was an intimation about the King Messiah, that he would not come until the sixth millennium." But if R. Akiba had known all this according to books and scribes, then there occurred with him something like what often occurs with every wise-hearted man who thinks and believes what his soul yearns and longs to be true. Thus, R. Akiba in his yearning for the salvation of God, when he saw the heroic feats of Ben Koziva and his success in battle, which were unlike the natural way of things, it occurred to him that this was from God and that he had rescinded his decree in order to show mercy to his people. Perhaps, too, Ben Koziva had said that he was of the seed of David; and if he were of the seed of Herod, as Rashi says in his commentary,[18] then there would be grounds for his [Ben Koziva's] claim, because Antipater, the father of Herod, was of the Judean nobility, according to what Joseph ben Gorion wrote, although Antipater's wife was an Idumean.

But see, our rabbis said to him [Ben Koziva], "Of the Messiah it is written that he smells and judges"—this means that among the attributes required of the Messiah ben David are these, that he be a great sage and prophet and that he delight in the fragrance of the fear of the Lord [Isa. 11:3], which is the spirit of wisdom and its attributes. And when they saw that this [wisdom] was not in him, "they killed him"—this means that they sentenced him to die like those who endanger their own lives, and so it was that the Romans killed him when they captured Betar.

The second [possibility] is that R. Akiba did not think that Ben Koziva would be king over Israel and the faithful shepherd guiding them, as the prophets stipulated about the Messiah, because Ben Koziva did not occupy himself at all with judicial matters at Betar, which is the role specifically assigned to the King Messiah, as it is said, *and with righteousness shall he judge the poor* [Isa. 11:4] and it says, *till he establishes justice in the land* [Isa. 42:4]. Rather, Ben Koziva would submit to the sages and listen to what they decided, as is mentioned in Midrash Lamentations Rabbati. Also, R. Akiba was aware that the King Messiah would be of the seed of David and that Ben Koziva in truth was not.

---

18. Rashi, commenting on b. Sanh. 93b, states: "Bar Koziva was one of the kings of Herod."

But it was R. Akiba's thought that Ben Koziva was the battle axe of the Holy One, Blessed Be He,[19] and that he made him in order to wreak vengeance upon his enemies for his people and the blood of his servants. Now see, those sent by the Holy One, Blessed Be He, to destroy his enemies are called "messiahs" (anointed ones) and "servants of the Lord," just as Nebuchadnezzar was called *my servant* [Jer. 25:9, 27:6, 43:10], and because Cyrus destroyed Babylon, it was said, *Thus says the Lord to his messiah Cyrus, whose right hand I have held, to subdue nations before him and undo the might of kings* (Isa. 45:1). And since it was traditionally accepted in the nation that the Messiah ben Joseph would come before the Messiah ben David, not to establish justice and righteousness, but only to fight the wars of the Lord and exact vengeance upon his foes; and Zechariah prophesied that he would die in battle, as it is said, *They shall look upon me, on him whom they pierced, and shall wail over him as over an only child* [Zech. 12:10]; and Scripture did not specify exactly how many years he would live and his wars would last—therefore, when R. Akiba saw the miracles (*nissim*) and the mighty feats (*ha-gevurot*) that Ben Koziva performed in all the Roman lands, he thought to himself that he was the agent (*shaliaḥ*) of Providence, the Messiah of the God of Jacob, concerned only with wars and vengeance upon his enemies. For see, our account of Ben Koziva is told very briefly and only a little part of it is found in the Talmud and Midrashim; however, in Roman history books, I myself saw his many mighty deeds in war and his heroic courage (*gevurat libo*) and his fierceness (*akhzariuto*) against his enemies, and that he went to Alexandria of Egypt and wreaked great vengeance upon the Roman populace there, and swept over all the kingdoms of Egypt and Babylonia, and no man could withstand him, and everywhere he went he would spill the blood of his enemies like water without mercy. They recounted all this in long stories in their books. Therefore, R. Akiba became his "armor-bearer" (*no-se kelav*)—meaning that he did not associate him with matters of justice and Torah study, which are the domain of the Messiah ben David who was yet to come. Rather, he considered him God's Messiah concerned with wars and vengeance alone.

But the rest of the sages of Israel did not accept his opinion that this was the Messiah ben Joseph, nor that his wars and acts of

---

19. Cf. Jer. 51:20—*mapeṣ atah li klei milḥamah*: "You are my battle axe and weapon of war."

vengeance were those destined to occur at the time of redemption, and therefore they said to him the words I cited above: "Akiba, Akiba, grass will grow from your jaws and the son of David will not yet have come." This means: you will die and be buried and grass will sprout up over you many years before the Messiah ben David comes. And it was well known to him [R. Akiba] that the Messiah ben Joseph would come close to the time when the Messiah ben David would come, and would prepare a path for him. Then how could it be thought that Ben Koziva was the Messiah ben Joseph? And who knows whether it was not through this sin that R. Akiba was put to death in a manner more painful than the deaths of the other sages executed by the [Roman] government?

In any case, nothing he did contradicts the periods for the coming of our Messiah which I explained earlier.[20]

Has Abravanel succeeded in solving the problems posed by the story of Bar Kokhba? First he tries to explain how R. Akiba would have been led to believe that Ben Koziva was the Davidic Messiah. Abravanel's primary concern here is with defending the concept of the messianic periods. He begins with the assumption that R. Akiba himself held to this structure of history, and argues that R. Akiba would not have thought the Messiah could come at that time except for two unusual conditions: first, Ben Koziva appeared convincingly to be the Messiah, and second, R. Akiba knew of two precedents for God's reducing the duration of a decreed period—God had shortened the Egyptian exile and had considered making Hezekiah the Messiah. But this new possibility, that God could have altered the periods to make Ben Koziva the Messiah, weakens Abravanel's argument against his Christian opponents: if God could have altered the periods for Ben Koziva, God could have done so for Jesus. Abravanel therefore argues against this possibility by showing that the rest of the sages unanimously disagreed with R. Akiba, and did so because they believed that the period precluding the Messiah had not been shortened. He further shows that even R. Akiba knew in his heart—having been instructed by R. Eliezer, according to the Zohar—that the Messiah could not arrive at that time.

Abravanel has now upheld the messianic periods, but he had to do so in such a way as not to undermine rabbinic authority. His claim that the other sages were right not only about the messianic periods, but about Ben

20. Abravanel, *Yeshu'ot Meshiḥo* 30b–31b.

Koziva, serves this purpose. As for R. Akiba, who was undeniably wrong about Ben Koziva, Abravanel tries to maintain respect for this sage by arguing that he had erred only for the most persuasive of reasons and worthiest of motives. Setting forth those reasons, Abravanel explains that Ben Koziva displayed supernatural powers and achieved military triumphs that could have come only from God. This, and the likelihood that he was a descendant of David, appeared convincing proof that Ben Koziva was the Messiah ben David. In regard to R. Akiba's motives, Abravanel argues that the sage's yearning for redemption—a worthy motive in itself—was so strong that it overcame his cognizance of the fixed time limits. "There occurred with him something like what often occurs with every wise-hearted man (*kol ḥakham lev*) who thinks and believes what his soul yearns and longs to be true."[21] In pointing to natural tendencies in human behavior and showing the emotions' influence on the intellect, Abravanel asserts a psychological causation. (Modern psychologists might call R. Akiba's thinking "wish-fulfillment" or "projection," but Abravanel avoids a pejorative implication by attributing this tendency to "every wise-hearted man.")

Abravanel thus portrays R. Akiba as a great and yet fallible leader whose mistakes deserve sympathy and even admiration. They were not doctrinal so much as psychological mistakes. From this psychological viewpoint, Bar Kokhba functions as an object of the continuing human desire for redemption felt by "wise-hearted" people throughout the generations, willing to maintain faith in "the salvations of His anointed" (*yeshu'ot meshiḥo*).

Yet Abravanel treats as only a possibility the hypothesis that R. Akiba meant the Davidic Messiah when he called Ben Koziva "Messiah"; he seems rather to have considered the alternate hypothesis more likely—that R. Akiba believed him to be the Josephite Messiah. Tradition portrayed the Josephite Messiah as a military leader who would appear prior to the Davidic Messiah and die in battle fighting the enemies of Israel.

In this second part of Abravanel's interpretation, most of the analysis is devoted to demonstrating the reasonableness of R. Akiba's action. Abravanel does this by proving that Ben Koziva exhibited, in an impressive manner, all the essential attributes of the Josephite Messiah. Abravanel reminds his readers that Ben Koziva was a great warrior who wreaked vengeance upon the oppressors of Israel and died in battle. Abravanel also shows in great detail, by reference to "Roman history books," the supernatu-

---

21. In Prov. 10:18, 11:29, and 16:21, and Job 9:4, the phrase *ḥakham lev* is virtually synonymous with "wise" (as the opposite of foolish), but it may denote here a mental tendency or virtue.

ral powers Ben Koziva exhibited and the astounding military victories he won, which could only have come from God. These are precisely the attributes of the Messiah ben Joseph. Even Ben Koziva's eventual death and failure did not disqualify him, but only furthered his similarity to the Josephite Messiah. The conclusion that Abravanel wants his readers to draw is that R. Akiba was eminently justified in believing Ben Koziva to be the Messiah ben Joseph.

Indeed, the single reason why R. Akiba was wrong, according to Abravanel, was the date. Abravanel explains elsewhere in *Salvations* that the Josephite Messiah would appear exactly seven years prior to the Davidic.[22] Hence, Ben Koziva had appeared several centuries too early. This means that except for the one missing condition, the date, Ben Koziva could actually have been the Messiah ben Joseph, whom he resembled perfectly.

Abravanel proceeds to defend the messianic time periods in the same way he defended them earlier, by trying to prove that the rest of the sages disagreed with R. Akiba and did so solely because of their adherence to the messianic periods. For evidence, Abravanel adduces R. Yoḥanan b. Torta's statement, presenting it as the opinion of all the sages and reading it in the following manner, as an argument based on the time limits: Ben Koziva is not the Josephite Messiah because the Davidic Messiah will not come until the period of messianic possibility, long after grass has grown from your jaws. Abravanel further asserts that R. Akiba also believed in the messianic periods and therefore knew in his heart that Ben Koziva could not be the Josephite Messiah. Abravanel may have intended his earlier psychological analysis to explain why R. Akiba ignored this knowledge.

But this time Abravanel does not excuse R. Akiba. For all Abravanel's earlier attempts to show how justifiable were R. Akiba's reasons and how worthy his motives, in the end Abravanel holds R. Akiba responsible for his mistake and guilty of a sin for which he was later punished by God. "Who knows whether it was not through this sin (*be'avon zeh*) that R. Akiba was put to death in a manner more painful than the deaths of the other sages executed by the [Roman] government?" In Abravanel's eyes, there was ultimately no excuse for his proclamation because he was aware of the time limits.

Abravanel has not succeeded, therefore, in solving the polemical problem presented by R. Akiba's proclamation—which was to save the messianic periods without undermining rabbinic authority. Recall Abravanel's claim

---

22. Abravanel, *Yeshu'ot Meshiḥo* 64a.

that the sages "had correct judgment that never failed" and that every rabbinic saying was true, binding, and in full accord with the rest of Jewish tradition. But however much Abravanel tried to mitigate the implications of R. Akiba's statement, he had to consider it a mistake because it contradicted the principle of the messianic periods—a principle fundamental to Abravanel's interpretation of all the other messianic statements of the rabbis and his defense of Jewish doctrine. Since, moreover, in upholding that principle, he had even argued that R. Akiba was ultimately cognizant of its reality, Abravanel had to consider R. Akiba's proclamation an intentional (though "wise-hearted") sin. As sin and as misjudgment, especially of a doctrinal nature, it contradicted Abravanel's notion of the unfailing, true, and unified nature of all rabbinic statements.

Let us take account, finally, of the way in which Abravanel's interpretation constitutes a reply to Maimonides, whose writings represented a central preoccupation of his intellectual life.[23] In the passage under consideration, the term "armor bearer" originates from the *Mishneh Torah*. In that work, as we have seen, Maimonides had assumed that Ben Koziva could have been the Messiah even though he lived during Abravanel's period of messianic impossibility, since Maimonides took into account only the candidate's eventual success or failure in fulfilling the messianic tasks. In reply, Abravanel argues that Ben Koziva failed not out of military or moral weakness, as Maimonides had to assume, but only for reason of having lived during the wrong messianic period. He had fulfilled, or could have, all Maimonides' requirements. Also in opposition to Maimonides, Abravanel tries to prove that R. Akiba was the only sage who supported Ben Koziva.

The False Messiah

Abravanel refers to Ben Koziva once elsewhere in *Salvations*, in a discussion of the Second Messianic Period, the era of "messianic possibility" that began in 469 C.E. Abravanel says that the rabbinic phrase "Days of the Messiah" refers to this period in the sense that it carried the possibility of the Messiah's arrival and also in the sense that people everywhere spent their days thinking about the Messiah.

---

23. Netanyahu, *Abravanel*, 17, 25, 32, 87.

But in those last millennia, the thoughts of people throughout the world... groped yearningly after the coming of the Messiah. Indeed, see: in the beginning of those last millennia, the disciples of Jesus of Nazareth arose and... promulgated it that he was the Messiah whom the prophets had specified, and their faith spread in those days throughout most of the world. Also, near that time, in Betar at the close of the fourth millennium, Ben Koziva made himself the Messiah. After them arose Muhammad, the prophet of the Ishmaelites, and said that the Lord had anointed him to tell and command nations.... And also in our exile, many men made themselves messiahs, as the great Master [Maimonides] described in his letter to Yemen. For at the beginning of the Ishmaelite dominion, a certain Jew arose in the East[24] and said that he was the Messiah. It was as though the nature of the time were bringing the thoughts of mankind to seek yearningly after the coming of the Messiah.[25]

During this period, the peoples of the world, rightly sensing that God was about to send them the Messiah, looked longingly for him to come at any moment, in the way that (in Abravanel's metaphor) people expecting a message from the king watch restlessly for his messenger. It was this tense expectation, according to Abravanel, which broke out into messianic movements.

He thus accounts for messianic movements through both historical and psychological causes (but with an essential theological dimension). Messianic movements were not mere instances of perversity but were rooted in and understandable through their historical context, and they had a psychological basis: "the thoughts of people." This psychological explanation resembles Abravanel's analysis of R. Akiba's messianic proclamation: just as R. Akiba "believed what his soul... longed to be true," so had "the

---

24. Literally, "beyond the river" (*be'ever le-nahar*). Abravanel is referring to a messianic movement described by Maimonides as occurring near Ispahan (which is east of the Tigris River) soon after the rise of "the Ishmaelite" (Muslim) kingdom, toward the end of the seventh century. According to Maimonides' *Epistle to Yemen*, a large number of Jews calling themselves "*benei 'ever ha-nahar*" (people from beyond the river) began a mass exodus toward the west under the leadership of "a man who claimed to be the Messiah" (known from other sources as Abu 'Isa). See Maimonides, "Epistle to Yemen," trans. Abraham S. Halkin, in *Crisis and Leadership: Epistles of Maimonides* (Philadelphia, 1985), 127, and Maimonides, *Iggerot*, Heb. trans. Joseph Kafih (Jerusalem, 1972), 56–57.

25. Abravanel, *Yeshu'ot Meshiḥo* 20a.

thoughts of mankind sought yearningly after the coming of the Messiah." R. Akiba had been caught up in this same fervor.

(We can now discern the gist of Abravanel's reply to an attack on R. Akiba of the kind found in *Pugio Fidei*, asserting that R. Akiba followed Bar Kokhba out of a demonically inspired madness. Abravanel presents R. Akiba as in no way mad but justifiably impressed by the truly messianic attributes actually exhibited by Bar Kokhba, as even non-Jewish sources proved. R. Akiba erred for only the worthiest of motives, his yearning for messianic redemption—a psychological-historical and not demonic motivation. For he lived in historical times that manifested widespread expectations of the Messiah, deluding also the followers of Jesus. Hence, R. Akiba was no more villainous, and indeed far better justified, than those who thought Jesus was the Messiah.)

The polemical effect of this psychological-historical interpretation of messianic movements is to discredit them, since they become the passing delusions of an era, while also confirming Abravanel's own expectation of the Messiah's arrival in his own days, since those earlier delusions emerged nonetheless out of an accurate apprehension that the true time was near.

Not only were they based on authentic expectation but they actually prepared the world to acknowledge the true Messiah when he arrived.

> This, too, came from God, in order to make known throughout the world the King Messiah who would come, and so that the hearts and mouths of all mankind would be filled with this [knowledge], even their false ideas and deceitful ways—so that when the time of his coming arrives . . . all the inhabitants of abomination and dwellers upon the earth will recognize and know that what they inherited from their fathers is untrue as regards the Messiah and this is our Messiah, for whom we [all] hoped throughout these years. . . . If before his coming the hearts of mankind had not turned after others [false messiahs], then at the actual time of his coming, the matter could not be verified and promulgated over all the world except with the greatest difficulty.[26]

The idea of false messiahs preparing the world for the true one derives from the *Mishneh Torah*, where Maimonides wrote, "Jesus of Nazareth and the

26. Ibid. 20b.

Ishmaelite [Muhammad] who came after him served only to clear the way for the King Messiah and to prepare the whole world to worship God with one accord."[27] False messiahs, in Maimonides' view, were part of a hidden process by which God used the accidents of history to further God's own will of redeeming Israel. Abravanel, however, conceives of false messiahs as part of a normal, even planned, development from within the decreed periods of history, with the final event, redemption, building cumulatively upon previous foundations.

Elsewhere in *Salvations*, Abravanel describes the arrival of redemption as "a natural process (*havayah tiv'it*)."[28] He compares it to the ripening of fruit and the dawning of the day, and speaks of the gradual accumulation of acts of oppression that finally bring down divine vengeance upon the nations of the world. Even the "travails of the Messiah," the catastrophic events expected immediately to precede redemption, follow nature's normal way of bringing change only through opposites, as famine precedes plenty, labor precedes birth, war precedes peace. When the Messiah comes, moreover, no radical break from the past will at first occur, but merely an increase in blessings and prosperity. Only after the miracle of resurrection, to occur at the end of the final messianic period of history, identified as "the World to Come," will human existence be transformed radically, through miracles and "great wonders outside the order of nature." Abravanel thus incorporated the radical changes of apocalyptic literature into his concept of history's natural development.[29]

Abravanel sees Ben Koziva, therefore, as part of this natural process of redemption, a moment within its fruition and dawning, a step in its unfolding. Ben Koziva, like other false messiahs, helped prepare the way for the true Messiah and was the object of expectations as redemption drew near. Abravanel explains Ben Koziva's messianic claims as a function of the same psychological dynamics that moved the other false messiahs: he was caught up in the mood of the times and thought he was the redeemer for whom everyone yearned. But Abravanel treats him more sympathetically than he does Jesus and Muhammad, both of whom he describes with the term, "false messiah" (literally, "imagined messiah": *mashiaḥ medumeh*), which he never applies to Ben Koziva; and he demonstrates how closely Ben Koziva resembled the Davidic and Josephite Messiahs, and clearly implies that his

---

27. *Mishneh Torah*, "Laws of Kings" 11, 4.
28. Abravanel, *Yeshu'ot Meshiḥo* 33b.
29. Ibid. 12a, 13b, 19b–20a, 56b–58a.

miraculous powers came from God. Ben Koziva truly did anticipate the Messiah of the future. He represented the heart's awakening to the dawn of the new age.

Agent of Divine Vengeance

Abravanel's discussion concentrates on R. Akiba, analyzing what he might have believed and why he was right or wrong. We have been told that Ben Koziva, though resembling the Davidic and Josephite Messiahs, was neither. But since we are also told that he performed true miracles, punishing God's enemies, he must have been more than merely a false messiah. Can we reach a more precise understanding of Abravanel's image of him? And what might that image have meant for the Jews of Abravanel's day?

We begin by distinguishing what Abravanel himself said about Ben Koziva from what he thought R. Akiba believed. This becomes clear from the following words:

1. "When he saw Ben Koziva's military success";
2. "When he saw the heroic feats (*gevurot*) of Ben Koziva and his success in battle, which were unlike the natural way of things (*lo keminhag tiv'i*)";
3. "When R. Akiba saw the miracles (*nissim*) and the mighty feats (*ha-gevurot*) that Ben Koziva performed in all the Roman lands";
4. "his wars and acts of vengeance."[30]

Abravanel expresses these statements as historical fact: he disputes the conclusions R. Akiba drew from the facts, but not the truth of what R. Akiba observed. Indeed, as proof of Ben Koziva's "miracles and heroic feats," he introduces the reports he found in "Roman history books." This passage is worth reviewing because it presents these reports as valid information about Ben Koziva.

> For see, our account of Ben Koziva is told very briefly and only a little part of it is found in the Talmud and Midrashim; however, in Roman history books, I myself saw his many mighty deeds in war and his heroic courage (*gevurat libo*) and his fierceness (*akhzariuto*)

---

30. Ibid. The first is from 30b, the last three from 31a.

against his enemies, and that he went to Alexandria of Egypt and wreaked great vengeance upon the Roman populace there, and swept over all the kingdoms of Egypt and Babylonia, and no man could withstand him, and everywhere he went he would spill the blood of his enemies like water without mercy. They recounted all this in long stories in their books.[31]

In this passage, Abravanel attributes his information to *divrei ha-yamim asher le-romiyim*, "history books of the Romans." The same phrase appears elsewhere in Abravanel's writings, but likewise without names of specific writers, and could refer to a variety of works available to him.[32] In this case, however, his "history books of the Romans" most likely refers to the world chronicle of Eusebius in Jerome's Latin adaptation, because Abravanel's account of Ben Koziva's wars matches precisely the sequence and locations of the Jewish uprisings reported in this Latin chronicle under the years 116 and 117 (see Appendix).[33] Moreover, Abraham Zacuto's story of Ben Koziva's wars, written at approximately the same time as *Salvations*, closely resembles Abravanel's account; and Zacuto explicitly identifies Eusebius as his source (as will be seen in the next chapter). Like Ibn Daud before him, Abravanel must have interpreted these separate Jewish uprisings as manifestations of a single, connected messianic movement, one led by a warrior who went unnamed in the chronicles but who, in Abravanel's mind, was clearly identical with the wondrous Ben Koziva of rabbinic legend. Abravanel thought the chronicles were filling in the details omitted from the legends.

Considering together Abravanel's various statements about Ben Koziva, we discover an image of a truly extraordinary military hero who exhibited supernatural powers in carrying out the will of God against the oppressors

---

31. Ibid. 31a.

32. Yitzhak Baer, in "Don Yizḥaq Abravanel Veyaḥaso el Ba'ayot Ha-Historiyah Veha-Medinah," *Tarbiẓ* 8 (1937): 241–59, on 246 n. 13, remarks that Abravanel's sources for Roman history are difficult to identify precisely. Abravanel studied the writings of numerous historians, classical and modern, in Latin and Spanish.

33. Abravanel may also have used later summations based on Eusebius. Less likely possibilities are Dio Cassius's Roman history (if translated into Latin), which limits the Jewish uprisings to Cyrene, Egypt, and Cyprus, mentioning no occurrences in Alexandria and Mesopotamia, and Orosius's *Seven Books of History against the Pagans*, which lacks some of the details appearing in Abravanel's story. Jacob Guttmann, in *Religionsphilosophische Lehren des Isaak Abravanel* (Breslau, 1916), 43 n. 3, suggested that "the history books of the Romans" mentioned by Abravanel in connection with Ben Koziva referred to "Hieronymus und Eusebius"; he believed, however, that Abravanel was thinking of the events listed in the Latin chronicle under the year A.D. 134 in relation to "Chochebas."

of Israel. Four main attributes distinguish this Ben Koziva of Abravanel's conceptualization. First, he was a great military hero of Israel's past, one who exhibited "heroic courage" (*gevurat libo*), "heroic strength" (*gevurah*), and military success. He was a gibbor, much in the sense of the rabbinic meaning of the word. Second, Abravanel's Ben Koziva was a conqueror, nearly invincible. He conquered a wide expanse of land and defeated the Roman armies throughout the East. Third, he displayed supernatural powers, performing "miracles" (*nissim*) and exhibiting strength and winning battles in a manner "unlike the natural way of things" (*lo keminhag tiv'i*). And fourth, Ben Koziva's wars were, in Abravanel's mind, "acts of vengeance." He "wreaked great vengeance" (*'asah neqamah gedolah*) upon his enemies, slaughtering them fiercely and unrelentingly, "without mercy."

Both the earthly and the transcendent combine in this exceptional warrior, Abravanel's image of Bar Kokhba. On the one hand, we can imagine him with bloodstained hands and heavy, clanging weapons, charging into the midst of battle. He plans strategy, shouts orders, and marches his men hard through foreign territory. We hear the location and sequence of his battles, sense the mood of his times. But Abravanel's Bar Kokhba also appears before us larger than life, more than human. Shining with an unearthly power, lifted by a mysterious splendor, he is moved by the vengeance of the Almighty, whose hand reveals itself in his spectacular victories.

The rabbinic legends had ascribed extraordinary strength to Ben Koziva and his army, but Abravanel's description goes further. He plainly calls Ben Koziva's victories by the name of *nissim*, miracles, picturing his powers as "unlike the natural way of things." This makes Abravanel's description exceptional in the history of Jewish images of Bar Kokhba. Ibn Daud and Maimonides had found nothing out of the ordinary about the man's abilities, nor do the sixteenth-century historians. Only the later kabbalists come close to portraying Bar Kokhba in as exalted a manner.

Let us examine further the supernatural powers ascribed to Bar Kokhba in Abravanel's account, and its new motif of vengeance.

What do those powers mean to Abravanel? They mean, on the one hand, that Ben Koziva exhibited one of the most important attributes of the Messiah as Abravanel envisioned him: miraculous powers. He envisioned both the Davidic and the Josephite Messiahs possessing such spectacular power and such a perfection of other attributes that these Messiahs would in themselves constitute two of the greatest wonders of the redemption.[34] The Messiah ben David, as described in *Salvations* and Abravanel's other writ-

---

34. Abravanel, *Yeshu'ot Meshiḥo* 56b.

ings, would be a perfect judge, prophet, and holyman, and a leader who guides Israel more as would a shepherd than a king. Two of his most impressive miracles would be to conquer the nations of the world "not with sword and spear" but "through the power of God," and then (according to some of Abravanel's statements) to convert those less wicked into worshiping the one true Lord.[35] But the Messiah ben Joseph, though likewise holy, pious, and powerful, would not possess these attributes to the same degree. As we have seen, Abravanel conceives of this second figure as a holy warrior empowered by God to punish the nations, and destined, in the process, to die fighting.[36] It is evident that Abravanel's images of the two Messiahs derive more from medieval apocalyptic literature, rabbinic legends, and prophetic metaphor than from the "rationalistic" conceptions of Maimonides. (Yet Abravanel explained the miracles of the "Days of the Messiah" in a naturalistic manner: those days would constitute a renewal of the era of Moses, David, and Solomon, a time of wonders when the *Shekhinah*, the presence of God, dwelt with Israel, and continuous blessings and wonders resulted "naturally" from such contact. Abravanel conceived of the messianic redemption as a repetition, though a more splendid one, of the miracles of the exodus from Egypt.)[37]

Attributing to Ben Koziva the supernatural powers that would be possessed by the Messiahs helps Abravanel justify R. Akiba's mistake. Indeed, most of the writers who speak of R. Akiba's proclamation explain it on the same grounds as Abravanel: that Ben Koziva truly did exhibit some of the essential attributes of the Messiah. It is worth noticing, furthermore, that as the image of the Messiah changed from one writer to the next (in our study), the image of Ben Koziva itself changed in a corresponding manner. Thus, Maimonides' Messiah achieves redemption without miracles, and Ben Koziva, as Maimonides imagined him, likewise achieved his military successes without miracles. The kabbalistic Messiah works in hidden, transcendental realms, and so does the kabbalistic Ben Koziva.

But on the other hand, despite Ben Koziva's supernatural powers, his role was not messianic. What, then, was it? His supernatural powers mean, at least, that God gave him those powers, since Abravanel ascribes all miracles to God. But he also tells us that Ben Koziva's wars were acts of

---

35. Ibid. 11b, 28b, 31a, 34b, 40b–41a, 49b, 56a–57b; Netanyahu, *Abravanel*, 238–39, 241; Sarachek, *The Doctrine of the Messiah in Medieval Jewish Literature* (New York, 1932), 269, 271, 280–83; L. Strauss, "On Abravanel's Philosophical Tendency and Political Teaching," *Isaac Abravanel: Six Lectures*, ed. J. B. Trend and H. Loewe (Cambridge, 1937), 108–9.
36. Abravanel, *Yeshu'ot Meshiḥo* 31a, 62b–64a.
37. Ibid. 57a.

vengeance; and we know from another passage in *Salvations* that he considered the Roman empire a wicked nation deserving punishment, because it had destroyed the Temple and oppressed Israel. We also know that Abravanel assigned to the Turkish people the role of punishing modern Rome (Christian Europe), and that he called the Turks "the agent [*shaliaḥ*] of the Providence of God sent to destroy the destroyers of his Sanctuary" (again equating Christian Europe with Rome). Abravanel likewise called Cyrus "the anointed of the God of Jacob sent to be an avenger of vengeance."[38] This is the same role Abravanel assigns to Ben Koziva—that of enacting vengeance against a nation that sinned against God and Israel. It is thus reasonable to infer that Abravanel, ascribing all miraculous power to God, considered Ben Koziva, too, an "agent of the Providence of God" (*shaliaḥ hashgaḥato shel hashem*, the term he applied to the Turks), empowered by God and serving God's will in punishing wicked Rome.

Adding this inference to Abravanel's other statements about Ben Koziva, including his idea about the psychological mood of the times, we arrive at a story like this: God gave a man named Ben Koziva the power to wreak vengeance upon the Roman empire, and this is just what Ben Koziva did, showing himself to be a magnificent gibbor, courageous, strong, and fierce in battle. But Ben Koziva lived during a time of intense messianic expectation, so that, caught up in this mood, he thought he was the Messiah whom the world was awaiting and that his wars were the wars of final redemption. Also caught up in this mood was R. Akiba, who, upon seeing Ben Koziva's miraculous conquests, forgot about the time periods and proclaimed this man the Messiah. In reality, the date made it impossible for this to be so. Nevertheless, Ben Koziva *was* an agent of God, an avenger of oppressions—which was as close as anyone at that time could come to being the true Messiah.

Such seems to have been Abravanel's understanding of the events. His account combines psychological interpretation with a theological viewpoint that perceives the transcendent and supernatural as fundamental causes in human history. History is here pictured as a complex interaction between earth and heaven—between, on the one hand, the natural emotions, thoughts, and political strivings of men, and on the other, the miraculous works and hidden but inexorable purposes of God.[39]

---

38. Ibid. 35a.
39. Cf. Netanyahu, *Abravanel*, 130–49; Isaac E. Barzilay, *Between Faith and Reason: Anti-Rationalism in Italian Jewish Thought, 1250–1650* (The Hague, 1967), 94–99, 118–26; Baer, "Don Yiṣḥaq Abravanel," 245–48, 257–59.

We saw that vengeance is a recurring motif in Abravanel's story of Bar Kokhba; it is also one of the most prominent themes in *Salvations* as a whole, and appears frequently in all three messianic books (but is muted in his biblical exegesis). Writes Netanyahu, "Indeed, there is no other subject in which Abravanel indulges so readily and which he discusses with greater zeal than the revenge upon Israel's enemies in the Messianic Age."[40] Redemption for Israel, according to Abravanel, will concomitantly bring "a great vengeance upon Israel's enemies," leading to "the destruction of the nations."[41] Abravanel pictures this vengeance as a terrible, fiery destruction that annihilates Edom (Christian Europe) totally and mercilessly. Its agent will be the Messiah, who will "avenge a great vengeance," "punish the nations," and "destroy them by wondrous means."[42] But Abravanel thought that divine vengeance had been manifested through some of the wars of former times, too, as when Cyrus destroyed Babylon, an enemy of God.

In the opinion of H. H. Ben-Sasson, this same hope for vengeance is a major theme heard in the writings of the generation of Jews expelled from Spain. He writes that the exiles nursed "thoughts of the vengeance that the Creator would wreak upon the towns in Spain where Israel had once lived." They usually assigned the role of initial avenger to the Turks and other Muslims. For example, R. Abraham b. R. Eliezer Ha-Levi wrote, "The End began when Constantinople was conquered by the great Turkish king . . . for at that time God began to wreak vengeance upon Edom and Amalek [Christian Europe] for persecuting his brethren [the Jews] by the sword . . . and it is right that God punish them through the Persians, who are the Turks."[43] Abravanel, too, expected the Turks to be the agents of the destruction of Christian Europe.

He spoke of oppressions accumulating until vengeance ripened like a fruit; the waiting made it all the sweeter when it came.[44] Like many of his generation, Abravanel thought they were living on the brink of redemption when they would be rescued and the people who had made them suffer would suffer in return. The time seemed ripe for revenge.

He was writing *Salvations* in 1497, five years after the Jews had been expelled from Spain and the very year when the Jewish communities of

---

40. Netanyahu, *Abravanel*, 226.
41. Abravanel, *Yeshu'ot Meshiḥo* 12a, 26a.
42. Ibid. 10b, 28b, 29a, 49b, 56b.
43. Ben-Sasson, "Galut u-Ge'ulah be-Eynav shel Dor Golei Sefarad," *Yitzhak F. Baer Jubilee Volume* (Jerusalem, 1960), 225.
44. Abravanel, *Yeshu'ot Meshiḥo* 12a.

Portugal were forced to convert under penalty of death. The Spanish exiles had lost their homes, wealth, and the land where they had lived for centuries; they had suffered death, abuse, and suspicion in their search for new homes; and now where they rested, they remained strangers dependent upon the fragile mercy of their new hosts. They felt abandoned and humiliated. Abravanel himself was living in Monopoli, his days of grandeur and power at the Spanish and Portuguese courts gone forever.

Netanyahu argues that the yearning for revenge felt by Spanish Jews derived from the distinctive character of this aristocratic community:

> In exalting the idea of revenge, Abravanel coined a phrase: "Revenge becomes great souls!" which epitomizes the psychological attitude of Spanish Jewry. The Spanish Jew was not only a highly civilized person, but also a person with a keen sense of pride. For centuries he had lived in Spain under conditions of semi-freedom and independence which, to be sure, he had to defend constantly, but which developed his self-consciousness and self-respect. The harrowing humiliations to which he was later subjected inflicted deep wounds upon that self-respect.... At the close of the long era of persecution which culminated in the expulsion, his soul was tormented by a burning hate and a fervent desire for revenge which was only intensified by the consciousness of his impotence.[45]

Of course, Spanish Jews did not invent the idea that wicked nations would suffer for their sins at the time of redemption. The earlier eschatological literature already contained this theme, interpreting it as divine judgment, punishment, recompense, as well as vengeance. Abravanel, however, raised the aspect of revenge to a central purpose of the messianic days.

This, then, is one meaning that Ben Koziva's wars had for Abravanel: they represented the manifestation of *neqamah*, vengeance, in Jewish history. Abravanel would likely have felt pride and satisfaction in discovering (as he

---

45. Netanyahu, *Abravanel*, 226–27. Netanyahu claims from limited data too much knowledge about "the soul of the Spanish Jew," but his basic thesis still holds, attributing the desire for revenge to these Jews' frustrated expectation of continued freedom and dignity. Stephen Sharot, in *Messianism, Mysticism, and Magic*, 71–75, compares the relatively passive Ashkenazi response to expulsions and riots with the response of Spanish Jews, which took the form of intense messianic expectations and a desire for revenge. Sharot discovers the essential difference in the particular feelings of "a people whose leaders had enjoyed wealth, status, and power, and who had been rejected by a society into which they had formerly been highly integrated, culturally and socially" (75).

thought) reports in the "Roman history books" about Ben Koziva's wars, which he easily interpreted as acts of revenge carried out in merciless fury. Those wars against Rome became for Abravanel the act of a Jew striking back (in the name of God) against his oppressors, oppressors like the Spanish and Portuguese kingdoms and representatives of the Church in his own time.

A further meaning that Abravanel seems to have discovered in Bar Kokhba is suggested by a statement appearing in the introduction to *Salvations*. There, as we saw, he explains that he wrote the book in order to offer hope and consolation to the Jews of his day who, suffering the agonies of expulsion and exile, had begun to doubt whether God cared about them and whether God would ever send the Messiah to save them.[46] In the now-lost *Ṣedeq Olamim* (*Eternal Justice*) of around 1493, Abravanel had addressed the question of whether God acts in history to execute justice; and to prove this he planned to write a survey of Jewish history, entitled *Yemot Olam* (*Days of the World*), showing the many times God had acted to save and to punish.[47] The brief reference to Bar Kokhba in *Salvations* teaches no distinct lesson about divine justice; the example's main consolation comes from proving the truth of Jewish messianic doctrine, especially the dates of the Three Messianic Periods (since these, if true, sustained messianic hope among the despairing exiles). The account does offer sufficient indication, however, that if Abravanel had written *Yemot Olam*, he would have included the wars of Ben Koziva as a prime example of how God had intervened to execute justice. If, as I have argued, Abravanel considered Ben Koziva an agent (*shaliaḥ*) of God wreaking vengeance, God was exacting justice in a world dominated by sinful governments. There is consolation in this idea because it shows that since God intervened in the past on Israel's behalf, God would intervene in the future, to redeem Israel and execute a full and final justice. By this reasoning, Ben Koziva, though a false messiah, becomes through his authentic fulfillment of divine justice a source of messianic hope.

Abravanel has used R. Akiba's error as proof of the imminence of redemption. By also presenting Ben Koziva's wars as an act of divine vengeance, despite their political failure, those wars are likewise transformed, for Abravanel's generation, into a promise of full and perfect judgment, raising up the lowly and bringing low the oppressor, at the time of final redemption.

---

46. Abravanel, *Yeshu'ot Meshiḥo* 4a.
47. Netanyahu, *Abravanel*, 65–66, based on statements in Abravanel's *Questions and Answers*, 8c, and his *Commentary to Kings*, introduction.

Abravanel's image of Ben Koziva—which is, ultimately, the image of a national hero and herald of the Messiah—shows the same national zeal and messianic fervor that pervade the whole of *Salvations*. There is a sense of urgency, excitement, and hope in Abravanel's words, which emphasize Ben Koziva's victories more than his defeats, his promise more than his warning, and the hopes of the future more than the failures of the past.

Changes in Abravanel's Image of Bar Kokhba

In *The Jew and His History* Lionel Kochan argues that Jewish historical thought, up until the sixteenth century, was structured around three primary themes: Israel's sacred relationship with God, the chain of transmission for rabbinic authority, and the coming of the Messiah. Such concerns are exemplified by the messianic speculations in the Talmud and *Megillat Ha-Megalleh* and by the histories of rabbinic authority which constitute most of *Seder Olam* and *The Book of Tradition*. In these writings, Kochan asserts, history was always charged with sacred meaning and it always called for a religious response from the community.[48] Looking specifically at expressions of Jewish "memory," Yosef Hayim Yerushalmi discovers only one genre of historical writing among medieval Jews, the "chain of tradition" books like *The Book of Tradition*. He points out that the memory of even recent sufferings merged with older memories of the recurring archetypal catastrophes of sacred history, such as enslavement in Egypt or exile from Jerusalem, so that prayers and ritual fasts commemorating medieval martyrs rarely mentioned specific names and events.[49]

Kochan's thesis fits the rabbinic and medieval accounts of Bar Kokhba. The rabbinic legends tell the story as an episode in the sacred history of God's relationship with Israel and call for repentance and renewed trust in the salvation of heaven. Neither Rashi nor Jacob b. Abraham of medieval France introduce significant changes into the story. Even Ibn Daud and Maimonides, who, representing a secularizing trend in Jewish thought, refashion the story in significant ways, nevertheless continue to place it within the framework of the sacred history of rabbinic tradition and God's involve-

---

48. Lionel Kochan, *The Jew and His History* (New York, 1977), chap. 2.
49. Yosef Hayim Yerushalmi, *Zakhor: Jewish History and Jewish Memory* (Seattle, 1982), 31–32, 42–52.

ment with Israel. They continue, too, to link Bar Kokhba with sacred doctrine, the belief in the Messiah. If we call these earlier images of Bar Kokhba "traditional" in the sense of expressing traditional historical concerns and categories as defined by Kochan and Yerushalmi, how "traditional" is Abravanel's discussion of Bar Kokhba? Does anything distinguish it from earlier tellings of the story?

I ask this as an issue separate from the oft-debated question of how Abravanel's thought is related to the intellectual currents of his day, particularly those associated with the terms Renaissance and Humanism.[50] The extent of debate over this question suggests an ambiguous and complex relationship, and a subject far beyond the scope of our examination of

---

50. Five scholars, in particular, represent this debate in its written form. It began in 1937, the five-hundredth anniversary of Abravanel's birth, with Yitzhak Baer's Hebrew article, "Don Isaac Abravanel and His Relationship to Political and Historical Issues." Baer's thesis was that Abravanel "drank from the newly opened springs of the humanist enlightenment," for evidence of which Baer claims to find the following elements in Abravanel's work: the citation of a wide range of classical literature, including Josephus, and an attempt to free the Bible and rabbinic tradition from the web of medieval Aristotelian interpretation, which Baer compares with the humanist rejection of scholasticism; the critical approach and historical method applied in Abravanel's biblical exegesis; a new feeling for life and practical reality expressed in his commentaries on the historical books of the Bible; Abravanel's political views, reflecting contemporary republicanism and the ideas of Seneca; and certain "realistic tendencies" in Abravanel's messianic writings. Baer concludes that Abravanel was "the first Jew to join the ideas of the Renaissance with the Torah of Israel and to begin to look at the tradition of the fathers through the enlightened perspective of an historical humanistic system." But also in 1937, L. Strauss, in "On Abravanel's Philosophic Tendency and Political Teaching" (in *Isaac Abravanel: Six Lectures*, 93–129), took issue with some of Baer's conclusions. Strauss argued that although Abravanel's "republicanism," historical methodology, and concern for the original sources of the tradition were indeed expressions of humanism, his thought nevertheless remained basically medieval, traditional, and anti-rationalist, differing from medieval writers solely in methodology. Then, writing in 1953, Benzion Netanyahu, devoting much attention to the question (*Abravanel*, 96–97, 116, 125–29, 248–49), took a position even further opposed to Baer's. He tried to show that Abravanel's thought was "typical of the Middle Ages" and, as such, "represents a revolt against the spirit of the Renaissance." Although Abravanel spoke "in the terms of Plato and Aristotle, Cicero and Seneca . . . his language as a whole was not that of the Renaissance, but of scholasticism." In *Between Faith and Reason*, 61–132, Isaac Barzilay argued that Abravanel's thought was fundamentally medieval, but belonged only to the "anti-rationalist" current of medieval Jewish thought (including Ha-Levi and Crescas), a current which, according to Barzilay, continued to find expression even during the sixteenth century. Abraham Melamed, in "The Perception of Jewish History in Italian Jewish Thought of the Sixteenth and Seventeenth Centuries: A Re-examination," *Italia Judaica—"Gli ebrei in Italia tra Rinascimento ed Eta barocca"* (Rome, 1986), 139–70, included Abravanel in his discussion of the degree to which Renaissance historiography influenced the perception of Jewish history among Jewish scholars of this period. Of Abravanel, Melamed notes that "despite his essentially medieval view of Jewish history, [he] at times utilized the natural laws of history as explanation" (145)—paralleling the new Renaissance "attempt to give natural and rational explanations to historical occurrences" (143).

Abravanel's image of Bar Kokhba. Contributing in no way to a resolution, our analysis is intended only to compare the earlier images we have studied.

Abravanel's image of Bar Kokhba exhibits a number of clearly traditional features. First, the fundamental questions that interest Abravanel, concerning rabbinic authority and messianic doctrine, are questions that were associated with Bar Kokhba from the beginning. Second, the primary texts that Abravanel discusses are texts concerned with messianic doctrine—the legends about R. Akiba's proclamation and Bar Kokhba's claim to be the Messiah. Of the two major rabbinic portrayals of Bar Kokhba, as a gibbor and as a false messiah, Abravanel devotes more space to the latter, although he integrates it with the former through the idea of the Messiah being a great warrior of vengeance. Abravanel's discussion of Bar Kokhba can be seen as a continuation of both rabbinic images of Bar Kokhba, defending, clarifying, and elaborating upon them. Furthermore, by making Bar Kokhba into a *shaliah* of God, Abravanel turns his wars into an episode in the sacred history of Israel's unique relationship with God, a central theme of Jewish historical thought: Bar Kokhba becomes a link between God and Israel, a channel for God's intervention in Jewish history. Indeed, Abravanel's telling of the story, in that it assumes God's direct and miraculous involvement in the life of Bar Kokhba, could be said to be *more* traditional, that is, closer to the original rabbinic conception, than the versions of Ibn Daud and Maimonides, who never mention God and miracles in their accounts and who conceive God's involvement in an entirely abstract and mediate manner. Finally, both the purpose of Abravanel's essay on Bar Kokhba and the response he tries to elicit from his readers fit squarely into the traditional structures of Jewish religious life: he tries to defend Jewish doctrine, to console his readers through hope and pride, and to encourage them to stand strong in their faith in "the salvations of His anointed."

Some ideational components of Abravanel's image of Bar Kokhba do differ a little from that of earlier images—portraying him against a framework of the ineluctable periods of messianic history and a "naturally supernatural" concept of redemption. But this remains well within traditional patterns of understanding the past.

Other elements in Abravanel's image, however, represent new features in the history of Jewish images of Bar Kokhba and deserve more attention.

One is the polemical context. Now, this is not new in itself; we have taken note of implicit political and ideological assertions in the rabbinic and medieval images of Bar Kokhba. Those arguments, however, were directed primarily to other Jews who, from the authors' viewpoint, were reading the wrong lessons from the Bar Kokhba rebellion. Abravanel, on the other hand, makes the polemical context a more explicit and significant concern, and he writes for Jews who must reply to Christian interpretations of the event. Bar Kokhba's story is thus told in a new context: directed partly to non-Jews, it cannot communicate sacred history in the way it can to members of the same sacred community. The polemical concern also alters the literary framework of the story, making Bar Kokhba into a topic under the heading of a specific issue in Christian-Jewish debates—whether the Messiah has yet arrived. Indeed, *Salvations* itself organizes the eschatological statements of the sages in accord with an abstract pattern of polemical questions that was foreign to the literary structures of rabbinic literature (organized according to Scriptural verse or legal topic). Abravanel was not, of course, the first to reorganize rabbinic eschatological traditions in this way; he elaborates on arguments and structures already developed by several polemical tracts written during the late Middle Ages. The *Mishneh Torah*'s image of Bar Kokhba might even be considered a more radical break from tradition, influenced as it is by Greek categories of thought for the purposes of a fairly abstract doctrinal argument. What Abravanel has thus done in *Salvations*, in the manner of scholastic argumentation, is apply similar abstract organizing and argumentative principles to traditional material and arrange it under categories derived from ideological contact between two religious traditions. It is also to be noted that however novel a framework this late medieval debate with Christians represented for Jewish thought, the debate yet remained within what must be considered rather traditional lines of thinking in the two religious communities.

Another new feature in Abravanel's discussion is his explicit reference to classical texts—"Roman history books" and Joseph ben Gorion (probably meaning Josephus but possibly only the author of the *Yosippon*)—in telling history. (Baer claims that Abravanel was the first Jew since the author of the *Yosippon* to have read the entire writings of Josephus, available in Latin translation.)[51] Indeed, references to the literature of classical antiquity abound in Abravanel's writings, apparently an influence of Renaissance humanism.[52] But if Ibn Daud had already made use of Latin sources to fill

---

51. Baer, "Don Yiṣḥaq Abravanel," 246.
52. Netanyahu, *Abravanel*, 13. In Abravanel's day, Italian humanism had already penetrated education in Spain and especially Portugal: see R. Weiss, "Learning and Education in Western Europe from 1470 to 1520," in *The New Cambridge Modern History*, I: *The Renaissance*, ed. G. R. Potter (Cambridge, 1957), and J. N. Hillgarth, *The Spanish Kingdoms, 1250–1516* (Oxford, 1978), 2:170–89.

out his story of Bar Kokhba, as I have suggested, he anticipated Abravanel in this; and Jewish medieval philosophers, mainly in Spain, had often cited Greek philosophers, with varying degrees of approbation, in their writings. Yet even so, Abravanel's story of Bar Kokhba represents a shift of perceptions: an account of an event in sacred Israelite history now explicitly cites "Roman history books" and obviously recommends them, even as non-Jewish books, as reliable sources of information. This means that though Abravanel is still presenting Jewish history as sacred history, the unique interaction between God and Israel, this has now become, in part, Jewish history seen through the eyes of Gentiles, history whose record is transmitted through untraditional sources of authority—indeed, sacred history supported and expanded and corrected by secular sources. In this sense, then, and probably without intention, Abravanel's telling of the history of Bar Kokhba has further approached the modern world of secular historiography. The similar citation of Eusebius in Abraham Zacuto's account of Bar Kokhba, written at this same time (to be examined in the next chapter), represents a similar shift in consciousness.

Abravanel also further develops the interest in geographical and political details that appeared first in Ibn Daud's account of Bar Kokhba. Abravanel names specific populations and locations, specific sequences of battles (but omits the Roman rulers who appear in Ibn Daud's account). The rabbinic account, in contrast, shows little interest in specific commanders, locations of the struggle, or sequence of events; it focuses rather on the theological core of the event, the age-old conflict between God and Israel and the specific Jewish factions in that struggle. The historical event has been crystallized into archetypes. What, then, is the significance of the political details in Abravanel's account? One thinks of the typical Renaissance interest in the geography of foreign lands, or the attempt to recover the classical past in its particularity—expressed also, it seems, in Abravanel's attention to such details in his exegesis of the historical portions of the Bible.[53] Yet in Abravanel's account of Bar Kokhba, these details appear totally subservient

---

53. Jacob Burckhardt, *The Civilization of the Renaissance in Italy*, trans. Ludwig Geiger and Walter Götz, 2 vols. (New York, 1958), "Part III: The Revival of Antiquity" and "Journeys of the Italians" (279–82). According to Moses Shulvass, *The Jews in the World of the Renaissance*, trans. Elvin I. Kose (Leiden, 1973), 307, this same interest in foreign geography motivated Abravanel's inclusion in his commentary to the Pentateuch of a "lengthy catalogue of the nations who descended from the sons of Japheth, trying to identify them with European and Asian peoples." Michael Mallett, in *Mercenaries and Their Masters: Warfare in Renaissance Italy* (Totowa, N.J., 1974), 210, notes that Italian humanist histories were preoccupied with battles and wars.

to his theological purpose of proving the intervention of God through the avenging destruction wreaked by Bar Kokhba. It is therefore difficult to draw any implication by comparison with earlier images of Bar Kokhba.

This holds true also for Abravanel's interest in a psychological underside to Bar Kokhba's story. Does his willingness to speak about the human emotions underlying the actions of R. Akiba, a figure of religious authority, reflect the characteristic interest in human behavior shown by Renaissance humanists like Petrarch and Menotti? Does it reflect "the tendency to express, or consider worth expressing, the concrete uniqueness of one's feelings, opinions, experiences," as found in the Italian literature and portrait-painting of the time?[54] Or should it be compared with Machiavelli's attention to the hidden human desires and apprehensions that govern political processes? But again the significance of Abravanel's retelling of the story remains unclear. He does not draw these portraits out of an interest in the persons themselves or to illustrate a lesson outside the normal range of traditional theological topics. Nor is astute psychological supposition new to Jewish thought, rabbinic or medieval. Compare the psychological insights into moral weakness and self-delusion found in Baḥya ibn Paquda's *Duties of the Heart* and Maimonides' "Laws of Repentance" in the *Mishneh Torah*, or the Zohar's theory of the several layers of soul, often in mutual conflict. Even the rabbinic story of Ben Koziva offers a psychological dimension: the gibbor was deceived by his own strength into thinking he could defend Betar without the help of God. How, then, does Abravanel's telling of the story differ? Like Ibn Daud (as I have argued), Abravanel explains R. Akiba's mistake on the basis of messianic attributes realistically displayed by Bar Kokhba. But Abravanel adds a concept of conflicting levels of consciousness: R. Akiba's noble yearning for redemption overcame his higher awareness of the truth, just as Ben Koziva's mind yielded to the messianic yearnings of the masses, the spirit of "the times." Does this theory serve merely the immediate polemical defense of the "Messianic Periods," or does it reflect an intellectual trend exhibited in the rest of Abravanel's writings? Further investigation is needed.

Also new in the history of images of Bar Kokhba is Abravanel's theme of *neqamah* (vengeance). Whereas Abravanel took obvious satisfaction in Bar Kokhba's wars against Rome, which he saw as wars of justifiable revenge, the rabbinic legends condemned the rebellion on grounds that military

54. Paul O. Kristeller, *Renaissance Thought* (New York, 1955), 20–21 and chap. 6.

action could not save Israel, and Ibn Daud likewise condemned it, emphasizing its disastrous consequences. But Abravanel, in striking contrast, never even mentions the destruction of Betar and proudly displays a list of Bar Kokhba's victories. His attitude toward the rebellion is far more favorable than the earlier literature.

Yet Abravanel never advocates that Jews take up arms against their oppressors—a position that would have represented a major change in Jewish political attitude. Although he writes approvingly of wars throughout *Salvations*, they are wars of the Messiah or of agents of God like Cyrus and the Turks. I have argued that he conceives of Bar Kokhba as such an agent. This Bar Kokhba has not initiated action himself to defend his people, but is only a passive instrument of non-human power. Abravanel's image of Bar Kokhba therefore works ultimately to encourage not political-military action but only a more faithful waiting for the divine vengeance that would soon begin with miracles from above. Baer, in *Galut*, his essay on the history of Jewish ideas about exile and return, voices wonder at Abravanel's lack of interest in practical solutions to the Jewish sufferings of his day: "On the other hand, so experienced and practical a man as Abravanel had not the slightest thought of making any effort either to improve the situation of the Jews or to make any outward preparations for their redemption. There was no point in trying to improve conditions, for redemption was already on its way. And God alone determines the individual stages of the process: The Jews were not permitted to free themselves from the Galut [Exile] before the appointed time."[55] For Abravanel, Bar Kokhba could be only a hero of divine vengeance, never a hero of human striving and political change. In this, Abravanel adheres to the rabbinic abhorrence of "forcing the end."

Finally, it remains to address briefly whether the unique features in Abravanel's image of Bar Kokhba reflect heroic images present in the non-Jewish societies in which Abravanel lived. Two considerations suggest such a possibility. First, Abravanel lived in close contact with the educated Portuguese, Spanish, and, later, Italian classes of his day, received a humanist education along with his Jewish one, and shows familiarity with and occa-

---

55. Yitzhak Baer, *Galut*, trans. Robert Warshow (1947; reprint, Lanham, Md., 1988), 67–68. Cf. Netanyahu, *Abravanel*, 235, considering Abravanel's stance representative of "the tragedy of a people who . . . breathed the atmosphere of dreams rather than reality. . . . Nevertheless, he regarded as futile any attempt on the part of the people to effectuate salvation by their own efforts. Sternly and repeatedly Abravanel warned that salvation would not come by human will and planning, but by divine power alone." Note the Zionist bent to both Baer's and Netanyahu's responses.

sional admiration for a number of non-Jewish societies.[56] Second, the type of hero implied by his image of Bar Kokhba—as in his vengeance, valor, widespread conquests, and fierceness or brutality—differs enough from heroic images in earlier Jewish traditions, at least in its combination of older elements, to allow for the possibility of non-Jewish influences.

The Italian mercenary captains, the condottieri, are unlikely models, not least because fame and fortune, rather than nation, vengeance, or God, motivated their wars.[57] But parallels can be drawn with the figure of the Spanish knight. *Poema de Mio Cid* and *Caballero Zifar*, though twelfth and fourteenth century works, respectively, as well as later romances modeled after them, were popular reading during Abravanel's days in Portugal and Spain. Themes of revenge, manly valor, and loyalty are prominent; in particular, the Spanish romances of religious chivalry, beginning with *Caballero Zifar*, acclaimed the virtues of, in Otis Green's words, "protecting the poor and weak, fighting always in a righteous cause, defending the Church and clergy, and constantly warring on the enemies of the Faith."[58] Could this image of the ideal knight of God, filtered through the apocalyptic mood of Abravanel's thoughts, have drawn him to themes of heroic valor, righteous battle, and vengeance on God's enemies in his reading of Bar Kokhba's story?

But this remains only a conjecture, difficult to verify. We would have to compare the rest of Abravanel's writings, examining the various contexts of these themes and the character of the men he held up as heroes. Nor can we overlook the medieval apocalyptic tracts that Abravanel would have known—in which the Messiah sometimes appears as a brutal warrior

---

56. Netanyahu, *Abravanel*, 13–15, 166–73 (on Venice), 184–86, 249.

57. They were most often men of unreliable moral character and not usually trusted or admired by the cities employing them. See Mallett, *Mercenaries and Their Masters*, esp. chap. 8, on the complex and changing relations between soldiers and citizenry. We also learn from this chapter, however, that some condottieri of the fifteenth century had become educated patrons and respected citizens of adopted cities, and that the humanist tradition glorified military action and praised valiant men; Italians read ancient treatises on war, invented new military devices, and created artistic portrayals of war. But could these cultural trends have touched and impressed Abravanel during his brief stay in Italy, before writing *Salvations*? How much had these social trends touched the Spanish social circles in which Abravanel moved?

58. Otis Green, *Spain and the Western Tradition*, vol. 1 (Madison, 1963), 10–15. Themes of brutal victory, loyalty to king, and revenge against family dishonor are important to El Cid, although more moderated than in the chivalric epics of France and Germany. See Gerald Brenan, *The Literature of the Spanish People* (Cambridge, 1953), 36–51, and on the popularity of the knightly romances in Abravanel's time, 125–31.

fighting God's final battle. And yet there remains a tone to Abravanel's portrayal of Bar Kokhba's heroism, perhaps in his *gevurat libo* (literally, his manliness or mightiness of heart), perhaps in the theme of revenge (though eschatological vengeance is found in several Jewish apocalyptic works, e.g., *Pirqei Mashiah*), which may well echo the brave knight of God admired in Abravanel's Spanish environment.

4

Bar Kokhba in Sixteenth-Century Historical Writings

The sixteenth century saw a notable increase in the composition of Jewish historical works. Because many of them show a particular concern with the misfortunes Jews suffered during their long history, several scholars have explained the appearance of such writings from a need to reflect upon one of the worst of those misfortunes, the recent expulsion from Spain and forced conversions there and in Portugal. Yosef Hayim Yerushalmi argues, moreover, that the increased eschatological interest aroused by the expulsion impelled Jews to search in history for signs of impending redemption.[1]

---

1. Yerushalmi, *Zakhor*, 58–60; Ben-Sasson, "Li-Megamot Ha-Qronografia ha-Yehudit shel Yemei Ha-Beinayim u-Be'ayotekha," *Historionim ve'Ascolot Historiot* (Jerusalem, 1962), 32–33; Michael Meyer, *Ideas of Jewish History* (New York, 1974), 17–19. It is to be noted that Ben-Sasson and Meyer explain the rise of Jewish historiography through a second concomitant cause: the influence of Italian humanism. Yerushalmi's theory of the commingling or coexistence of messianism and historiography in the sixteenth century appears in "Messianic Impulses in Joseph ha-

Some Jewish historical writing, furthermore, seems to have been particularly stimulated by contact with Christian humanists expressing an avid interest in history and foreign nations.[2] Indeed, increasing contacts with Christians generally in Italy and Prague apparently inspired attempts by a number of Jewish writers to understand their relationship with their non-Jewish neighbors from a historical perspective.

Yerushalmi identifies as new elements in these works a broader chronological and geographical scope, a new prominence and appreciation given to Jewish life in exile, and an increased interest in the history of other nations; but he thinks they failed to attain the level of critical skepticism toward historical evidence that was current in non-Jewish historiography, or to overcome traditional Jewish methods of understanding history.[3] Robert Bonfil, too, recognizes "a truly novel type of Jewish literary production," but in only three or four historical works of the time, the others failing to transcend traditional conceptualizations because the Jewish political status in Europe deprived Jews of the kind of subject matter, the exploits of kings and warriors, which the Renaissance concept of history considered essential.[4] Both Yerushalmi and Bonfil, moreover, note the meager production of historical works compared with other kinds of Jewish writing at this time, and the relative lack of interest shown by the general Jewish public in new forms of Jewish historical writing, especially in comparison with older histories like *The Book of Tradition*, the *Yosippon*, and *Seder Olam Rabbah*, or with

---

Kohen," *Jewish Thought in the Sixteenth Century*, ed. Bernard D. Cooperman (Cambridge, 1983), 482–84. Lester Segal, *Historical Consciousness and Religious Tradition in Azariah de' Rossi's Me'or Einayim* (Philadelphia, 1989), chap. 1, stresses the endeavor, found in most historical works of sixteenth-century Jewish writers, to record the recent and continuing calamities of Jewish life in order to bring about or foresee a practical (i.e., messianic) resolution.

2. Robert Bonfil, in "How Golden Was the Age of the Renaissance in Jewish Historiography?" *History and Theory* 27 (1988): 78–102, argues that Renaissance ideas were the only important stimulus to Jewish historiography. See also Bonfil, "The Historian's Perception of the Jews in the Italian Renaissance: Towards a Reappraisal," *Revue des Etudes Juives* 143 (1984): 59–82.

3. Yerushalmi, *Zakhor*, 61–63. Cf. Meyer's (1974) assertion that the historical writing of the time differed "in a broadening of historical horizons, in a turn to secular interpretation, in historical criticism of traditional texts, and in a new regard for chronological sequence" (19). Abraham Melamed, "The Perception of Jewish History in Italian Jewish Thought," 139–70, addresses the question of how Jewish writers of the sixteenth and seventeenth centuries in general, not only historians, conceived of Jewish history. He argues that a number of these writers adopted significant Renaissance concepts of history: the use of natural, in place of theological, explanations for historical events; increased interest in ancient non-Jewish history and familiarity with, including quotation from, classical authors; and the critical evaluation of traditional sources of information through reasoning and evidence from non-Jewish sources.

4. Bonfil, "How Golden," esp. 93–95.

legendary fantasies such as *The Gests of Alexander* or tales of the Ten Lost Tribes.

In this chapter we shall examine the image of Bar Kokhba in six historical works of the sixteenth century, asking whether it has been influenced by any new purposes and methods adopted by the writers, or by their memory of the Spanish expulsion.[5]

Samuel Usque:
Consolation for the Tribulations of Israel (1553)

Samuel Usque, a friend of Isaac Abravanel's son, Samuel, grew up as a *converso*, a member of a converted Jewish family of Portugal. During his youth, the Jewish communities of Spain and Portugal endured several crises: the Portuguese King John II deported Jewish children to "reeducate" them, King Emanuel III forcibly baptized large numbers of Jews, conversos were butchered by mobs in 1506 and during the 1520s, and the Portuguese Inquisition was gradually gaining power, reaching full authority by 1544.[6] These events, particularly as they affected the faith of Portuguese Jews, became the primary concern of Usque's single literary work, *Consolation for the Tribulations of Israel*, written after his escape from Portugal and his wanderings through eastern Mediterranean cities and central Europe. He wrote the book while living in the Italian city of Ferrara in the 1550s.

The *Consolation* is written in Portuguese in the form of a pastoral dialogue carried on among three shepherds, a literary form much in vogue among the cultured classes of the Renaissance, to which many Portuguese conversos belonged.[7] The shepherd named Ycabo, representing the people Israel, recounts a full chronicle of Jewish sufferings from biblical times to the present. Pointing to Israel's sins, he expresses his fear that God has

---

5. I limit my study to these six writings because of their accessibility and this mixture of tradition and innovation that appears in them, heralding in some ways, as Yerushalmi and Meyer have suggested, the emergence of a modern historiography. I have searched for references to Bar Kokhba in other historical writings of the sixteenth century, but have not searched historical works of the seventeenth, such as Yosef Sambari's *Divrei Yosef* (1672), nor non-historical works such as Abraham Portaleone's *Shiltei Gibborim* (1612) or Simon Luzzato's *Discorso circa il stato degli ebrei* (1638).

6. Martin A. Cohen, trans., introduction to Samuel Usque, *Consolation for the Tribulations of Israel* (Philadelphia, 1977), 5–17.

7. Ibid., 10.

abandoned Israel—a fear that may show the effect of Christian contentions that God had abandoned the Jews for rejecting Jesus. In Ycabo we hear the despair of Portuguese Jewry, beaten down by expulsions, inquisitions, and polemical attacks. Usque speaks to them through the words of the other two shepherds, Numeo and Zicareo, the prophets Nahum and Zechariah sent to earth to comfort Israel. They console Ycabo by explaining the true cause of Israel's suffering, demonstrating God's continuing mercy and concern, and citing prophetic utterances that promise God's sure and imminent salvation.

It is in the set of Ycabo's speeches about the period of the Second Temple that Usque tells the story of Bar Kokhba, a primary example of Jewish suffering.

> And forty-eight and a half years after the destruction of the holy Temple, there arose in the city of Betar in Judea a Jew by the name of Bar Koziva. His knowledge surpassed that of most people in his day, and he announced that he was the true Messiah whom we await, and offered amazing proofs of his identity. In short, his ways and manner were so effective that he incited the people of this city to rebel against the Roman empire. Hadrian Caesar, who was then emperor, learned of the rebellion and attacked the city with a mighty army. After the siege that lasted three and a half years, he captured it and inflicted such a cruel and frightful massacre upon its people that our enemies' horses wallowed up to their mouths in Israelite blood, and the current of the blood was so great and powerful that it swept large and heavy stones along as it coursed to the sea, four thousand paces from the city. Finally, a third part of the two rivers which flowed in the area of Jericho ran red with the blood of forty-five thousand men who were slain, and for seven years the heathens round about fertilized their vines with the putrid blood of Jews. Among those slain was Bar Koziva; his head had been cut off by a Roman soldier.[8]

In Usque's story, Bar Koziva's most distinguishing features are his extraordinary knowledge and his ability to offer amazing proofs of his messianic claims, which convince the people of Betar. Usque does not tell us clearly what those "amazing proofs" were. They could be proofs of his knowledge, but what was "amazing" about it? Or they might be merely a warrior's feats

---

8. Usque, *Consolation*, 150–51. All passages from *Consolation* are translated by Martin Cohen.

of strength, as found in the rabbinic legends—but this would have no connection with Bar Koziva's "amazing knowledge." If we compare the messianic movements current in the early sixteenth century (to be examined briefly below), we find messianic prophets or claimants authenticating their claims by predicting events, as in the case of Solomon Molko, or we find followers believing that prophets or claimants have performed miracles, as conversos thought David Reubeni and the "Messiah of Setubol" had. Do Bar Koziva's "amazing proofs," then, refer to astounding predictions, similar to the way that Molko accurately predicted floods and comets? If so, the connection between such predictions and Bar Koziva's knowledge remains obscure. Yet if there is a connection between his knowledge and the proofs, what could it be?

A Speculation: Knowledge and Magic

In the absence of clear answers from Usque's story of Bar Koziva, I propose to compare Usque's one other account of a false messiah, David Alroy. The parallel that immediately catches our attention is Alroy's possession of extraordinary knowledge. The sequence of events is also similar: knowledge is followed by messianic acclamation and then rebellion. In the excerpt from Usque's account below, I include passages that illustrate the content of Alroy's knowledge.

> In Hamaria there lived an Israelite named David Alroy. He had studied under Chisdai, the most learned Jew in all the Diaspora, and later under the head of the academy in the city of Baghdad. He thus became an expert in Talmud and in all other disciplines, including witchcraft and magic. Made conceited by his knowledge, he assembled a large group of Jews living on Mount Chaphton and informed them that he was the Messiah. They joined him in a rebellion against the king, and killed many of the king's troops.... The king questioned him, asking if he had really proclaimed that he was the messiah whom the Jews were awaiting, and who would perform many miracles.... David, [later] deceived and imprisoned, availed himself of his wisdom. He used his magic so effectively that he broke his fetters, and freed himself, and left the prison grounds after demolishing a strong wall with a mere word.... He came before them, invisible.... He removed his turban, spread it over the river Gozan, and crossed to the other side.... On that day, David traveled the

equivalent of a ten-days' journey by skillfully harnessing the power that resides in God's ineffable name.[9]

When we further compare this account with Usque's literary source, the story of David El Ro'i in Benjamin of Tudela's travelogue, we discover that Usque has accentuated the motif of magic in the story and has added his own explanation for Alroy's messianic claim, namely, that Alroy had become "conceited" over his exceptional knowledge. Usque learned from Benjamin's account that El Ro'i's knowledge included Talmud, "the profane sciences," and "the books of the magicians and enchanters." He learned, too, that the Persian Jews had proclaimed El Ro'i the Messiah because of the "signs by false miracles" (*simanim be 'otot sheqer*) he had performed.[10]

In both stories of the false messiah David Alroy, knowledge is closely connected with "proof" of being the Messiah. In Benjamin's account, knowledge includes the magical knowledge enabling El Ro'i to perform the false miracles that convinced people that he was the Messiah. In Usque's account, this knowledge made Alroy so conceited that he thought he was the Messiah. His knowledge of "witchcraft and magic" gave him, specifically, the powers of strength, invisibility, riding across water, and speedy travel.

Furthermore, the king in Usque's story of David Alroy associates the Messiah of Jewish expectation with the ability to perform miracles. Comparing these words with Benjamin's story, we learn that they are Usque's own addition, a description of the Messiah apparently intended as an accurate perception on the king's part. That miracles were part of Usque's cosmology is shown by the numerous instances of them in his book.

Usque's two accounts of false messiahs, David Alroy and Bar Koziva, present them both as men of great knowledge. We should then infer that just as Alroy's knowledge led him to proclaim himself the Messiah, Usque's Bar Koziva, also possessing great knowledge and also proclaiming himself the Messiah, acted from the same delusion.

I suggest that these parallels carry over to the "amazing proofs" in the story of Bar Koziva. Since Usque thought the Messiah would perform miracles, and since the people of Betar are convinced by Bar Koziva's "amazing proofs"; and since those messianic proofs are unlikely to have been demonstrations of a warrior's might or a scholar's expertise (being

---

9. Ibid., 174–76.
10. Benjamin of Tudela, *Mas'ot shel Rabbi Benyamin: The Itinerary of Rabbi Benjamin of Tudela*, text ed. and trans. A. Asher (Elkam Adler), 2 vols. (New York, 1840), 77–79 of Heb. text.

neither "proofs" nor "amazing" in relation to a miracle-performing Messiah), Usque most likely intended Bar Koziva's "amazing proofs" as miraculous or magical phenomena, perhaps even predictions about the immediate future. The simplest way, then, to explain the new features in Usque's story of Bar Koziva, his extraordinary knowledge and his amazing proofs of being the Messiah, is to infer a connection between them of the kind that appears in Usque's story of David Alroy, such knowledge including the "witchcraft and magic" (Usque's words in Alroy's story) needed to perform the "amazing proofs" (words from Bar Koziva's story) which convinced people that these men were the Messiah.

If this line of reasoning is probable, it leads us to an image of Bar Koziva and David Alroy as scholar-magicians. This image combines two images of false messiahs appearing in medieval Jewish history and literature—the image of the false messiah as magician, and the image of him as a deluded scholar.

The most famous example of the first type, the guileful magician, is the image of Jesus of Nazareth appearing in the medieval book *Toldot Yeshu* (History of Jesus).[11] The book presents Jesus as a shameless heretic who acquires magical powers by learning the Ineffable Name of God (*Shem ha-Meforash*). Then he claims to be the Messiah, and for proof performs many apparent miracles using the power of that name—curing the lame, healing lepers, riding across the Sea of Galilee on a millstone, and flying through the air. As a result, many young men believe his messianic claims, and a false religion is founded.

The second type of messianic claimant reflected in Usque's stories, the scholar who comes to believe he is the Messiah or messianic prophet, has a number of representatives in late medieval Jewish history: the kabbalist Abraham Abulafia in the late thirteenth century, Moses Botarel in the late fourteenth, Solomon Molko and R. Asher Lammlein in the early sixteenth, and after Usque's time, in the seventeenth century, Shabbatai Ṣevi.[12] Usque must have been familiar with Solomon Molko, and especially interested in him, because Molko was a Portuguese converso who had returned to Judaism. Although he seems not to have studied magic, his example—a converso who became a Jewish scholar, had visions and made prophecies, and who briefly stirred up intense messianic hopes—may have reinforced Usque's desire to point out the danger of "conceited" scholars who think they are the

11. See translation by Hugh Schonfield, *According to the Hebrews* (Oxford, 1937), 35–61.
12. See Silver's summary in *Messianic Speculation*, 87, 108–9, 143–48.

Messiah or heralds of the Messiah. One way Usque could have done this was by reproducing Benjamin of Tudela's story of David El Ro'i and introducing motifs from it into the legend of Bar Koziva.

The *Consolation*'s inclusion of two stories about scholar-magicians may also be related to the great interest that European scholars were then taking in magic and the occult. "High magic," writes Richard Cavendish, "reached its apogee in the Renaissance with the revival of Neoplatonism, the rediscovery of the Hermetica, and the Christian adoption of the Cabala."[13] Along with the humanist interest in the literature and philosophy of classical antiquity came a new interest in what were considered the ancient magical texts—Plato and the Neoplatonists, the Pythagorean tradition, Orphic hymns and the Hermetica, as well as kabbalah and Egyptian hieroglyphs. Italian philosophers like Marsilio Ficino and Pico della Mirandola formulated new syntheses of these traditions and defended the practice of magic, and men like Agrippa von Nettesheim, Paracelsus, and Johann Tritheim gained reputations as practitioners. Johannes Faust, the most infamous of the scholar-magicians of the sixteenth century, was a contemporary of Samuel Usque. Whatever the actual Faust did or did not do, he was known as an evil magician, astrologer, and alchemist; scholars denounced him as a charlatan, and Protestant leaders called him a servant of the devil. We do not know whether Usque, in his many travels or during his sojourn in Italy, ever heard of Faust, but the legends about this man show the cultural milieu in which Usque wrote. It included savage witch-hunts; people accepted the efficacy of the magic arts and feared their misuse. The popularity of the Faust legends, in which a scholar's pursuit of knowledge becomes perverted by cravings for unlimited power, shows that the figure of the scholar-magician aroused anxiety in the hearts of many sixteenth-century Europeans. The Italian version of Faust is "the universal man," the student of all subjects both holy and profane who attempts to experience and master all things. From a traditional Jewish or Christian viewpoint, this ideal manifests a blasphemous arrogance.[14] Usque's portraits of the false messiahs, Bar Koziva and David Alroy—though apparently based on Benjamin of Tudela's earlier story of a scholar-magician claiming to be the Messiah—may also convey a warning against the scholar-magicians of the late Renaissance.

---

13. Richard Cavendish, *A History of Magic* (London, 1977), 83.
14. Ibid., 83–107; D. P. Walker, *Spiritual and Demonic Magic from Ficino to Campanella* (Notre Dame, Ind., 1975).

Betar and the Millenarian Movements of Usque's Time

We can be more certain that Usque directed the story's warning against messianic claimants in general, regardless of the kind of proof they offered. Usque would have had a number of events in mind, for messianic hopes repeatedly manifested themselves among the converso population of Spain and Portugal throughout the first half of the sixteenth century, Usque's whole lifetime. Several converso prophets had arisen in Spain around 1500. An uneducated "Maiden of Herrara," believed by many conversos, claimed to have been taken to heaven where she heard voices of souls who had been burnt as martyrs. Other converso prophets claimed to have seen portents or ascended to heaven and heard messianic promises or even to have met Elijah and the Messiah. Converso communities responded by fasting, returning to Jewish law, and dressing in holiday clothes to await the Messiah—but were soon imprisoned and executed by the Inquisition for thus revealing their Jewish faith.

In Portugal, conversos rejoiced at the arrival of David Reubeni in 1528. Claiming to represent the king of one of the Ten Lost Tribes, this stranger sought the Portuguese king's help in "liberating" the Holy Land—an eschatological goal in the eyes of Christians and Jews alike. Conversos perceived in this man a herald of the imminent messianic era when they would be free. In his journal, Reubeni asserts that he had to tell conversos that he would conquer the Holy Land by military might and not, contrary to their expectations, by signs or miracles (*lo be'ot velo bemofet*).[15] Also around this time, Solomon Molko, mentioned before, received visions commanding him to leave Portugal. Traveling to Turkey and Palestine, he met other Jews eagerly awaiting the Messiah. In 1529 he announced the year 1540 as that of the Messiah, and in Rome, astir with millenarian prophecies related to the invasion of the German Charles V, he preached apocalyptic warnings to packed synagogues, also impressing church officials, and successfully predicted floods, comets, and earthquakes.[16] Another messianic figure, Luis Dias, an uneducated converso tailor, came to consider himself first a prophet and then the Messiah around 1540. This "Messiah of Setubol" attracted a following of conversos in Setubol and

---

15. Elkan Nathan Adler, comp., *Jewish Travellers* (London: 1930), 284–315 (David Reubeni's diary on his sojourn in Portugal); Aescoly, *Messianic Movements*, 360–65; Silver, *Messianic Speculation*, 145–47.

16. Silver, *Messianic Speculation*, 147–50; Aescoly, *Messianic Movements*, 273–76, 376–79, 386–97.

Lisbon; they believed he worked miracles and they kissed his hand as they would the hand of a king.[17]

Beyond the converso community, too, groups of Jews and Christians continued to see signs of the end. Abravanel had predicted that the Messiah would come in 1503, and in 1502 a German Jew, Asher Lammlein, appeared in Venice and proclaimed that if Jews engaged in penance and gave charity for six months, Christian churches would fall and the Messiah would arrive; Venetian Jews proceeded to do as he urged.[18] Usque seems also to have visited Safed soon after its rise as a new center of kabbalah; Scholem says of Safed at this time that it "numbered more inspired enthusiasts and devout seekers of mystical salvation than any other city."[19] Then, before returning to Italy, Usque visited Prague, where he would surely have heard of Thomas Muntzer's peasant rebels (1524–25) fighting what they considered the Final Battle preceding the Second Coming, or the Anabaptists' attempt to inaugurate a New Jerusalem at Munster in 1534, or ongoing waves of similar millenarian sentiment.[20] Virginia Reeves, in *The Influence of Prophecy in the Later Middle Ages*, describes numerous and frequent millenarian expectations among Catholic visionaries of the time—seeking the "Last World Emperor" in various French and German kings or an "Angelic Pope" who would appear after the tribulations of the Antichrist to renew the church and the world. Guillaume Postel, for example, whose writings were taken seriously throughout Western Europe, had a vision in Venice around 1551. It indicated that he was the first-born of the New Age, a "lower messiah" whose mission was to found a universal empire that would bring all peoples from all faiths into one Christian order so that the whole of creation could return to its pristine glory.[21] Furthermore, Jews and Christians alike found eschatological significance in the rise of the Protestant movement, which split the Christian world; in the increasing power of the Ottoman Empire, which conquered Hungary in 1547; and in the discovery of the New World, pointing (as Columbus envisioned it) to a universal conversion that would inaugurate Christ's return, or (as Jews hoped) to the

---

17. Cecil Roth, *A History of the Marranos* (Philadelphia, 1932), 146–48.
18. Silver, *Messianic Speculation*, 143–44.
19. Scholem, *Sabbatai Ṣevi*, 19; Scholem, *Kabbalah* (New York, 1974), 72–74; Cohen, introduction to Usque, *Consolation*, 14.
20. Norman Cohn, *The Pursuit of the Millennium*, rev. ed. (New York, 1970), chaps. 12–13.
21. Virginia Reeves, *The Influence of Prophecy in the Later Middle Ages* (Oxford, 1969), 479–81.

discovery of the Ten Lost Tribes and their imminent return to the Land of Israel at the end of days.[22]

In this ideological and emotional climate, full of passionate hopes and frequent disappointments, among conversos as well as many European Jews and Christians, Usque, too, believed that redemption was near. The last pages of the *Consolation* comforts readers by explaining why redemption would soon begin: in each age of history, says Numeo, Israel's cries had reached progressively higher into the heavens, each tribulation sending prayers of pain one step closer to God, so that now the cries of the Portuguese Jews had reached finally into the highest heaven, and God, hearing them, soon would act: "You have begun to attain the final stage of your preparation for redemption."[23] The Messiah would come, but Usque is careful not to declare a date. Martin Cohen suggests that Usque remembered the failure of Abravanel's prediction of the year 1503;[24] he may also have known how the calculations of the exiled Spanish Jew, Abraham Ha-Levi (for the year 1530), and of Solomon Molko (for 1540), had likewise disappointed hopes.[25]

If Usque, too, thought that redemption was imminent, what did Betar's destruction and Bar Koziva's delusions about redemption mean to him? One would think that such disastrous consequences of messianic belief would give Usque cause to reconsider his own hopes.

The "cruel and frightful massacre" of Betar, told in grim and relentless detail, constitutes more than half of Usque's account. It is one of the many tribulations filling Usque's history of Israel. And this one, like all the others, comes as divine punishment for sins. All the subjugations, oppressions, massacres, and expulsions of Jewish history were, according to the *Consolation*, "misfortunes which the Lord wishes to give us, persecutions which their sins bring on, a scourge with which the Lord chastises them." Ycabo, representing Israel, exclaims, "We see clearly that the multitude of our sins have delivered us into the power of Your wrath, and that we have persisted in these same iniquities, for if it were not so, our affairs would have a happier and more favorable end."[26] One of Usque's goals was to answer the Christian contention that Israel's tribulations signified God's punishment

---

22. Ibid., 359–60; McGinn, *Visions of the End*, 284–85; Silver, *Messianic Speculation*, 112–14.
23. Usque, *Consolation*, 236–38.
24. Ibid., 276.
25. Silver, *Messianic Speculation*, 130–35.
26. Usque, *Consolation*, 213, 223.

for Israel's rejection of Jesus. Usque thus identifies for each of the tribulations a pattern of specific actions (other than that rejection) which brought it about.

Ycabo acknowledges that he deserved the tribulations "because I was disobedient, like Adam in the terrestrial paradise, I abandoned God." Indeed, for Usque (as Martin Cohen argues in his introduction to the *Consolation*), the sin of abandoning God was the one fundamental sin that united all the specific instances of transgression in Israel's history. Of most concern to him, and given central importance in the *Consolation*, was abandoning God through assimilation, apostasy, and lack of faith in God's salvations—which Usque saw as the particular way in which Portuguese Jews had sinned. Worst were those conversos who had escaped Portugal but still "persevered in their error; like rebellious limbs, they refuse to attach themselves to the body of Israel" because of "the illusions of great ease and wealth with which the world entices them."[27]

What, then, were the sins for which Betar was being punished? To begin with, Bar Koziva had sinned in proclaiming himself the Messiah. At the end of David Alroy's story, Usque cites specific scriptural verses that brand false messiahs as sinners and define their sin. The verses cited from Jeremiah and Ezekiel declare that false prophets wrongly claim divine authority, arouse empty hopes, and lead people away from God. The verses also declare that all false prophets will be destroyed for their sins.[28] These statements are intended to apply to all (false) messianic movements.

Like the rabbinic legends and Ibn Daud's account, Usque's account warns against false messiahs. But in comparison with earlier accounts, Usque's presents Bar Koziva's rebellion as totally futile, a foolish misjudgment with catastrophic consequences, since he exhibits no military abilities and he leads only one small city against a powerful empire.[29] It is also startling to find that Usque has completely omitted R. Akiba from the story—in contrast to Abravanel, who had worked hard to defend him, and Maimonides, who had focused his argument on him. Usque, it seems, was

27. Ibid., 56, 224, 206–7.
28. Ibid., 176.
29. If, according to Cohen, ibid., 272, Usque had read Dio Cassius's writings, he read Dio Cassius's account of the Jewish revolt in Judea and Galilee (see Appendix), the leader of which goes unnamed. This is the war we today call the Bar Kokhba rebellion, but Usque apparently thought Dio Cassius was describing a later war than the one described in Midrash Lamentations, which mentions only one town, Betar, led by a man named Ben Koziva. Usque inserts this war (our "Bar Kokhba rebellion") in the *Consolation* as a later one, led by an unnamed Jewish leader, unrelated to Betar and Bar Koziva, and quashed by the Roman general Severus rather than Hadrian (152–53).

not concerned with the polemical issues raised by R. Akiba's proclamation. For this reason, he also did not have to discover anything positive about Bar Koziva to justify R. Akiba's support.

But the people of Betar are being punished as well. Usque places the story of Betar at the end of his Second Dialogue, devoted to the subject of the Second Temple (which Christian polemicists claimed was the Temple of messianic times). Usque shows that Jews suffered greatly during the period of the Second Temple (thus it could not be the messianic era), and that they suffered as punishment for the principal sins of that time. Ycabo declares, "And because I did not acknowledge Him but remained obstinate by flouting His precepts and living in this Second Temple with discords, jealousies, and bloodshed, I received His cruel punishments through the Romans."[30] The destruction of Betar, like the million people who died in Jerusalem and the destruction and profanation of the Temple, was punishment for this same general sin of that era—although Usque lists many specific sins of the cruel tyrannous leaders of Jerusalem, especially the Sicarii, for which the whole city was punished. Notably, Usque gives far more space to the downfall of Jerusalem than to that of Betar.

But beyond whatever the Jews of Betar did, Hadrian is also named "responsible for the extermination of your people in the regions of Syria and Jerusalem." Hadrian, and all the other non-Jewish oppressors who throughout history brought suffering to the Jews, were "instruments of punishment for your iniquities," agents of God's wrath (as in Isaiah's concept of Assyria's role); and yet repeatedly in the *Consolation*, these agents seem to act in ways that exceed their role of punishment, adding to it an unnecessary cruelty and hatred for their victims—a "malice with which they have inflicted the penalty for your iniquities." The Jews are sinners being punished, but the non-Jewish persecutors are eager malevolent executioners. Often in the book, especially in the medieval accounts, the Jewish victims even appear as helpless innocents. Hadrian, then, as punishment for his unnecessary cruelty to the Jews, was "plagued by the Lord with a painful illness for your vengeance," until he killed himself to gain relief.[31] This divine vengeance on oppressive enemies (again the motif of vengeance) was interpreted by Usque as a sign of God's mercy and special concern for Israel, and was intended to console the suffering conversos who felt abandoned.

30. Ibid., 163.
31. Ibid., 161, 163, 228, 161.

But did Usque have in mind a more specific sin committed by the people of Betar? Bar Koziva led the people away from God; this was his sin, but are we meant to discern sin in the way the people of Betar acquiesced to his "amazing proofs" and false promises—thereby deserving their terrible massacre? Set beside the fundamental themes of the *Consolation*, their acquiescence seems to take on the shape of apostasy, a turning away from God to embrace the empty words of a man who had set himself up in place of God's Messiah.

By showing his readers, "the gentlemen of the diaspora of Portugal," what was sinful about the actions of Bar Koziva and the Jews of the Second Temple Period (and perhaps also the people of Betar), Usque is asking those readers not to repeat the same sin. He is teaching them through history that sin brings suffering, faith brings salvation. Thus, the story of Betar, as part of the chain of sins and rebellions during the Second Temple Period, conveys an implicit call for repentance—a call for turning back to God and trusting in God's salvation. He addresses particularly those conversos he describes as "vacillating in their faith, resigning themselves unnecessarily and succumbing to their afflictions"—most of whom did so "out of too little constancy," an age-old weakness of the Jews. As Usque states near the end of the *Consolation*, "The compassion of the heavens is prepared to give infinitely as long as there is room for it in the recipient." Usque therefore urges his readers to make room for God's compassion: "Keep unshaken faith in Him in all your misfortunes, because he wishes the hour to arrive in which His liberal compassion will reach you."[32]

We can feel in this sentence, as throughout the *Consolation*, a sense of urgency and tense expectation. God was about to redeem Israel; all that was needed was for Jews to turn to God in faith and in obedience to the Torah. The free conversos should return to Torah and those in Portugal should at least keep their ancient faith constantly in mind.[33] This is why it is so important to Usque that his readers repent and understand the lessons of history.

Betar, as a story of the consequences resulting from a generation's flouting of God and Torah, and also perhaps a story of the deluded faith a city places in merely human promises, taught one of those lessons Usque wanted his readers to learn. The crucial human task, yet the most difficult of the time, was to wait and keep faith, and not be distracted by amazing proofs

---

32. Ibid., 38, 39, 260.
33. Ibid., 206–7.

or precarious calculations of messianic dates or the passing gains to be gotten by apostasy.

Yosef Ha-Kohen: *The Vale of Tears* (1575)

Most modern students of *The Vale of Tears* (*Emeq Ha-Bakha*), beginning with Samuel David Luzzato in 1852, have identified the *Consolation* as a major influence on it.[34] Yosef Ha-Kohen does indeed mention several times "the book of the Portuguese, Samuel Usque,"[35] and *The Vale of Tears* takes for its subject the same type of events, the misfortunes of Israel, with which the *Consolation* is concerned. Yosef's aim, however, is not so much to console as to cause weeping.

Ha-Kohen writes, "The expulsion from Spain aroused in me the decision to write this book: let the Children of Israel know what our enemies have done to us ... for the day will come."[36] This sentence reveals two major motives for writing the book. First, *The Vale of Tears* tells "what our enemies have done to us," recounting all the misfortunes Jews had suffered at the hands of foreign nations, from the time of Betar, the beginning of the Diaspora, until 1575, when the book was published. The second purpose, eschatological in nature, appears clearly in the following sentences from his introductory paragraph: "Let everyone who reads it [this book] be astounded and gasp. Let him raise his eyes, two wells of tears, on high and, putting his hands to his loins, ask, How long, Oh God? My God, may the days of our mourning come to an end. May he send us the just Messiah and redeem us soon, for the sake of his love and mercy. Amen, amen!"[37] Ha-

---

34. Samuel David Luzzato, preface to *Vale of Tears*, ed. M. Letteris (Vienna, 1852), xi–xii; Meyer Waxman, *A History of Jewish Literature* (New York, 1933) 2:473; Israel Zinberg, *A History of Jewish Literature*, trans. and ed. Bernard Martin (Cincinnati, 1974), 4:77; Tryggve Kronholm, "The Vale of Tears: Remarks on the new edition of Joseph hakkohen's Sefaer Emaeq habbaka," Orientalia Suecana 30 (1981): 154. Karin Almbladh, however, in her recent edition of *Emeq Ha-Bakha*, credits Ha-Kohen's reliance on the *Consolation*, but finds its primary inspiration in the immediate sufferings of the Italian Jewish communities in which he lived: see Almbladh, ed., *Sefer 'Emeq Ha-Bakha (The Vale of Tears), with the chronicle of the anonymous Corrector* (Uppsala, 1981), 20 (English section); see 26–29 for discussion of sources.
35. Yosef Ha-Kohen, *The Vale of Tears*, trans. Harry S. May (The Hague, 1971), e.g., 50 and 52.
36. Almbladh, ed., *'Emeq Ha-Bakha*, 62.
37. Ibid., 9.

Kohen wanted his reader, from learning this history, to weep not only in repentance for the sins that had caused such punishments, but also in grief over Israel's sorrows past and present. Then the reader's cries, joined by all the tears of other Jews remembering this anguished history, would move God at last to avenge and redeem Israel.[38] "For the day will come" (from the sentence quoted above)—the day of messianic redemption. Yerushalmi convincingly argues that Yosef Ha-Kohen's earlier book, *Divrei Ha-Yamim le-Malkhei Ṣarfat u-Malkhei Beit Ottoman ha-Togar* (History of the Kings of France and of the Ottoman Turkish Sultans), sustains messianic hope by showing readers the events of world history that are leading to the final messianic wars.[39] *The Vale of Tears*, however, goes further: Ha-Kohen hoped that this book, by moving God to redeem the Jewish people, would itself work to change history: "Oh Lord, witness this. . . . We raise our eyes to you." "See our suffering . . . champion our battle." "Oh God of vengeance, vindicate the blood of your servants."[40]

Bar Kokhba and Betar

In his story of Bar Kokhba, Yosef Ha-Kohen seems to have combined Ibn Daud's account of the three Kozivas with Usque's portrayal of Bar Koziva as a false messiah.[41] Ha-Kohen mostly follows Ibn Daud. Thus, the Kozivas appear as a line of three kings who rebelled against Rome, conquered Egypt, and stirred up a widespread messianic movement involving great numbers of Jews. But Ha-Kohen adds certain details that introduce new motifs and accentuate old ones in new ways. In the following translation of Ha-Kohen's story of the Kozivas, I italicize those words representing significant elements not found in Ibn Daud's account:

> Koziva arose in Betar and said, "I am the Messiah ben David." He rebelled against King Domitian, and killed his viceroy in Judea. But Domitian could not act strongly against him because he was still

---

38. On the call for repentance and the anger of God, see Ha-Kohen, *Vale of Tears*, 17, 22, 35, 39; on awakening God's mercy, 1, 39, 88.
39. Yerushalmi, "Messianic Impulses in Joseph ha-Kohen."
40. Ha-Kohen, *Vale of Tears*, 88 (from the writer who completed *Emeq Ha-Bakha*, who calls himself "the Corrector"), 39; on vengeance, 17, 24, 33, 53, 67, 87, etc.
41. See Almbladh, *'Emeq Ha-Bakha*, 43, for her identification of Ha-Kohen's sources as Ibn Daud's *Book of Tradition* and *History of Rome* and Usque's *Consolation*. She characterizes Ha-Kohen's account of Bar Kokhba and the succession of the Roman emperors as "fantastic."

young. Koziva reigned in Betar in the fifty-second year after the destruction of the Temple of our God. When Koziva died, Rufus (meaning "red"), his son, reigned in his stead. When Rufus died, Romulus, his son, reigned in his stead. Many Israelites gathered around Koziva and his sons, from all the places where they had been scattered: *he raised up foot soldiers and cavalry, and rebelled against the emperor. Tidings went out to every land,* and they fought with the nations in surrounding areas, and overpowered Egypt. Thus, Koziva and his son and grandson reigned over Betar *and its surroundings,* until the days of Hadrian I; *and the nations obeyed them.* . . .

Romulus ben Koziva congratulated himself, saying, "I am the Messiah of God," and many obeyed him. Then the wrath of Hadrian burned against them, and he went out with a large army and a strong hand, and besieged Betar three years, and the city was captured on the ninth day of the fifth month in the seventy-third year *after the expulsion of Judah from its soil.*[42]

Yosef's additions to Ibn Daud's text introduce motifs related to two particular themes. The first is that of the wicked messianic claimant. Yosef writes that Romulus ben Koziva "congratulated himself" after he and his father and grandfather won spectacular military victories, and then announced himself as the Messiah. Conceit generated dangerous messianic delusions.

The ultimate source of this theme might have been the legend in b. Sanhedrin that Bar Koziva (read literally as a "son of Koziva") claimed to be the Messiah. But the closest text is the *Consolation*, which explicitly presents his announcement as a delusion born of conceit over his power. It seems, then, that Ha-Kohen adopted this idea most directly from Samuel Usque and tried to reconcile it with Ibn Daud's account of the three Kozivas. Ha-Kohen thus arrives at the image of a false messiah who is not a magician-scholar but a charismatic military leader deluded by his own success.

None of the false messiahs of the sixteenth century exactly matches this image. But Romulus's military power does bear some resemblance to the claims made by David Reubeni, who presented himself as a powerful Jewish prince come to establish an alliance with the European states (and perhaps to aid Europe in its conflict with the Ottoman empire). Ha-Kohen portrays him in *The Vale of Tears* as a charlatan who won people's trust through ingenious

---

42. Ibid., 3–4.

lies and symbolic gestures. Another false messiah of the sixteenth century, Asher Lamlein, Ha-Kohen calls "a false prophet, lunatic, and bag of wind"[43]—attributing to him, even more so, the same self-delusion and empty promises he ascribes to Romulus ben Koziva. It thus seems that Ha-Kohen intended his portrait of the Kozivas to stand as a warning against the messianic charlatans of his day. Yet we must take note, as Yerushalmi reminds us, that Ha-Kohen did indeed expect the Messiah to arise in his days and was himself deeply moved by the mission and words of Shlomo Molkho.[44]

The second theme conveyed in Ha-Kohen's additions is the military and political power of the Kozivas: "he raised up foot-soldiers and cavalry . . . tidings went out to every land . . . [they] reigned over Betar and its surroundings . . . and the nations obeyed them." These statements, which may be interpretations of Ibn Daud's text, augment the Kozivas' power and add realistic details, and they might especially interest readers living among Italian city-states involved in attempts to expand alliances and amass conquered territories.

Yosef Ha-Kohen goes on to narrate the downfall of Betar. He mostly follows Usque's version of the legends of Midrash Lamentations, but he again diverges from his sources, this time adding phrases not found in Ibn Daud's and Usque's versions that amplify the horror and suffering (indicated in italics):

> *Much blood was spilled there. The aged were not spared, mothers were dashed near their children, on that day of God's wrath*; and the horses in the streets walked through blood of the slain that reached as high as their bellies, *at that time of violence*. A torrent of blood issued out rushing to the sea, and washed away great rocks *that can still be found at Jericho*; and the rivers turned to blood, *and their stench rose to the heavens*. The number of the dead was forty-five thousand. Also Romulus ben Koziva they killed with the others slain *on that violent day. Those who remained alive, Hadrian expelled to Spain: these are the exiles of Jerusalem who have lived in Spain to this day.*[45]

The number and emotional intensity of Ha-Kohen's additions suggest that this segment of the story, the massacre of the Jews at Betar, was for him the

---

43. Ha-Kohen, *Vale of Tears*, 73–74, 76–77.
44. Yerushalmi, "Messianic Impulses," esp. 471–72.
45. Almbladh, ed., *'Emeq Ha-Bakha*, 4.

most important part of the history of the Kozivas. In the framework of *The Vale of Tears* as a whole, Betar represents the first episode in the long history of Jewish suffering that is the subject of the book; and the effect that Betar's destruction works on readers is reinforced and amplified by the history of later calamities in the rest of the book.

How did Yosef Ha-Kohen intend this story of Betar's destruction to affect readers? First, his use of the phrase, "day of God's wrath," and his portrayal of Romulus's sinfulness indicate that he was defending the justice of God and calling for Jews to repent. "The wrath of God" is a phrase that recurs often in *The Vale of Tears*—partly as a stock metaphor, but also because it explains the cause of Jewish suffering: "God has found Israel guilty; therefore did he pour out his wrath." At the same time, however, *The Vale of Tears* puts the greater blame for Jewish suffering upon the Gentiles. They are portrayed as envious, hateful, and cruel, and they appear in the book as mobs, murderers, and slanderers, whereas Jews most often appear as innocent victims: "The blood of your servants was shed . . . though they had done no evil."[46] (Malevolent apostates comprise a notable exception.) By and large, Ha-Kohen portrays Jews as faithful servants of God, helplessly given over to Gentile violence and hatred. And except for the sinful Kozivas, that is the way Jews and Gentiles are portrayed in the story of Betar. Hadrian is a cruel, violent murderer, and the Jews are innocent victims: old men, mothers, and children who die in the massacre.

Thus, a second effect that Ha-Kohen intends for the story is to arouse anger at Gentiles for the way they treated Jews at Betar, and he especially wants it to arouse God's wrath and punishment, just as he intends other stories in the book to do so. Describing a German attack on Jews in the 14th century, he wrote, "They suddenly rose up and killed many with the sword; others were flagellated with whips and burned. Behold this, Oh Lord; witness it and champion their cause!" Regarding Pope Pius V, a persecutor of Jews in Ha-Kohen's own day, he pleads, "Oh Lord of Hosts, righteous Judge, let me witness your anger with him."[47] Like Abravanel and Usque, Yosef Ha-Kohen writes often of revenge; he wants God to wreak a terrible vengeance upon the Gentile nations who over all those centuries had inflicted suffering upon the Jewish people.

A third object of this passage is to move readers to tears of grief, horror, and pity for the victims at Betar. The destruction tales of Midrash Lamenta-

---

46. Ha-Kohen, *Vale of Tears*, 39.
47. Ibid., 52–53, 102.

tions already do this, but Ha-Kohen adds new details that reinforce this effect: the stench of the blood, the helplessly slaughtered infants and mothers and old men, and the expulsion of the survivors *to* Spain—all recall the horrors of the recent expulsion *from* Spain. Ha-Kohen inserts the phrase, "that day of violence" (*yom hanimar hahu*), twice, like a lament and its echo.

Viewing the story of Betar within the context of the general content and purposes of *The Vale of Tears*, we recognize how it furthered broader functions of the book. Together with all the other examples of Jewish suffering, this event showed readers that Jewish suffering and Gentile persecutions were fundamental components of Jewish history; that Jews had suffered ever since the time of Betar, when they were expelled from their land; and that only God could save them from the cruel power of the Gentiles. As Ha-Kohen states in the book's introductory poem, readers are to respond to this history by turning to the mercy of God. Their tears would then move God to raise up the desperately awaited Messiah to redeem them from their suffering and punish their oppressors.

History of Suffering

Does anything in Ha-Kohen's story suggest a shift in historical perception? The story has a tone and emphasis that would not fit, for example, into Ibn Daud's *Book of Tradition*, and yet none of the motifs of the story is new in itself. The difference seems to issue from the meaning that Betar's suffering acquires within the framework of *The Vale of Tears* as a whole. The *Memorbücher* (memorial books) of the Middle Ages had described single incidents of Jewish persecution in specific areas during a limited number of years; Nuremberg's *Memorbuch*, for example, tells of persecutions in Germany and France from the First Crusade of 1096 to the Black Death of 1349. The so-called "martyrological" sections of these books were read aloud in synagogues during memorial services for the dead—probably to acquire the merit generated from those who died as martyrs (by *kiddush ha-Shem*, sanctification of the Name), and to recall those exempla of the loyal deaths that circumstances might demand from later Jews.[48] *The Vale of Tears*, although it might be loosely considered a *memorbuch* or even a martyrology, had an activist intent, to prevent further Jewish deaths by moving God to

---

48. See recent discussions in Yerushalmi, *Zakhor*, 46; Meyer, *Ideas of Jewish History*, 91–102 (introduction to the Crusade chronicle of Solomon bar Simeon, with translated excerpts); "Memorbuch," EJ 11:1299–1301.

bring immediate redemption; it also had a much larger scope, weaving together occurrences of Jewish suffering in many locales into a total history of Jewish life in the Diaspora.

From that perspective, Jewish history is no longer an internal story of the transmission of revelation and rabbinic authority culminating in the messianic redemption. *The Vale of Tears* characterizes Jewish history as suffering culminating in redemption, as the relations between Jews and Gentiles, which now become part of the ancient theme of sin, punishment, and salvation found, for example, in the Deuteronomic writings. But that biblical structure is here broadened, extended outward, and qualified by new causalities and concerns on a social level, as political power and Gentile hatred become significant historical causes. In this respect, *The Vale of Tears* resembles Ha-Kohen's other historical work, *Divrei Ha-Yamim*, which despite its eschatological motivation, usually demonstrates an interest in political causality.

Samuel Usque's *Consolation* represents a similar change in perception, because of the attention it gives to Israel's suffering at the hands of foreign nations, who appear in it as primary actors in Jewish history.

This framework of suffering lends special meaning to Ha-Kohen's story of the Kozivas and Betar. Rather than a defense of rabbinic authority or a clarification of messianic doctrine, the emphasis falls on the suffering of the inhabitants of Betar and the cruelty of the Romans. The Kozivas, as false messiahs, come to signify a lesson about the relationship between Jews and Gentiles—a lesson of how false messiahs, with their wish for illegitimate power, arouse latent Gentile violence against the Jewish people.

Abraham Zacuto:
Book of Genealogies (1504)

We come now to the first of three chronicles of the sixteenth century that were written in annalistic form and refer to Bar Kokhba. Like *The Vale of Tears*, these annals too speak of the non-Jewish world, but in a different way—by recounting the history of non-Jewish nations and correlating that with prominent events in Jewish history.

We begin with the chronicle written by Abraham Zacuto (1450–1515), an astronomer who served several Spanish and Portuguese courts before fleeing Portugal in 1497; his astronomical tables were widely used by the Portuguese and Spanish explorers of the time. *Book of Genealogies* (*Sefer Yuḥasin*), completed in Tunis during his wanderings (seventy-one years before *The Vale of Tears* appeared), is divided into six sections, the first five of which present a history of the rabbinic chain of tradition—the transmission of revelation and authority through the rabbis—from its beginning until Zacuto's own day.[49] Zacuto states as the purpose of such knowledge the facilitation of the study of Jewish law and its authorities.[50] This is the time-honored goal of Jewish scholarship, and fits squarely within the framework of traditional Jewish thought. In the sixth section, at the end of the book, however, Zacuto adds a brief account of Gentile history and scientific progress, correlated with the major events of Jewish history. He defends his inclusion of this material on the grounds that a knowledge of Gentile history would benefit Jews in two ways: it would strengthen their faith in God's control over history, and it would "assist Jews dwelling among Christians to argue with them about their religion."[51] These are pious goals, but at the same time they represent an opening into a secular arena of discourse.

Zacuto speaks of Bar Kokhba in both portions of the *Book of Genealogies*—the portion recounting the internal history of Jewish tradition, and that recounting the external history of the nations. According to whether Bar Kokhba appears in the context of Jewish history or world history, different but related characteristics distinguish him. In the context of Jewish history, R. Akiba's messianic proclamation is the most important topic; whereas what stands out in the context of world history is Bar Kokhba's character as a powerful opponent of the Gentiles.

Let us look first at what Zacuto writes of Bar Kokhba in the section of the *Book of Genealogies* dealing with internal Jewish history:

> Rabbi Moses ben Maimon, at the end of *Mishpatim*, said that he [R. Akiba] was the armor-bearer of Ben Koziva, king of Betar, because he thought he was the Messiah. However, in the *midrashot*, we do not find that he was his armor-bearer. Rather, because he was of the tribe of Judah, and was fighting wars and performing heroic feats (*gevurot*) and succeeding, he thought that he was the Messiah, and expounded *A star shall step forth from Jacob* (Num. 24:17). But when

---

49. Zacuto begins with a brief outline of biblical events, but his chief interest is with the rabbinic tradition.
50. Abraham Zacuto, *Sefer Yuḥasin Ha-Shalem*, ed. Zvi Filopowski (Frankfort-am-Main, 1924), 1–3.
51. Ibid., 231–32.

he saw that he could not smell out wicked men, as it says *And he shall smell the fear of the Lord* (Isa. 11:4)—he became disappointed with him. This is a major text against the Gentiles.[52]

Zacuto brings in both of the rabbinic traditions about Ben Koziva, the tradition of the messianic gibbor and that of the false messiah, and combines them in a unique manner by giving them a chronological sequence. That is, he assumes that the legends in Midrash Lamentations portraying Ben Koziva as a gibbor who earned R. Akiba's support refer to an earlier time than the events told in the legend of b. Sanhedrin, in which Ben Koziva fails to pass a messianic test. Zacuto interprets the two traditions as episodes in a single story of how R. Akiba at first supported Ben Koziva and afterward repudiated him.

Zacuto's chief interest in this is to defend R. Akiba, apparently against a Christian attack allowed by Maimonides' interpretation of the events. Christian polemicists could point to Maimonides' statement of R. Akiba's support for Ben Koziva (as his "armor-bearer") as evidence for the failure of rabbinic leadership to recognize the Messiah. Zacuto's reply was first to repeat Maimonides' argument that R. Akiba had good reason, on the basis of Ben Koziva's lineage and military success, to think that Ben Koziva was the Messiah, but then to show, contrary to Maimonides, that R. Akiba soon discovered the truth about Ben Koziva and withdrew his support.[53]

The other side of Ben Koziva, that which affects foreign nations, appears in the last section of the book, in Zacuto's chronicle of world history. Here Zacuto presents Ben Koziva in the role not of messianic claimant but of "a great gibbor":

> In a Christian chronicle is presented the account of Ben Koziva the Jew, who reigned over Israel in the time of Hadrian, 5318 years after Creation, when Hadrian was reigning, fifty-two years after the Destruction. He [Ben Koziva] was a great *gibbor*, and brought death and destruction upon the Christians, as Eusebius said, author of the chronicle. He vanquished them fiercely in all their countries, as well as the Libyans and Philistines. He made war upon them and de-

---

52. Ibid., 37.
53. Abraham Neuman, "Abraham Zacuto Historiographer," in *Harry Austryn Wolfson Jubilee Volume* (Jerusalem, 1965), 2:611–12, discusses Zacuto's frequent disagreements with Maimonides in matters of history.

stroyed their countries, until Hadrian came and rescued them. Koziva likewise went to Egypt and destroyed two kingdoms, Sedon and Taviner; and came to Alexandria of Egypt, and fought with it, but Hadrian defeated him. Then a great number of people died in Alexandria. Koziva went from there to the Land of Mesopotamia, which is Aram Naharaim, and the Land of Israel. The Jewish people lived there, and there he fought a great war with Hadrian, and Hadrian killed a great number of Jews. This is found in books, and agrees closely with the words of the sages, who said in [Tractate] Gittin, "He killed many Jews in Alexandria." Then he [Hadrian] went to the Land of Israel and destroyed Betar. From this, it appears that Betar was destroyed by Hadrian Caesar fifty-two years after the Destruction—and not seventy-three years, as the author of *Seder Olam* says. It was also not mentioned [in Eusebius's chronicle] that Koziva had been killed, although the sages record this. Hadrian died sixty-five years after the Destruction.[54]

Zacuto's major source of information in this second picture of Bar Kokhba is Jerome's Latin adaptation of the world chronicle of Eusebius, who here becomes the first foreign historian to be named explicitly in Jewish writings about Bar Kokhba. (The similarity between what Zacuto and Abravanel say about Bar Kokhba's conquests in Egypt and Mesopotamia thus suggests that one of the "Roman history books" used by Abravanel was the Latin chronicle of Eusebius.) The difference between the accounts of Eusebius and Zacuto is, of course, that Eusebius does not portray the battles in Egypt and Mesopotamia as a single war led by a single leader; this interpretation, and the connection with Bar Kokhba, are Zacuto's. He has followed Ibn Daud and Abravanel in drawing the same conclusions from the same material.

In this second discussion of Bar Kokhba, Zacuto retells the events told by Eusebius and then tests this account against Jewish traditions about the same events. In regard to the massacre at Alexandria, Zacuto shows that Eusebius and the sages agree; in regard to the date given by Seder Olam for the fall of Betar, Zacuto uses Eusebius to refute it on grounds that Hadrian was not alive at that time;[55] and in regard to the death of "Koziva," Zacuto

---

54. Zacuto, *Sefer Yuḥasin*, 245.
55. No known manuscript of Seder Olam specifies the date of Koziva's death as seventy-three years after the destruction; but Ibn Daud's *Book of Tradition* (which Zacuto usually calls *Book of the*

points out that this information, omitted in the chronicle, was supplied by the sages. Zacuto is thus trying to synthesize the various historical traditions in order to find the kernel of historical truth in them; he arrives at this truth by discovering where the Christian and Jewish sources agree and by evaluating the logic of their statements.

In his analysis of the traditions about Bar Kokhba, Zacuto gives as much weight to the statements of Eusebius as to those of the sages; and this is indicative of a general attitude seen throughout the last section of the *Book of Genealogies*. What Christians say about Jews is important to Zacuto. Though he accords them less authority than Jewish sources,[56] especially rabbinic writings, and sometimes even curses the Christian authors, they nevertheless affect the way he looks at Jewish history, including Bar Kokhba.[57] Abravanel and Zacuto were not the first Jewish writers to use non-Jewish sources of information about Bar Kokhba, but they were the first to consciously give credit to those sources and so to construct an image of Bar Kokhba that depended, in significant measure, on what non-Jews said about him.

From that information Zacuto presents Ben Koziva in the image of a great gibbor doing battle against Gentiles and conquering foreign lands. For a brief period in the past, a Jewish king played a role on the stage of world history, and wielded formidable political and military power.

By citing his sources and evaluating them, Zacuto's conclusions acquire the appearance of bare factuality. Yet a comparison with Eusebius and Abravanel offers clues to what Zacuto may have felt about Ben Koziva's story. One clue shows up in the way he interprets Eusebius's report of the Jewish uprisings in Egypt and Mesopotamia of 116–117 C.E. Turning these uprisings into bloody wars fought by a powerful Jewish warrior, Zacuto exaggerates the extent of the Jewish victories and, though Eusebius never mentions Christians in connection with the wars, Zacuto adds them to the story: Ben Koziva "wreaked death and destruction upon the Christians ... vanquished them fiercely (*be'akhzar*) in all their lands." Indeed, Zacuto's

---

Generations) does. Is, then, Zacuto referring to Ibn Daud, or to a lost text of Seder Olam—perhaps the one that Ibn Daud utilized as the basis for his own dating of the death of the last Koziva?

56. Zacuto, *Sefer Yuḥasin*, 231.

57. Salo W. Baron, in "Azariah de' Rossi's Historical Method," *History and Jewish Historians* (Philadelphia, 1964), 227, remarks on the curse, *yimaḥ shemo* (may his name be obliterated), which Zacuto frequently attached to the names of the Christian writers he cited, particularly sainted ones like Augustine and Isidore, and explains this from the painful memory Zacuto bore of recent persecutions.

picture of Ben Koziva has a similar feeling to Abravanel's, which also calls Ben Koziva "fierce" and portrays him as a magnificent warrior. Abravanel considered Ben Koziva's wars "acts of vengeance." Add to this the fact that Zacuto was an exile of Abravanel's generation, many of whom longed for God to work his revenge upon Christian Europe, and what we find is a number of clues which together suggest that Zacuto sympathized with Ben Koziva's wars and perceived in them acts of revenge or at least the actions of a Jew fighting back against his Christian oppressors.

In the sixth section of the *Book of Genealogies*, Zacuto says nothing about Ben Koziva's messianic aspect, presenting him only in his character as a "great gibbor." Such a picture represents a significant departure from the way he had always been portrayed in the past. The rabbinic legends told of his military feats primarily to show their inadequacy and to advocate an alternative approach to redemption, through piety and prayer. Ibn Daud, Maimonides, and Abravanel were interested in his military success mainly to prove that the sages had good reason to think he was the Messiah: the important topics are rabbinic authority and messianic doctrine. In this earlier literature, Bar Kokhba's military aspect always had meaning in relation to internal sacred history and redemption. Zacuto himself follows this pattern in his presentation of Bar Kokhba in the first section of the *Book of Genealogies*. But in the last section, Zacuto removes Bar Kokhba's military aspect from its traditional themes and associations, and Bar Kokhba appears only as a Jewish warrior who played a role in world history and whose life pertained exclusively to issues of national power and Jewish-Gentile relations.

Azariah de' Rossi: *Light to the Eyes* (1573)

A significant though brief linguistic analysis of the names "Bar Kokhba" and "Ben Koziva" appears in *Light to the Eyes* (*Me'or Einayim*), one of the more remarkable Jewish books of the sixteenth century. Its major section, entitled "Words of Understanding" (*'Imrei Binah*), consists of a series of discrete essays on a broad range of historical problems raised by classical Jewish literature—for example, Philo's relation to rabbinic thought, the chronology of the Persian period of Jewish history, the vestments of the

Temple priests, ancient Hebrew script, the meaning and historical value of rabbinic legends, and, in an extended analysis, the history and validity of the Jewish practice of dating events from the time of creation. Unlike all other Jewish historians of the time, this book's author, Azariah de' Rossi (1511–1578), makes no attempt to narrate a sequence of events, much less the whole history of the Jewish people, or to discover the import of recent history. Following a number of other Italian writers, Azariah wrote solely about "antiquities."[58] In addition, *Light to the Eyes* utilized, and gave respectful credence to, a far greater range of non-Jewish sources than any other Jewish historical work written up to that time.[59]

De' Rossi's remarks about Bar Kokhba appear in chapter 12 of "Words of Understanding":

> From the Babylonian Talmud and the Jerusalem Talmud, Ta'anit, and likewise from Midrash Lamentations on the verse *They hunt our steps* (Lam. 4:18), it has already been established that the war of Betar did not occur until fifty-two years after the destruction. And this date points to the years of Hadrian, who was without a doubt the destroyer of Betar. He killed Ben Koziva, according to the words of our sages in the places I have mentioned. Many historians recounted this also, and especially Platina, Chapter 7, as I said. Orosius in his book, and also Eusebius, Book 4, Chapter 6, of his history, said that this Ben Koziva pretended that his name was Bar Kokhba, which is close to the sages' exegesis of the verse *A star shall step forth* (Num. 24:17), according to Midrash Lamentations Rabbati, on the verse *The Lord swallowed* (Lam. 2:2). According to the Jerusalem Talmud, Chapter *Bisheloshah Peraqim*, however, because he was like a failure (*akhzav*) in the war with Hadrian, they called him *Ben Koziva*. And all this is clearly found too in the history books of all the Caesars, in the life of Hadrian Caesar. In my opinion, the sages said concerning him [Hadrian], at the end of the Gemara, and Tosefta Sota . . . that after the complete destruction that occurred in his days, the Jews

---

58. Baron, ibid., proposes that Azariah found his models for the essay form in the works of Gellius, Rhodiginus, and Alexandro d' Alexandro (210–11), and his models for antiquarian interest in the school of Flavius Blondus, still active in Azariah's day (208–9).

59. See the comparisons of Azariah with other Jewish historians in Lester Segal, *Historical Consciousness and Religious Tradition in Azariah de' Rossi's Me'or Einayim* (Philadelphia, 1989), 6, 47, 79.

never again raised their head, and never again raised a sword against a foreign nation.[60]

In this same chapter of *Light to the Eyes*, Azariah mentions Ben Koziva again in only two brief statements: "In the Jerusalem Talmud, Chapter *Bisheloshah Peraqim*, and in Midrash Lamentations on the verse *The Lord swallowed*, is narrated at length the story of Betar and Ben Koziva"—and, "The writer Platina . . . recounted that Hadrian had destroyed Betar and killed Ben Koziva."

The Names

The topic of Ben Koziva's name has arisen only incidentally. Azariah is in the process of solving a problem raised by several rabbinic statements that contradict each other as to which foreign ruler had devastated Alexandrian Jewry,[61] and then incidentally, which Roman Caesar, Vespasian (according to b. Gittin 57b) or Hadrian, had destroyed Betar. In the course of investigating that question, Azariah came upon another problem—the inconsistency between rabbinic and Christian texts as to the name of the Jewish commander defeated at Betar. Eusebius and Orosius (see Appendix) use the names "Barchochebas" and "Chochebas," whereas the sages (in Midrash Lamentations and the Jerusalem Talmud) call that commander "Ben Koziva." What is the relationship between the two sets of names?

Azariah's solution is this: Orosius and Eusebius "said that this Ben Koziva pretended his name was Bar Kokhba, which is close to the sages' exegesis of Num. 24:17, according to Midrash Lamentations Rabbati." But Orosius and Eusebius never mention the name "Ben Koziva." Rather, it is Azariah himself who asserts that the man called "Ben Koziva" in Jewish literature is the same man whom Orosius and Eusebius called "Barchochebas."[62] The two names

---

60. Azariah de' Rossi, *Me'or Einayim*, ed. D. Cassel (Vilna, 1864–66), 1:187.
61. See Segal's discussion of Azariah's analysis of this question in *Historical Consciousness* (137–39).
62. Jerome/Eusebius and Orosius do not actually use the name "Bar Chochebas" in the Latin chronicles; they use the brief form, "Chochebas." Rather, the full name, "Barchochebas," appears only in Eusebius's *Ecclesiastical History*, Book 4, Chap. 6—the exact location that de' Rossi specifies in Eusebius's *"divrei ha-yamim."* Hence, Eusebius's Greek-language *Ecclesiastical History* rather than the Latin chronicle appears to have been Azariah's source, although he may have consulted an Italian translation (he does derive several etymologies in *Light to the Eyes* from Greek, but admits [1:146] to deficiency in his knowledge of Greek). No previous Jewish writer had consulted the *Ecclesiastical History* with its more complete spelling-out of the name "Barchochebas"; and this alone

are connected by the assumption that "Ben Koziva pretended that his name was Bar Kokhba."

Azariah de' Rossi, therefore, was the first scholar, Jewish or Christian, to make this connection between the Greek and Aramaic names—recognizing that the Greek name "Barchochebas" was a transliteration of the Aramaic name "Bar Kokhba," and that this name was implied by Num. 24:17, the verse R. Akiba cited in proclaiming Ben Koziva the Messiah. Seeing that the name "Barchochebas" had a messianic meaning, Azariah goes on to seek the meaning of the name "Ben Koziva," and concludes, in parallel with Judah Ha-Nasi's bitter remark in Midrash Lamentations 2.5, that "Ben Koziva" signifies "failure, disappointment" (of that messianic hope), from its possible derivation from the word *akhzav*.

It is also noteworthy that Azariah de' Rossi was the first Jewish scholar to have connected the Ben Koziva of rabbinic legend with the Judean rebellion that began in 132 C.E. As we saw, previous writers who made use of the Latin chronicles—Ibn Daud, Abravanel, and Zacuto—believed Ben Koziva to be the unnamed leader of the Jewish uprisings that the chronicles reported occurring in Egypt and Mesopotamia in 116–117. But Azariah—through his linguistic analysis of the name "Barchochebas," and his identification of it with R. Akiba's exegesis of Num. 24:17, and also through his familiarity with the life of Hadrian, which he learned from "the history books of all the Caesars"—discovered that the war which Ben Koziva had led could only have been the uprising in Judea that Roman historians and Eusebius date to the latter years of Hadrian's reign. This is the same conclusion, of course, held by scholars today.

Since Azariah, in explaining Ben Koziva's name, states as a fact that he was a "failure in his war with Hadrian," that appears to be the way he pictured Ben Koziva—as an unsuccessful warrior. Azariah must also have inferred that "the sages," because they had applied Num. 24:17 to Ben Koziva, mistakenly believed him to be the Messiah. But Azariah does not judge the validity of Eusebius's allegation that Ben Koziva, with malicious intent, had "pretended his name was Bar Kokhba," nor does he seek to determine the relationship of that claim to the sages' belief that he was the messianic star (*kokhba*) promised by Num. 24:17. Whatever other thoughts Azariah may have had about Bar Kokhba, he does not state them. This hardly constitutes an "image" at all. Azariah tells no story and suggests no

---

could explain why de' Rossi was the first scholar to make the connection between the Greek and Aramaic names.

motives; he neither teaches a lesson nor derives doctrine. Instead, he presents us with a solution to a discrete intellectual problem.

Azariah de' Rossi's Method

Our understanding of Azariah's image of Bar Kokhba will be determined, in part, by how we interpret the general aims of *Light to the Eyes*. These have now become, however, a matter of debate. Salo Baron, in three masterful essays written in the 1920s, portrayed Azariah opening up traditional Jewish literature to the critique of medieval Christian writings and the Renaissance interpretation of classical antiquity, and yet compromising his investigations repeatedly by his own medieval worldviews and a need to defend Judaism to the outer world.[63] But Robert Bonfil, in a recent reconsideration of *Light to the Eyes*, proposed that "the apologetic trend is the principal and pervading force" in the book, determining its entire scope and direction. He sees Azariah responding to the Counter-Reformation's increasingly sharp polemics, which adduced the Talmud's inconsistencies and mistaken historical reports as evidence of its deficiency; the novelty of Azariah's defense lay in his decision explicitly to recognize those passages as mistakes in an attempt to distinguish important Jewish doctrine from the personal opinions of the sages.[64] Most recently, however, Lester Segal has argued that Azariah was mainly pursuing an antiquarian attempt to open rabbinic legends to comparative critique, partly with the aim of recovering the meaningful core of rabbinic legends for those Jews influenced by Renaissance values of humanistic learning.[65] Whereas Bonfil connected the aims of *Light to the Eyes* specifically to the Counter-Reformation, Segal places them more in the context of Renaissance syncretism and the "rationalistic" stream of medieval Jewish thought. Yet both agree that Azariah's methodological originality lay in the extent to which he brought to bear the scholarly standards and documentary resources of Late Renaissance Italy in the critical examination of rabbinic legendary material (*aggadah*).

---

63. These essays appear as "Azariah de' Rossi: A Biographical Sketch," "Azariah de' Rossi's Attitude to Life," and "Azariah de' Rossi's Historical Method," in *History and Jewish Historians*, 167–239. For this picture of de' Rossi, see especially 202, and for Azariah's apologetic aims, 187, 212.

64. Bonfil, "Some Reflections on the Place of Azariah de Rossi's *Me'or Enayim* in the Cultural Milieu of Italian Renaissance Jewry," in *Jewish Thought in the Sixteenth Century*, esp. 37–42.

65. See Segal, *Historical Consciousness*, esp. 47, 74–79, and 165. Replying to Bonfil on 31, 41 n. 24, and 84 n. 28, Segal argues that Bonfil's few citations from *Light to the Eyes* are irrelevant to Azariah's explicit and numerous claims to be pursuing the truth per se.

It is difficult to discern how Azariah de' Rossi's brief reference to Bar Kokhba, limited to an analysis of names, expresses any general apologetic aims, although one might imagine Azariah's satisfaction in being able to mention an example of failed messianic hopes and their disastrous consequences, since he considered the messianic ferment of his day, intensely focused upon the year 1575, to be a "stumbling block" to his people.[66] Yet de' Rossi's words about Bar Kokhba do issue directly out of his method of studying history, so that the relationship between this "image" (if we may call it that) and his approach to the Jewish past can be examined with some benefit.

We have already noticed that Azariah limits his discussion of Bar Kokhba to an explanation of the two names. Unlike many writers before him, he neither defends R. Akiba nor clarifies messianic doctrine. This choice of subject matter derives from a radical distinction that Azariah tried to maintain throughout *Light to the Eyes* between the holy "discourse" of revelation, which included the topics of messianic doctrine and rabbinic authority, and "secular discourse," under which he classified all questions of history, including his own investigations.

He held rabbinic tradition absolutely authoritative in regard to revelation—which he defined as all laws and doctrines transmitted in the name of Moses, derived from the Torah by proper hermeneutical rules, and instituted as a "fence around the Torah." The historian had no right to raise questions about this realm.

> However, [we must deal differently with] matters which, by their very nature, could not have been announced to them [the sages] on Sinai, such as events which happened thereafter, and with other data about which we are certain that they stated them as their own opinion without the backing of Scripture. Wherever it is possible for us to harmonize them with what has been established as true by later scholars we should do so.... But when it is impossible, we must assume that they [the sages] did not report a tradition from the Prophets but merely heard it from the scholars of their own time.[67]

---

66. Ibid., 31 and 40 n. 24. Azariah hoped that his chronological studies would "remove the stumbling block from the path of our people" (*Me'or Einayim* 2:276) when Jews discovered that traditional chronological figures, being faulty, could not support any messianic calculations whatsoever. David Tamar discusses the messianic ferment among Italian Jews directed toward a date two years subsequent to the completion of *Light to the Eyes*: "Ha-Ṣipiyah be'Italyah Li-Shnat Ha-Ge'ulah 5335," *Sefunot* 2:(1958) 61–88.

67. Azariah de' Rossi, *Me'or Einayim* 2:269–70; trans. Baron, *History and Jewish Historians*, 171.

Moving beyond earlier endeavors by scholars such as Maimonides and Naḥmanides to rationalize or relativize the *aggadic* (narrative, non-legal) portions of rabbinic literature, Azariah claims not only the freedom but the responsibility "to investigate the correctness of these matters ... because we are concerned that the words of the sages in narrating noted events should not contradict each other."[68] Azariah's distinction between sacred and secular rabbinic statements thus allows for error in the secular (historical) ones.

These errors provide one of Azariah's stated justifications for the historical study of rabbinic literature: so that (in Segal's words) its "historical flaws and inconsistencies may be revealed, clarified, and rectified and even its conflicts with the realities of nature rationally analyzed and explained."[69] For Azariah believed that behind the apparent fallacies in rabbinic statements lay a profound wisdom and purpose, often formulated as metaphor and story.[70] His goal was to discover this wisdom by exposing the historical or scientific fallacies that deflected the modern reader's (or the religious opponent's) attention.

Azariah justifies his historical studies in a second way, repeatedly explaining them as a search for truth in itself (*ha'emet be'aṣmo*): "The beautiful soul will yearn in all things to know the truth." "Howsoever we follow the quest for wisdom, benefit may be hoped for, because by way of this study ... we will acquire forces of understanding, and ... it is in man's nature and sweet to the soul." Quoting Quintilian, he adds that the study of history brings delight and preserves from weariness.[71] The search for truth thus possesses value apart from any service it renders to Jewish tradition. A secular pursuit, it provides the secular benefits of training the mind and giving pleasure.

In the context of *Light to the Eyes*, then, Bar Kokhba appears as a secular topic, clearly distanced from the "serious" topics of holy law and doctrine. He appears as part of an attempt to clarify the historical kernel in rabbinic *aggadot* (legends), and also as an object of the pure quest for truth. Neither the analysis of his name nor the determination of the Caesar who destroyed Betar teaches a significant "lesson of history"—in sharp contrast to other

---

68. Azariah de' Rossi, *Me'or Einayim*, 1:182.

69. Segal, *Historical Consciousness*, 77. See also Baron, *History and Jewish Historians*, 180, 200, 221, 225, and Kochan's discussion in *The Jew and His History*, 50–55.

70. Azariah de' Rossi, *Me'or Einayim*, 35, 179, 192, 206, 208. See Baron, *History and Jewish Historians*, 225 and 435 n. 123, for some translations.

71. Azariah de' Rossi, *Me'or Einayim*, 1:189, 80; trans. Kochan, *The Jew and His History*, 51–52. For other examples see Segal, *Historical Consciousness*, 32–34, 74–75.

Jewish writings about Bar Kokhba as well as Renaissance historiography in general.[72] Thus, Azariah's Bar Kokhba, lacking meaning for the present, belongs more to the past. This, too, was a consequence of Azariah's distinction between revelation and history. Precisely because he thought the Torah and commandments had "turned all the darkness before us into light," he thought there was nothing of serious importance left for the Jewish historian to teach.[73] He claimed his role was merely to clarify historical problems in the relatively unimportant realm of the secular, which would sometimes result in exposing the hidden wisdom of aggadic statements.

Another method followed by Azariah affects his portrayal of Bar Kokhba: his use of the essay form to investigate discrete historical questions. Instead of an actor in the drama of historical events, Bar Kokhba figures into the essays of *Light to the Eyes* only insofar as his life raises a question for secular scholarly analysis—as names, accompanied by shadows of action, and the pretension, acclaim, or failure that those names happen to cast.

Azariah's presentation of Bar Kokhba is shaped also by his encyclopedic knowledge of a vast amount of Jewish, classical, Christian, and contemporary Italian literature, reflecting the syncretistic tendency of the early Renaissance, and by the way he uses those texts to reach his conclusions. De' Rossi is careful to base his findings only upon primary sources, which he names explicitly in his argument; comparing the various sources for their information on a question, he tries to discover the historical kernel to which they point.[74] In matters of history and science, moreover, Azariah usually gives as much weight to the opinions of non-Jewish texts as to those of Jewish texts, though he tries to salvage the underlying "wisdom" in the intentions of any Jewish passages found to be in error.[75] Such respect for foreign literature represents a more accepting attitude in general toward the non-Jewish world than we have seen in the Jewish historians we have so far studied.

---

72. On the teaching aims of Renaissance historiography, especially Plutarch, see Myron Gilmore, "The Renaissance Conception of the Lessons of History," in *Facets of the Renaissance*, ed. William H. Werkmeister (New York, 1959), 73–86. Segal, *Historical Consciousness* (6, 34, 47, 79), sees this "non-utilitarian" nature of Azariah's work as a significant distinction from all other Jewish historical works of the time; its "utility" lay in clearing up inconsistencies in Jewish literature that might undermine the faith of Jews broadly involved in Italian culture. From Bonfil's viewpoint, the very pointlessness of Azariah's critique of rabbinic legends was meant to shelter them from Christian attempts to derive doctrine or undermine the authority of the Talmud.

73. Azariah de' Rossi, *Me'or Einayim*, 2:264. See Kochan, *The Jew and His History*, 54–55, Baron, *History and Jewish Historians*, 196.

74. See Baron, *History and Jewish Historians*, 216f. and 230f.

75. See Segal, *Historical Consciousness*, 165.

Segal thinks that it also "reflects much of the humanist zeal for the idea of the unity of truth, expressed earlier by figures such as Marsilio Ficino and Pico della Mirandola."[76] Just such syncretism distinguishes, for example, Azariah's study of the name "Bar Kokhba." He joins together two different traditions of knowledge, Christian and Jewish, to learn something new about Bar Kokhba's name that neither side alone could provide.

As a result, Azariah's picture of Bar Kokhba is a composite of what both internal Jewish sources and external Gentile sources, sacred literature as well as secular literature, say about him. The image of Bar Kokhba thus becomes universalized, in the sense that it derives from what both Jews and Christians see in him, and it depends upon non-Jewish sources for completeness. Segal even argues that Azariah's use of non-Jewish sources to expand the meaning of Jewish sources blurred the traditional division between sacred and profane—implying a relativism toward the aggadic portion of tradition.[77]

Furthermore, by Azariah's open acknowledgment of his sources of information, his work as a historian enters into his picture of Bar Kokhba. Earlier writers—the rabbinic storytellers, Ibn Daud, Samuel Usque, and Yosef Ha-Kohen—all told their accounts as though they were transmitting unarguable truths from the past. But de' Rossi, and Abravanel and Zacuto as well, acknowledge and evaluate their sources. In this way, they imply that their conclusions, being dependent on those sources and their reading of them, are conditional. Their image of Bar Kokhba, too, becomes conditional, and consequently more accessible to the reader, who now perceives its relation to the historian's mind. The reader sees the historian no longer as a passive transmitter of authoritative truth, but rather as an active investigator into that truth. Our knowledge of Bar Kokhba thus takes on the appearance of being a product of what past observers reported and what contemporary minds concluded about those reports.[78]

In the process, then, the role of the contemporary thinker rises in stature relative to the ancient tradition. Through his application of external sources, Azariah has aspired to evaluate the historical accuracy of the Talmudic traditions as to which Caesar destroyed Betar. His claim to have learned

---

76. Ibid., 49–50.
77. Ibid., 121–22.
78. Cf. Segal, ibid., 164: "Consequently in his work ancient Jewish historical situations are often no longer what the rabbinic classics had described them to be but rather what the 'modern' scholar Azariah has attempted to reconstruct after having subjected the relevant sources to critical evaluation."

more than the ancient sages knew about this matter attributes distinct value to the secular attainments of the modern researcher. Elsewhere in *Light to the Eyes* Azariah likened modern scholars to the familiar figure of a dwarf standing on the shoulders of a giant, while insisting that moderns nevertheless have an advantage over the ancients in matters depending on reflection and empirical investigation.[79] Such reservations about the Jewish sages resemble those upheld in humanist circles in regard to the classical ancients.[80]

Yet we must recall Azariah's disparagement of the knowledge gained through historical inquiry in relation to the final truth already available from the holy Torah and transmitted inerrantly by the sages. For all that Azariah has discovered new about Bar Kokhba, he considered it merely ancient history having limited contemporary relevance.

Gedaliah ibn Yaḥya: *The Chain of Tradition* (1587)

We now look briefly at a second annalistic chronicle, *The Chain of Tradition* (*Shalshelet Ha-Kabbalah*), written by Gedaliah ibn Yaḥya (1522–1578), who lived most of his life in the papal cities. This book is significant for the wide reading it received among the Jewish masses, becoming one of the most popular chronicles written in the sixteenth century.

Ibn Yaḥya's story of Bar Kokhba is derived exclusively from Jewish sources: Midrash Lamentations, Ibn Daud, Maimonides, and Azariah de' Rossi. He introduces some motifs of his own, which are italicized in the translation below. Notice the dramatic quality of the events Ibn Yaḥya selects to tell, but also the occasionally confusing storyline of the account:

> Fifty-two years after the destruction, a certain man arose, named Bar Kokhba, for thus they applied to him the verse, *A star shall step forth*, according to Midrash Lamentations Rabbati. But afterwards, because he rebelled against the emperor Hadrian, they called him Ben Koziva, from the words, *sheqer* and *kazav* [lie and falsehood]. He made himself Messiah, and *all the Jews in Betar followed after him, and especially R. Akiba, who would run before him with king's regalia in*

---

79. Azariah de' Rossi, *Me'or Einayim*, 1:196.
80. Segal, *Historical Consciousness*, 154–58. Cf. Baron, *History and Jewish Historians*, 200–201.

his hands. Three generations of them [Kozivas] reigned over Israel, last of whom was Romulus ben Rufus ben Koziva. Hadrian Caesar went up against Romulus on the Ninth of Av in the seventy-third year after the destruction, which is fifty-two years after the destruction plus eighteen. This was the year 3920 after creation, according to the chronology of Rabbi Abraham ben David [Ibn Daud]. And he killed a great number of Israelites, *and among them were R. Akiba and his companions.* He destroyed the city, *and its site became afterwards unknown.* It says in Midrash Lamentations that five hundred schools were in Betar and that in the smallest of them were more than three hundred children. And Midrash Lamentations also says that Betar's misfortune happened because they rejoiced over the destruction of the Temple because the kings of Jerusalem compelled the inhabitants of Betar to stand before them, and reigned over them against their wills.

And these are the destructions of the Jews.[81]

As we see from the italicized sentences (aside from the biblical verse), Ibn Yaḥya added a number of ideas of his own. These were not mere invention, but explanations, interpretations, and actions inserted to make the story more dramatic or comprehensible to his readers.

In the preface to *The Chain of Tradition*, Ibn Yaḥya describes the book's subject matter: "I choose to divide all this compilation into three parts: the first will be the order of the transmission of the Torah from Adam until today, and the second will be my informing you a little of some of the laws of the spheres and the heavenly world, the creation of the newborn in the womb, and what happens to him at the end, and magic . . . , and the third will be the chain of the sages of the nations and the evil decrees against Israel and the fine inventions born in every generation."[82] Our passage on Bar Kokhba appears in the first part of the book, in the middle of a long history of R. Akiba, who is one of the links in the chain (*shalshelet*) of the Torah's transmission (*kabbalah*). Bar Kokhba's rebellion appears as one episode in R. Akiba's life. Indeed, the most striking scene in the passage is the one picturing R. Akiba, "with king's

---

81. Gedaliah ibn Yaḥya, *Shalshelet Ha-Kabbalah* (Warsaw, 1881), 13b.
82. Based on the translation in Abraham David, "R. Gedalya ibn Yahya's *Shalshelet HaKabbalah* ('Chain of Tradition'); A Chapter in Medieval Jewish Historiography, Introduction," trans. Bruce Lorence, *Imanu'el* 12 (1981): 60–61. I was unable to consult Professor David's dissertation, "The Historiographical Accomplishment of Gedaliah ibn Yaḥya, Author of *Shalshelet Ha-Kabbalah*" (1976).

regalia in his hands," running ahead of Bar Kokhba in a triumphal procession reminiscent of the processions held in Italian cities in Ibn Yaḥya's own time.[83] This picture of R. Akiba carrying the king's "paraphernalia" or "weapons" (*klei ha-melekh*) is an interpretation of the term *no-se kelav* (arms bearer), appearing in Maimonides' discussion of Ben Koziva. Ibn Yaḥya took Maimonides to mean that R. Akiba was Bar Kokhba's *no-se kelav* in the sense of carrying his regalia, which implied R. Akiba's wholehearted endorsement of Bar Kokhba's messianic claims.

Two further additions to the story would have special meaning to Jews living in sixteenth-century Italy: Ibn Yaḥya's interpretation of the enmity between Betar and Jerusalem as a political struggle between competing city-states, and his picture of Bar Kokhba in the role of a king who rules over a single, powerful city, Betar, the inhabitants of which crown him and obey the rule of his family for three generations.

The image of Bar Kokhba that readers meet in *The Chain of Tradition* is that of a family of rulers who reigned over a Jewish city-state. The first Koziva convinces the citizens that he is their messianic king, is hailed as such by R. Akiba, and persuades them to throw off the yoke of Roman rule. But the name "Koziva" reminds readers that his claims were false. Readers are thus presented with a Bar Kokhba in the roles of rebel-ruler and false messiah, but not in the role of a powerful warrior fighting Rome and conquering foreign lands. Ibn Yaḥya accentuates the political side of Bar Kokhba at the expense of the military (which is what impressed writers like Abravanel and Zacuto), so that the history of Betar becomes the story of an ill-fated attempt on the part of a Jewish city-state to gain political autonomy.

The piteous consequences of this attempt are played up in the story: the venerable R. Akiba dies along with "a great number of Israelites"; numerous innocent schoolchildren are slaughtered; the city is totally destroyed, no traces remaining to show its location. This is the theme of "the destructions of the Jews," the phrase appearing at the end of the story. It is also one of the three topics Ibn Yaḥya assigns to the third part of his book, where he depicts the tribulations suffered by Jews since the fifth century C.E. The destruction of Betar is told there, too, in the section on world history, and without reference to Bar Kokhba:

> In the days of R. Akiba, approximately 3,860 years after creation and approximately fifty-two years after the destruction of the second

---

83. See Jacob Burckhardt, *The Civilization of the Renaissance in Italy*, 2:416.

Temple, the destruction of Betar occurred, at the hands of Hadrian Caesar. He brought more evil to Israel than had occurred with the destruction of the Temples, and he killed twice the number of those who left Egypt, and those people who remained, he expelled in revenge.[84]

The words "evil," "revenge," and "expulsion" stand out in this telling, along with the great number of victims. These words are associated with Hadrian, who appears here as the murderous villain of the story.

According to the preface to *The Chain of Tradition*, Gedaliah wanted his readers to gain two benefits (*to'alot*) from reading these tales of suffering. One was to realize "how merciful God is" in allowing Jews to survive despite "our sins [which] caused our destruction." The second (and partly contradictory) benefit was to be inspired with new faith when they saw how Jews in the past "delivered themselves in martyrdom or suffered affliction and exile, and despite all this, did not sin or commit heresy against God."[85] Gedaliah, like Azariah de' Rossi, lived during difficult times for Italian Jews. Jewish communities suffered great political insecurity in all the Italian states except the Este and Gonzaga dominions, particularly from the threat of expulsion. Ibn Yaḥya himself was among those expelled from the Papal territories in 1569, and Jews were being forced to wear badges, reside in ghettos, and relinquish their sacred books for burning. The Counter-Reformation was in full sway, manifesting some of its fervor and anxiety in aggressive missionary activity toward the Jews.[86] The theme of the "destructions of the Jews" had an immediate relevance.

We can see how the story of the destruction of Betar worked to produce the two effects set forth in the book's preface. The story clearly specifies the sin that caused Betar's defeat—rejoicing over the destruction of the Temple—while the deaths of the innocent schoolchildren and R. Akiba serve as inspiring examples of martyrdom.

The story of Bar Kokhba in *The Chain of Tradition* resembles the stories in the *Consolation* and *The Vale of Tears* in their emphasis on suffering. It differs, however, in offering as exempla specific Jews who died at Betar, to be admired and if need be, emulated by readers. Like the *Consolation* but

---

84. Gedaliah ibn Yaḥya, *Shalshelet Ha-Kabbalah*, 48a.
85. David, "A Chapter in Medieval Jewish Historiography," 69–70.
86. Bonfil, "The Place of Azariah de Rossi," 32–35. David, "A Chapter in Medieval Jewish Historiography," 66; Baron, *A Social and Religious History of the Jews*, vol. 14, chap. 40.

not *The Vale of Tears*, no military power is depicted in connection with Bar Kokhba; but unlike both those books, *The Chain of Tradition* does not clearly ascribe conceit or sinful intention to Bar Kokhba, and he is even honored by the great R. Akiba himself.

As stated before, Bar Kokhba enters the book mainly as an episode in the life of R. Akiba, a link in the sacred history of the transmission of the Torah. But Ibn Yaḥya also connects Betar with the history of Jewish suffering—sacred history insofar as it refers only to Israel's relationship with God, but secular insofar as it involves other causes, blames non-Jews, and recounts "the destructions of the Jews" against the background of world history.

David Gans:
Sprout of David (1592)

David Gans (1541–1613), like a number of other Ashkenazi Jews of his time, undertook serious studies of astronomy, mathematics, geography, and history. He wrote on all these subjects but became best known for his chronological annal, *Sprout of David* (*Ṣemaḥ David*), written while he lived in Prague. The most cosmopolitan city in German-speaking lands at that time, Prague was not only a center of European renaissance and humanism, but of Jewish learning, in traditional subjects as well as secular ones. Both of Gans's famous teachers—R. Judah Lowe, who stood out above the many famous rabbis of the city, and R. Moses Isserles of Cracow—had investigated (with differing conclusions) European science, history, and philosophy.[87]

In the introduction to *Sprout of David*, Gans states that he wants to provide "a general chronological outline" for Jewish householders of his generation who had no time to study the original texts. To this end he lists in summary form what he considers the major events in Jewish and world history, arranging them according to the year they occurred. "In order to separate the holy from the profane" (*lehavdil bein haqodesh uvein haḥol*), moreover, Gans divides his book into two parts: the first "deals with the

---

87. See Otto Muneles, ed., *Prague Ghetto in the Renaissance Period* (Prague, 1965), esp. Otto Muneles and Vladimir Sadek, "The Prague Jewish Community in the Sixteenth Century (Spiritual Life)"; André Neher, *Jewish Thought and the Scientific Revolution of the Sixteenth Century: David Gans (1541–1613) and His Times*, trans. David Maisel (Oxford, 1986), 19–44; Mordechai Breuer, "Modernism and Traditionalism in Sixteenth-Century Historiography: A Study of David Gans' *Tzemaḥ David*," in *Jewish Thought in the Sixteenth Century*, 50–54.

living God," that is, with Jewish history, and the second "deals with mankind," world history.[88] Like Zacuto, Gans gives Bar Kokhba a place in both parts of his annal, but the account of Bar Kokhba appearing in the second part constitutes merely a brief summary of the lengthy account in the first.

The discussion of Bar Kokhba in Part I includes a long excursus on the chronology of the events:

> [The year] 3870: Ben Koziva, who was called Bar Kokhba, rebelled against the Romans and made himself Messiah. He was therefore called Bar Kokhba, because he expounded [Scripture] and said that concerning him it was said, *A star shall step forth* (Num. 24:17), and R. Akiba himself, when he saw him, said about him, "This is the King Messiah," as it says in Midrash Lamentations Rabbata on the verse, *The Lord has swallowed* (Lam. 2:2). The Jews who were in Betar anointed him and crowned him king over them. They cast off the yoke of the Romans from upon their neck, and they made a great slaughter among the Romans and Greeks who lived in Africa, a people great and large as the sand upon the seashore that cannot be counted. Likewise, in Egypt also, the inhabitants of Alexandria of Egypt—they, too, killed many Romans; according to the words of the master of *Light to the Eyes*, Chapter 12: more than 200,000 people. And the Jews who were in Gefri (which is *Cypern* [German for Cyprus])—they, too, killed all the Gentiles "until no survivor was left of them" [Num. 21:35]. Until Caesar Trajan sent against them the commander of his army, his nephew Hadrian, who made a great slaughter among them such as was never heard or seen before, not even in the days of Nebuzarradan or in the days of Titus. Already our rabbis, may their name be for a blessing, differed in opinion, in the chapter Ha-Nezikin [b. Gittin 57b] about the great slaughter made at that time, when they said: "*The voice is the voice of Jacob*": this is Vespasian Caesar, who killed in the city of Betar four hundred myriads"—although the destruction of Betar occurred at least fifty-two years after the destruction [of the Temple] by Titus, the son of Vespasian; also, four Caesars reigned after Vespasian before Betar was destroyed. In any case, we find in many places that the kings and Caesars were called by the name of the previous Caesar, as will be explained in Part Two in many places. In the

---

88. David Gans, *Sefer Ṣemaḥ David*, ed. Mordechai Breuer (Jerusalem, 1983), 6–7.

Jerusalem Talmud, in Ta'anit, and in Midrash Lamentations Rabbata, on the verse, *The Lord has swallowed*, will be found [an account of] the destruction of Betar and the deeds of Ben Koziva; also in Midrash Genesis, in the section "The Generations of Isaac"; and in the *Book of Tradition* of Abraham ben David [Ibn Daud]; and in the *Book of Genealogies*, pages 32, 35, and 142; and in *Light to the Eyes*, Chapter 12.

Concerning the date of the deeds of Ben Koziva and the destruction of Betar, there are differing opinions. According to the opinion of R. Abraham ben David, the beginning of the reign of Ben Koziva occurred in the days of Caesar Domitian, the brother of Titus, in the fifty-second year after the destruction of the Temple; and he wrote that this Koziva died in his kingship, and that his son, Rufus, reigned in his stead, and after him, Romulus, the son of his son, reigned, who was also called by the name of his grandfather, Koziva; and he wrote that it was in his [Romulus's] days that the great slaughter occurred at Betar, in the seventy-third year after the destruction of the Temple, even though, according to his words, the duration of the kingdom of Koziva and his descendants was twenty-one years. This is not in opposition to the statement of the sages, may their memory be for a blessing, who said in *Seder Olam*, Chapter 30, that Ben Koziva reigned for two and a half years, and likewise they said [the same thing] in Chapter Ḥelek [b. Sanhedrin], because it is possible to say that the sages, may their name be for a blessing, were referring to the last Koziva. However, as to what he [Abraham ben David] wrote, that the end of the kingdom of Koziva and the great slaughter occurred in the seventy-third year after the destruction of the Temple—it seems that this calculation does not correspond either to the dates of the lives of the Caesars Trajan and Hadrian nor, in my opinion, to the end of the days of R. Akiba, who was slain at that time, for on the day when R. Akiba died, Rabbi [Judah Ha-Nasi] was born. Therefore, I placed the end of the kingdom of Ben Koziva and the destruction of Betar in the fifty-second year after the destruction of the Temple, in accord with the words of Seder Olam Zuta, and in accord with the words of the master of *Book of Genealogies*, on pages 32, 35, and 142, and in accord with the master of *Light to the Eyes*, Chapter 12; and see Part Two, in the year 3870.[89]

89. Ibid., 90–91.

Now the brief account in Part II:

> 3870 [years since creation]; 120 [according to the Christian calendar]. Bar Kokhba, called Ben Koziva, rebelled against the Romans and made himself Messiah, and the Jews slew the Roman and Greek peoples, a population great and numerous as the sand of the sea. Until the emperor sent against them the commander of his army, his nephew Hadrian, and he slew many thousands of souls from Israel, defeating them. This was the year 3870, as explained in Part I.[90]

Gans's discussion of Bar Kokhba in Part I takes the form, first, of a narrative account of important deeds and then, of an analysis of problems in the sources. This analysis, together with Gans's lengthy listing of his sources, takes up by far the greater portion of the passage, and are representative of the interest in exact, measurable matters that Gans expresses in the rest of his book.

Gans's Method

Gans's primary document for his information is Midrash Lamentations; his secondary sources are *The Book of Tradition, The Book of Genealogies, Light to the Eyes,* and probably at least one non-Jewish chronicle.

The reason for thinking that Gans consulted a non-Jewish chronicle is that his story of the Jewish uprisings of 116–117 differs from the Jewish sources he names: like the account of Dio Cassius, Gans limits the rebellion to North Africa, Egypt, and Cyprus—omitting the battles of Mesopotamia found in earlier Jewish accounts, including the *Book of Genealogies*.[91] Also like Dio Cassius and Eusebius, Gans characterizes the violence in Alexandria and Cyprus as separate outbreaks of rebellion rather than, as in previous Jewish accounts, attacks by the army of Bar Kokhba as it marched to Jewish settlements throughout the Near East. Where Gans differs from these classical sources, of course, is in still interpreting the rebellions outside Judea as messianic movements stirred up by the news of Bar Kokhba's victories. Gans could read only German and Hebrew historical works, and

---

90. Ibid., 220.
91. The *Ecclesiastical History* of Eusebius similarly limits the rebellion to Egypt and Cyrene (unlike the Latin *Chronicum* and Orosius's *Seven Books*). Could "Cyrene" have been confused with "Cyprus"—the German-language *Cypern* of *Sprout of David*?

Mordechai Breuer names his source in this instance as the *Chronologia auch Anatomia* by Laurentius Faustus, whom Gans credits frequently for information about classical rulers, persecutions of the early Christians, and various plagues and deaths.[92]

In regard to the rabbinic sources, Gans combines Zacuto's interest in R. Akiba's proclamation with de' Rossi's narrow focus on conflicting rabbinic reports. Contrary to Zacuto, Gans omits the rabbinic tradition from b. Sanhedrin telling how the sages rejected Bar Kokhba, which was important to Zacuto for its hint that R. Akiba had later forsaken Bar Kokhba. This omission from Gans's account parallels the lack of serious interest in doctrinal issues and Christian-Jewish debates that we find elsewhere in *Sprout of David*. But in contrast to de' Rossi, Gans attempts to save the honor of the rabbinic tradition that names Vespasian the conqueror of Betar. The rabbis, he argued, were not mistaken; they were only following a Roman practice in the nomenclature of Caesars. Here we see Gans taking a more deferential attitude than de' Rossi toward the historical portions of rabbinic literature.

In the matter of the date of Betar's fall, he does break openly with Ibn Daud, but he appeals to the authority of Zacuto and de' Rossi, who had also disagreed with Ibn Daud's dating of the event. Gans adds one argument of his own, based on the chronology of the lives of the sages. It appears, moreover, that Gans rejected Ibn Daud's idea of there having been three Kozivas: in Gans's own narrative account, in both Parts I and II, he speaks of only one man. Yet he does not fail to append Ibn Daud's story of three Kozivas and even to defend its chronological logic. We thus learn about David Gans what he claimed in his introduction: that he considered his role a modest one, more that of a compiler and neutral mediator of information than an explorer of new territories like de' Rossi.[93]

We can recognize even in these two entries about Bar Kokhba some of "the co-existence of the old and the new ... wavering between their devotion to tradition and their inclination to criticism, between germinating scientific attitudes and age-old religious beliefs" that Mordechai Breuer

---

92. Gans, *Ṣemaḥ David*, 90. I have been unable to verify this assertion. See Breuer's list of Gans's citations from Faustus, 479. My discussion of *Ṣemaḥ David* is particularly indebted to Professor Breuer's insightful articles and his edition of the book. Jirina Sedinova, "Non-Jewish Sources in the Chronicle by David Gans, 'Tzemah David,'" *Judaica Bohemiae* 8 (1972): 10, 13, discusses Gans's use of Faustus's historical works, adding that Gans also utilized Hubert Golzius's *Keyserische Chronik* for material on the history of the Roman empire from Julius Caesar onward.

93. Gans, *Ṣemaḥ David*, 6.

discovers in the writings of David Gans in general and of the scholars of his generation.[94] Our passages show an intense interest in chronological problems and inconsistencies in the Jewish texts and earlier Jewish historical works; bring to bear outside knowledge of Roman history (the nomenclature of the Caesars); and convey a more accurate reading of the classical accounts of the uprisings of 116–117 than had yet appeared in Jewish literature about Bar Kokhba. But unlike de' Rossi, Gans is content mostly to collate and reconcile texts without critical evaluation, and he fails to name his non-Jewish sources (this being his general policy in Part I of *Sprout of David*), with the result that his image of Bar Kokhba appears to derive entirely from internal Jewish tradition.

Gans's Image of Bar Kokhba

Sprout of David, written in a relatively tranquil environment for Jews, Prague of the late sixteenth century, expresses a generally friendly attitude toward the Christian world. In the introduction to Part II, listing nine benefits to be gained from reading about non-Jewish history, Gans includes the "favor and goodwill" that Jews would win from Christians in being able to converse knowledgeably with them about world history. Such a goal expresses the desire for good relations with Christians and a concern for their opinion. In addition, the book speaks of non-Jewish rulers with frequent admiration—especially for the Holy Roman emperors of Gans's day, Maximilian II and Rudolph II, but even for traditional villains like Titus.[95] Hadrian, despite his bloody conquest of Betar in Part I, is described in Part II "making peace" with all kingdoms and extending Roman territory by "pleasing words" instead of sword and bow.[96] Furthermore, Part II is of equal length with Part I, and contrary to Gans's professed division of sacred from profane, he intermingles the two histories, Jewish and Gentile, throughout. Typically, the account of Bar Kokhba in Part I makes use of non-Jewish sources (without naming them), as well as information about non-Jewish culture, to clarify Jewish history; the same Bar Kokhba of holy Jewish history appears again in the supposedly profane realm of world history.

Sprout of David shows little bitterness, furthermore, about the history of

---

94. Breuer, "Modernism and Traditionalism," 63.
95. Ibid., 71–72. See Ben-Zion Degani, "Ha-Mivneh shel Ha-Historiyah Ha-'Olamit u-Ge'ulat Yisra'el be-Ṣemaḥ David le-R. David Ganz," *Ṣiyon* 45 (1980): 180–83, on "the German Kaisers."
96. Gans, *Ṣemaḥ David*, 220, 221.

Jewish exile. In striking contrast to the Ashkenazi *Memorbücher* filled with martyrs, and also in contrast to the Spanish and Italian Jewish history books we have examined, Gans's chronicle mentions persecutions only briefly and even omits some. The book's aim, according to the title page of Part II, is rather to "show the mercy that accompanied the humble in our many wanderings." First among the lessons of world history is its "abundant evidence of Divine Providence watching over the people Israel. . . . God, the Blessed and Exalted, protected us and did not let us be devoured. . . . Praised be the Lord who has bestowed His wondrous love upon us."[97] In telling Jewish history, then, the emphasis falls on Jewish survival and success. Moreover, argues Breuer, Gans "dwelt at length on any event which was likely to enhance the prestige of the Jewish people among the Gentiles."[98] He devoted long passages, for example, to Alexander's meeting with the elders of Israel, the heroic deeds of the Hasmoneans, and the Jewish rebellion against Rome in the first century.

Breuer specifically includes Gans's account of the Bar Kokhba rebellion among the passages meant to enhance Jewish prestige. Indeed, the prominent action in our passage's narrative portion is Bar Kokhba's slaughter of huge numbers of Greeks and Romans in Africa, and the forceful Jewish rebellions in Alexandria and Cyprus. The destruction of Betar, on the other hand, receives only a perfunctory repetition of Ibn Daud's statement about a "great slaughter . . . such as was never heard or seen before." Compare that with the horrifying destruction tales of Midrash Lamentations, Gans's primary source. Recall, too, that Samuel Usque and Yosef Ha-Kohen not only repeated these tales in their entirety but amplified them into long, gruesome plaints over Israel's sufferings at the hands of Gentiles, and Gedaliah ibn Yaḥya told of the slaughter, "evil," and "revenge" committed by Hadrian at Betar. In *Sprout of David*, then, the story's emphasis falls more heavily on the rebellion of the Jews than the retaliation of the Gentiles, and as a result, Gans's account shows off Jewish strength without arousing hostility against non-Jews.

The story fulfills another aim of *Sprout of David*, which was "to bring joy to householders"—that is, to merchants, shopkeepers, and craftsmen rather than men of learning—as they "rest from their labors by reading of matters new and old."[99] To amuse working men, *Sprout of David* offered the kind of

---

97. Ibid., 165; trans. Meyer, *Ideas of Jewish History*, 129.
98. Breuer, "Modernism and Traditionalism," 74.
99. Gans, *Ṣemaḥ David*, 165.

sensational news items that excited many Europeans of the time, eager to hear of the interreligious violence, geographical discoveries, and technological inventions constantly occurring. This is why, Breuer asserts, we find in *Sprout of David* so many natural disasters, technological inventions, geographical facts, and episodes of human violence in the form of war, rebellion, religious persecution, and crime, described with graphic bloodshed and fantastical quantities of victims.[100] The story of Bar Kokhba's violent rebellion, the number of Roman and Jewish victims, and the information about the African population satisfied such desires for sensational news. How different this is from the story's older function of arousing grief and repentance or reinforcing faith in messianic doctrine or defending rabbinic authority against Karaite or Christian attack!

But perhaps the most important benefit Gans names as coming out of the study of world history, particularly the political and military history of the Gentile nations, was a change in the future course of world history. Gans writes, "When the reader . . . comes upon the might and power of kings and emperors, while we in our exile have neither king nor ruler, he will pray to God to restore our judges as of old and to plant the Sprout of David [*Ṣemaḥ David*, i.e., the Messiah] in Jerusalem."[101] Gans hopes that examples of political freedom and power from the past will move his readers to yearn and pray for redemption, which will in turn move God to hasten the arrival of the Messiah. Breuer identifies a strong messianic motive in *Sprout of David*, evidenced "in many passages that point to the proximity of the Messiah's coming and bear testimony to alert messianic expectations."[102]

Gans's story of Bar Kokhba, although it does not tell of foreign kings, is nevertheless basically a story of "the might and power of kings and emperors," because it concentrates on Bar Kokhba's rise to power and his victories rather than his defeat. It is thus possible that Gans may have thought the story would have the same effect as the military history of foreign kings—inspiring readers with an example of political power. And since Bar Kokhba was a Jew, he could serve also as an example of the power once wielded specifically by Jews. Gans conceived of redemption as a transformation in the realm of political and military power: God would grant Jews "the might and power of kings," the same freedom, power, and national life that

---

100. Breuer, "Modernism and Traditionalism," 65–66. Cf. Degani, "Ha-Mivneh," 173–74.
101. Gans, *Ṣemaḥ David*, 167.
102. Breuer, "Modernism and Traditionalism," 74–77. See esp. Degani, "Ha-Mivneh," who focuses on this issue.

Gentiles now enjoyed. But unlike Bar Kokhba the rebel, Jews would gain this power only through prayer, not by taking up arms. Bar Kokhba exemplified the power for which Gans yearned, but not the proper means of attaining it.

Insofar as the story functions in this way, moving readers to yearning and prayer, it takes on a traditionally sacred dimension, as it does also through Gans's citations of exclusively Jewish sources and his placement of the longer account of Bar Kokhba in Part I of *Sprout of David*. At the same time, however, the actual content of the story exhibits significant marks of secularization. Gans's main subject is not Bar Kokhba's messianic claims but his rise to power and his victories against Rome and "Africa." The story's explanation of events solely through military and political causes, its entertainment value, the important theme of Jewish-Gentile relations, and Gans's far greater interest in questions of chronology and textual discrepancies than in doctrine, eschatology, or religious authority—these together tend to secularize Gans's image of Bar Kokhba.

Persecutions, Eschatology, and History

The image of Bar Kokhba in sixteenth-century historical writings reflected the persecutions, eschatological fervor, and some of the new historical viewpoints of the time.

It was particularly in response to the Spanish and Portuguese expulsions, as well as later Italian persecutions, that Samuel Usque and Yosef Ha-Kohen wrote their histories of Jewish suffering and Ibn Yaḥya assembled his list of "the destructions of the Jews." For them Betar was one of the first and most horrifying examples of the persecutions that Gentiles had inflicted upon Jews all through the centuries. Usque and Ha-Kohen both blamed Bar Kokhba for instigating the rebellion, but the emphasis of all three stories falls more heavily on what the Gentiles did afterwards—the bloody massacre of most of the inhabitants of Betar and the expulsion of the remainder. Betar foreshadowed Spain. Not since the destruction tales of Midrash Lamentations, composed soon after the event itself, had writers been so moved by this part of the story.

Like the rabbinic storytellers, Usque and Ha-Kohen perceived in Bar Kokhba a desire for illegitimate power, the paradigmatic sin of false messiahs, calling down divine punishment. Bar Kokhba thus continued to have meaning as a figure in the ongoing story of Israel's sins and punishments, but now in a consciously historical framework that sought to comprehend the entire history of Israel's relationship with God. He also acquired a new meaning in relation to the history of Jewish-Gentile interactions: his sin activated Gentile hatred, a pretext for Gentile armies, mobs, and inquisitors to attack the Jewish people.

All the authors we studied (including Zacuto, it appears) were moved by messianic yearnings, which were reinforced by the dramatic changes occurring in Europe and Jewish life in those days, and all our writers were aware of the false messiahs, prophets, and messianic calculations that had recently appeared. Usque and Ha-Kohen tell the story of Bar Kokhba in ways that clearly imply a warning against contemporary claimants, while Azariah de' Rossi and Ibn Yaḥya connect the name "Koziva" to falsehood and disappointment, and Zacuto pointedly shows that the sages eventually rejected Bar Kokhba's claims. Yet none of these writers saw the falsehood of messianic claimants as justifiable reason for abandoning messianic hope.

An intense desire for revenge fills not only the *Consolation* and *The Vale of Tears*, composed around the middle of the sixteenth century, but also the *Book of Genealogies*, written by a Spanish exile at the beginning of the century, which pictured Bar Kokhba as a fierce warrior vanquishing the Christians of his day. In contrast, *Sprout of David*, written in end-of-the-century Prague, with its friendlier atmosphere, gave only brief mention to the destruction of Betar, or to other persecutions of the Jews. Bar Kokhba seems, instead, to have served Gans as a positive model of Jewish political and military power, if not the proper means of acquiring it.

The image of Bar Kokhba took on non-traditional features through some of the new methods and viewpoints adopted by Jewish historians in the sixteenth century. When Bar Kokhba acquired a role in the martyrological history of the interactions between Jews and Gentiles, he became part of a new kind of history, a more secular one, in which non-Jews played a significant part. His image was secularized, too, insofar as historians portrayed him as a political and military figure whose life had meaning for its role in world history (as in Zacuto's and Gans's books), and also insofar as the events in his life were told as psychological, social, or political facts without reference to God or Torah. We also saw how Azariah and Gans presented Bar Kokhba as an object of explicitly secular goals in historical study, that is, as a facet of truth in itself, a topic of conversation between Jews and Christians, or a source of entertainment. Azariah's treatment of Bar Kokhba's name as a topic in the realm of secular historiography, moreover, separated Bar Kokhba distinctly from the sphere of sacred truth and authoritative doctrine. Finally, the image of Bar Kokhba changed when Abravanel, Zacuto, and Azariah all cited Gentile literature as valid sources of knowledge about him: their images of Bar Kokhba thereby came openly to include what non-Jews, the secular world, saw in him. Indeed, the newly discovered name, "Bar Kokhba," itself depended on recognizing the authority of those secular texts.

5
Bar Kokhba in the Later Kabbalah

While Jewish scholars in Prague and the Italian peninsula were turning to the study of history for new perceptions of Jewish existence, kabbalists in Italy, Safed, and elsewhere were also seeking new paths of understanding. For them, however, history was only the surface-reflection of hidden events taking place on a cosmic dimension, in the life of the Divine. Kabbalists explained history against a complex structure of transcendent forces, processes, and configurations whose outlines they tried to apprehend.

We shall look at two sets of texts from the Kabbalah of the sixteenth and seventeenth centuries—one written by Ḥayyim Vital (1542–1620), the most influential disciple and interpreter of the great sixteenth-century visionary Isaac Luria, and the other written by the prophet of the Shabbatean messianic movement, Nathan Ashkenazi of Gaza (1644–1680). These two writers held an image of Bar Kokhba that differed significantly from all previous images, not only because of the distinctive Lurianic ideas that shaped their perception of him, but also because they accorded him near-messianic status.

Two concepts in particular, *gilgul* and *tikkun*, give the kabbalistic image of Bar Kokhba its distinctive features. *Gilgul*, in its kabbalistic context, refers to the transmigration of souls, their rebirth, or metempsychosis; and in the terminology of Lurianic Kabbalah, a *gilgul* is also one particular embodiment of a soul in the course of its being reborn from generation to generation. According to this idea, as we find it formulated by Ḥayyim Vital, there exist only a limited number of souls, all of which once constituted the spiritual body of the primordial, cosmic Adam. When this Adam sinned, his cosmic "body" fragmented into a multitude of lesser souls and derivative sparks, most of which then entered into a process of transmigration from generation to generation. This process, *gilgul*, allows souls to rectify sins committed in earlier lives, and eventually the original stain caused by the transgression of that primordial Adam, until ultimately they succeed in restoring the purity and exalted nature they originally possessed. Kabbalists believed that in the meantime, during this era of transmigration, every soul-spark bears into each new life the effects, both good and bad, of what they did in previous *gilgulim*, so that every living person exhibits certain character traits and affinities related to his or her earlier lives.[1]

According to Lurianic thought, moreover, the fragmentation of the primordial Adam is part of (and in some senses, constitutes) the disarray of the entire cosmos, the good enmeshed with evil, sparks of divine light scattered, as in Gnostic myth, amidst black dross. Israel's exile among the nations is one particularly painful manifestation of this general fragmentation. The sins that Israel commits daily cause even further fragmentation, but Israel has also been given the power to repair the damage and restore the lost unity of the universe. Indeed, this is Israel's sacred role in the Lurianic drama of existence. This process of restoring and purifying the universe is called *tikkun*; it continues on from generation to generation, souls being reborn repeatedly through *gilgul*, until the process is finally completed. *Tikkun* is effected through performance of the commandments, prayer, the meditative intentionality (*kavvanah*) that accompanies these actions, and special meditative rituals. On the historical level, *tikkun* also makes possible the messianic redemption of Israel. That is to say, not until the *tikkun* is completed can the

---

1. Gershom Scholem, "Gilgul: Seelenwanderung und Sympathie der Seelen," in *Von der mystichen Gestalt der Gottheit* (Zurich, 1962), 193–247, esp. 225–37 on the Lurianic formulations. See also the English summary in Scholem, *Kabbalah*, 344–50.

Messiah appear and redeem the nation (since, as was said, historical events correspond to hidden cosmic processes). Thus, as Gershom Scholem observes in regard to the Lurianic concept of redemption, "The messianic king, far from bringing about the *tikkun*, is himself brought about by it."[2]

Sefer Ha-Gilgulim

In *Sefer Ha-Gilgulim*, Ḥayyim Vital applies the concept of *gilgul* to the histories of biblical and talmudic figures, explaining the events in their lives on the basis of their previous *gilgulim*. We are told, for example, that R. Akiba's death as a martyr served to repair the damage caused by an earlier *gilgul* of his soul, in the form of the patriarch Jacob, who had sinned by endangering Joseph's life (Gen. 37:13); R. Akiba's death centuries later finally undid the harmful effects of this sin.[3] In the course of explaining R. Akiba's death—and there are other reasons for it—Vital mentions Bar Kokhba, and he proceeds to explain Bar Kokhba's life, too, on the basis of previous *gilgulim*.

Shelah and Shiloh

In the first part of the explanation, Vital reveals a hidden link between R. Akiba and Ben Koziva.

> R. Akiba ['Aqiva] was a spark of the Messiah, because the letters in *'AQYVA* are the same letters as in the name *Ya'AQoV* plus an aleph ['*A*], which signifies *'Adam Ha-Rishon* [the Primordial Adam]. The sages also said in Midrash Lamentations and at the end of Maimonides' Laws on Kings that R. Akiba was the arms-bearer of Ben Koziva, because he was so strong that he could catch catapult stones and they could not prevail against him. This was because he was of the nature of Judah, and was in Lod. He and R. Akiba were one entity (*davar eḥad*). Not without significance was he called "Ben Koziva," and not without significance was R. Akiba his arms-bearer.

---

2. Scholem, *Sabbatai Ṣevi: The Mystical Messiah*, 46. See Scholem's extensive discussion of these Lurianic concepts in their larger framework, 18–102.

3. Ḥayyim Vital, *Sefer Ha-Gilgulim* (Premisla, 1875), 25b (Part II, Chap. 8).

> It is established that the Messiah is from Judah, and Er and Onan [two disobedient sons of Judah and older brothers of Shelah] are his *qelipot* [husks, waste-matter], and hence they died. But Shelah alone was truly of the same spark as the Messiah, although not entirely—and therefore, Scripture said: *And he was in Keziv when she bore him* (Gen. 38:5). "Keziv" and "Keziva" are identical.[4]

Before proceeding to the rest of Vital's analysis, let us examine a few points in the passage above.

Vital is speaking about the *gilgulim* of the soul-spark of the Messiah. He tells us that Jacob and Judah had possessed this soul, and that Judah's third son, Shelah, received it after them. This means, as we shall learn, that Shelah could potentially have been the Messiah. But he was not, and as the messianic soul was reborn again and again, in successive *gilgulim* through the centuries, it reached the generation of R. Akiba. Then it split into two sparks, becoming the men we know as R. Akiba and Ben Koziva. Vital tells us that they were *davar eḥad*, one entity in the sense of being two sparks from the same soul, both thus sharing the nature of that soul. Vital finds in this common origin and affinity between the two men an explanation for R. Akiba's proclamation of Ben Koziva as Messiah: being a spark from the same soul, R. Akiba recognized the messianic character of Ben Koziva's soul.

Notice the way Vital proves this: since the name "Koziva" has the same consonants as the name of the town "Keziv," where Shelah was born, Ben Koziva is a *gilgul* of the same soul that had dwelt in Shelah, the messianic soul. As such, Ben Koziva exhibits the same nature as Shelah—who, in the continuation of Vital's exposition, becomes the archetype for all potential messiahs, for all those men into whom Shelah's soul passed in later generations.

Vital now interprets Gen. 38:11:

> *Judah said to Tamar his kallah* . . . —this indicates the Shekhinah, for she goes with us in Exile after all the wicked generations were killed according to the example of Er and Onan, who died for their sins. He said: *Remain a widow in your father's house* . . . —in the manner of what Scripture says: *How is she become like a widow* (Lam. 1:1). Surely it must mean that she was a widow in the exile of "your father's house"—meaning that of the Holy One Blessed Be He. She will not

---

4. Ibid.

return . . . *until Shelah has grown.* For he was yet small—meaning: until the *yud* is completed, which is the transcendent light, as Scripture says: *Behold I make you small among the nations; you are greatly despised* (Obad. 1:2). For now Shelah remains in exile until "Shiloh" is complete, who is the Messiah and Moses.[5]

Vital interprets Gen. 38:11 as a reference to the Shekhinah in exile, which he finds symbolized in Scripture by Tamar's widowhood. The Shekhinah (divine presence) is one of the ten primary manifestations of God that the kabbalists call *sefirot*, and is often thought of as a bride, *kallah*. (Though the Hebrew word *kallah* means "daughter-in-law" in the literal context of Gen. 38:11, Vital has uncovered its kabbalistic import by reading it through another of its meanings, "bride.") Here, Vital tells us that the Shekhinah has accompanied the people of Israel into exile, which for her (a widow-bride like Tamar) is a period of grief and bereavement. In Scripture, Shelah is supposed to save Tamar from widowhood when he grows up, by marrying her in conformity with the practice of levirate marriage (*yibbum*), wherein the brother of a deceased man serves as the redeemer, *go'el*, of the widow; and Vital interprets this to mean that the Messiah will redeem the Shekhinah from exile—but not until the messianic spark has "grown" fully into the Messiah. In the meantime, the spark is still incomplete, like the name "Shelah," which in Hebrew lacks the *yud* necessary to spell "Shiloh," the name of the Messiah (according to the traditional exegesis of Gen. 49:10). Vital thus considers Shelah the archetype for all the men over the centuries in whom the messianic spark lodged but who nevertheless did not "grow" into Shiloh and redeem the Shekhinah. Vital next explains why these men never attained full messianic stature.

> The reason that it was decreed that she remain a widow is this: *Lest he also die like his brothers* (Gen. 38:11). The reason is that in every generation there comes into the world a spark of the Messiah by the will of Heaven. If the generation is worthy, it is revealed who he is; but if not, he dies or they kill him by Sanctification of the Name [martyrdom], as occurred to R. Akiba in the time of Ben Koziva, and many others hidden from us. However, it is necessary that in every generation he comes in *gilgul* either to redeem Israel if they are worthy, or to give merit to the generation, or to teach them Torah if

5. Ibid.

they walk in darkness. To this, Scripture referred when it said: *Lest he also die like his brothers*—meaning: he will come in every generation; therefore, do not marry him until he grows and comes by the will of God to redeem Israel.[6]

According to Vital, the reason why the men bearing the messianic sparks failed to attain full messianic stature is that the generations in which they lived did not merit redemption. In the context of Lurianic kabbalah, this means that those generations failed to bring about the final *tikkun*. If they had effected *tikkun*, the incomplete messianic spark would have attained full messianic stature and redeemed Israel; or in Vital's symbolism, Shelah, the incomplete messiah, would have become Shiloh, the full Messiah.

According to Scholem, this "idea that a spark of the messiah-soul is present in a number of . . . 'messianic' men throughout the generations is fairly general in the writings of the Safed kabbalists."[7] Later interpreters of Lurianic kabbalah continued to teach the idea. Naftali Bacharach, in *Emeq Ha-Melekh* (c. 1648), claiming to quote a Lurianic homily, states, "In every generation he [God] creates one perfectly righteous man, worthy like Moses . . . provided that also his generation merits it. . . . He will redeem Israel, but everything depends on the transmigration of souls (*gilgul*) and their purification." Likewise, in *Tuv Ha-'Areṣ* (c. 1655), Nathan Shapira of Jerusalem writes that this messianic soul is sent into the world "to redeem [Israel] if they repent, or to preserve the world in evil times, as in the generation of the great [Hadrianic] persecution, or else to enlighten the world in the period of exile through his Torah."[8] (This last formulation of the idea resembles Vital's in part; Shapira even alludes to R. Akiba's martyrdom during the Hadrianic persecutions, as Vital does in the passage under study.) What all the various statements of the idea assume, Scholem argues, is that the messianic soul undergoes a fundamental change at the time of redemption. Before then, the Messiah's *nefesh, ruaḥ,* and *neshamah*, the three levels of soul attainable by all people, undergo *gilgul* from generation to generation; but at the consummation of the general *tikkun*, the Messiah

6. Ibid.
7. Scholem, *Sabbatai Ṣevi*, 57.
8. Ibid., 56. Scholem's note 73 states his inability to find the homily that Shapira claimed to cite. Bacharach (in Frankfurt) and Shapira were two seventeenth-century interpreters of Lurianic kabbalah whose writings had a particular influence on the Shabbatean movement. See Scholem, *Kabbalah*, 394–95; and *Sabbatai Ṣevi*, 365–66.

receives the highest level of his soul, the *yeḥidah*, which only he can attain.⁹ The *yeḥidah* makes him the Messiah. This is what Vital means when he speaks of Shelah becoming Shiloh: the incomplete messianic soul gains the *yeḥidah* that distinguishes it as the true Messiah.

This cannot occur, however, until the generation is worthy—meaning that the people of the generation must purify their souls and effect *tikkun*. Then and only then can the messianic spark be completed, enabling the Messiah to bring the *tikkun* to its fulfillment in the realm of history.

The Unfinished Messiah

Applied to Ben Koziva, these ideas mean that he was the Shelah of his generation. Had his generation been able to effect *tikkun*, he would have received the *yeḥidah* and attained full messianic stature; but because they failed to do so, redemption was impossible, and what they needed instead was to be taught Torah and provided merit through the death of a righteous man. This, according to Vital, was the alternate role of the messianic *gilgul*, and it was therefore allotted to R. Akiba, who, as teacher and *ṣaddiq* (saint), embodied this role.

Vital thus gives Ben Koziva a high status indeed: in Vital's eyes, Ben Koziva was a genuine spark of the Messiah, a man whose soul could potentially have attained full messianic stature. This was indicated both by his name, which connected him to Shelah, and by his historical character as an invincible *gibbor* performing supernatural feats. He failed to redeem Israel not because he himself had sinned, but because his generation had. Only for this reason did Ben Koziva become a false messiah instead of a true one.

This image of Ben Koziva stands as both a warning and a promise to Vital's readers.

As a warning, it shows how easily a Shelah can be mistaken for a Shiloh. That is the implication Vital draws from his exegesis: "He [Shelah] will come in every generation; therefore, do not marry him until he grows and comes by the will of God to redeem Israel." For Tamar to marry the young Shelah would mean that the Shekhinah (here representing Israel) would embrace Shelah's *gilgul* as her redeemer before he has grown into the Messiah. The problem is that Shelah's *gilgul* might, in the words of Gen. 38:11, "die like his brothers"—that is, the messianic spark might not grow

---

9. Scholem, *Sabbatai Ṣevi*, 57.

into Shiloh, the true Messiah capable of redeeming the Shekhinah. Instead, if the generation is unworthy, Shelah's *gilgul* may have to die like R. Akiba.

Vital is therefore cautioning his readers not to embrace false messiahs. He is warning them not to force the end before its time, but rather to continue their acts of *tikkun* until the general *tikkun* is completed, when the messianic spark would be transformed into the Messiah. The references to R. Akiba and Ben Koziva in this regard suggest that Vital thought their generation had forced the end, or perhaps only R. Akiba had done so, by embracing Ben Koziva as Messiah.

The idea that a generation's unworthiness delays redemption, an idea found often in the kabbalistic literature of Vital's time, means that Israel is responsible for its own fate. To them is given the task of effecting *tikkun* and the power to turn the Shelah in their midst into the Shiloh able to redeem them. Vital's words, therefore, by showing readers how their sins delay redemption and by setting before them the possibility that their acts of *tikkun* would bring the Messiah, imply not only a call for repentance and spiritual effort, but also a promise of redemption if they respond.

The Safed kabbalists believed that the time of redemption was imminent and that theirs were the final generations. Vital, too, believed this, and perhaps we can recognize in the passage under study a feeling of messianic expectation and excitement. Along with much else in Vital's writings, this passage urges readers to devote all their energies to completing the process of redemption, because it could occur in their lifetime. The same messianic spark that had manifested itself as Ben Koziva was present in the reader's own day, impatient to step forth, waiting only upon the moment when *tikkun* would be completed.

In a sense, Ben Koziva was still alive. The concept of *gilgul* changes our relationship to people of the past: they are no longer confined to the past. There is an aspect of Ben Koziva that is present through all historical time—the messianic spark; it exists even now, in our very midst. As an archetype, Vital's Ben Koziva manifests a messianic potentiality that is renewed over and over again, until it at last succeeds in attaining its ultimate end, to become the Messiah. Ben Koziva represents the state in which the messianic soul exists during the time of exile and waiting. He also attests to the present deficiency of existence, the incompleteness of *tikkun*, and the failings of the Jewish people. He is Shelah, the unfinished Messiah. By portraying Ben Koziva in this way, Vital has extracted from the life of Ben Koziva what continued to be valid and accessible: the active possibility of messianic redemption alongside the continuing failure of human effort.

The process of *gilgul* gave Ben Koziva, in addition, a specific, personal relationship to the living man in whom the same soul-spark now dwelt. Vital had long believed that he himself bore the messianic soul in his generation, and Luria had confirmed this by telling Vital that he bore the soul of R. Akiba—which is the messianic soul.[10] Ben Koziva, then, as a *gilgul* of that same soul, was, in a sense, alive in Ḥayyim Vital himself. The idea of *gilgul* had, so to speak, "activated" Ben Koziva for Vital's generation, both as paradigm and as reborn soul.

The Problem of Recognizing the Messiah

Gen. 38:11, according to Vital's interpretation, alludes to the danger of embracing as Messiah a man in whom the messianic soul is still incomplete. Stated in Vital's metaphors, it is the problem of distinguishing Shiloh from Shelah. Vital censures R. Akiba for proclaiming Ben Koziva the Messiah, because even though Ben Koziva was indeed the messianic spark, he never became the fully grown Messiah. In *Sha'ar Ruaḥ Ha-Qodesh*, Vital writes that R. Akiba had to rectify this error in later *gilgulim*.[11]

The problem of identifying the Messiah arises, in part, from the nature of the evidence. In kabbalistic thought, the significant events occur beyond the world of history, which is only a pale reflection of the hidden, inner processes of the universe. As Rachel Elior points out, kabbalists claimed that those events could be discerned only through inspired kabbalistic interpretation of the hidden depths of the Torah, as in Vital's uncoding of Gen. 38:11, or through private visions and meditations.[12] What was important about Ben Koziva, from this perspective, was not what he did as a warrior, but rather his soul, which gave him, through *gilgul*, a suprahistorical relationship with Shelah. Ben Koziva's soul made him messianic, prior to anything he did in his life. Moreover, he would attain full messianic stature only upon the consummation of the general *tikkun*, an occurrence also difficult to perceive.

To be the Messiah, then, according to the later kabbalists, means primar-

---

10. Vital, *Sefer Sha'ar Ruaḥ Ha-Qodesh*, ed. Shmuel Vital (Tel Aviv, 1963), 131f. On messianic identifications of Luria and Vital, see Scholem, *Sabbatai Ṣevi*, 54–57 and Joseph Dan, *Gershom Scholem and the Mystical Dimensions of Jewish History* (New York, 1987), 257–59, based on the content of Vital's *Sefer Ha-Ḥezyonot*. Vital seems to have considered Luria the Messiah ben Joseph and himself the Messiah ben David.

11. Vital, *Sefer Sha'ar Ruaḥ Ha-Qodesh*, 106.

12. Elior, "Messianic Expectations and Spiritualization of Religious Life in the Sixteenth Century," *Revue des Etudes Juives* 145 (1986): 45.

ily to be the messianic soul and participate in the hidden process of *tikkun*. This is very difficult to discern and verify from a public and historical perspective.

This issue and Vital's warning anticipate some of the debates that would occur over Shabbatai Ṣevi. Let us turn now to three documents in *The Fading Flower of Ṣevi* to examine how Nathan Ashkenazi and his opponents drew Bar Kokhba into the debate over Shabbatai Ṣevi's authenticity.

Nathan's Letters

The largest messianic movement in Jewish history reached its climax in the summer of 1666 and involved Jewish communities in Asia Minor, Palestine, Africa, and Europe.[13] Their hopes were centered upon a man named Shabbatai Ṣevi, who was himself a kabbalist, as were his closest supporters. The leading intellectual exponent of the movement, Nathan b. Elisha Ashkenazi, was a particularly brilliant student of Lurianic ideas.

Unlike all previous writers on Bar Kokhba, Nathan invoked his example to gain support for a living messianic claimant. Ibn Daud and Samuel Usque, on the other hand, who also had experienced or heard about messianic movements in their own days, turned the incident of Bar Kokhba into a warning against messianic claimants. Likewise in Nathan's time, too, an opponent of the Shabbatean movement named Jacob Sasportas employed the example of Bar Kokhba to dissuade people from believing in Shabbatai Ṣevi. Here is what Sasportas wrote in his anti-Shabbatean book, The Fading Flower of Ṣevi (*Ṣiṣat Novel Ṣevi*), a collection of documents concerning the Shabbatean messianic movement:

> And if Rabbi and R. Akiba erred in the case of Ben Koziva, in that they saw him fighting the wars of the Lord and conquering in a supernatural fashion, and with one of his knees hurling back the catapult stones; and if in regard to this, Rabbi applied to him the verse: Koziva *shall step forth out of Jacob;* nevertheless, R. Yoḥanan b.

---

13. Scholem, *Sabbatai Ṣevi*. See Stephen Sharot's review of Scholem's evidence and Sharot's categorization of the various Jewish communities into three degrees or types of response, with the communities of Central Europe, particularly Poland, showing the lowest level of interest: Sharot, *Messianism, Mysticism, and Magic*, 88–91.

Torta replied, "Grass shall grow out of your jaws, and still the Messiah will not have come." Did they not doubt him and make a mistake about this possibility, and get angry at him, even though they had something upon which to rely? But as for us—what deed did we see that we should err about him [Shabbatai Ṣevi]? . . . And why do we not doubt more than R. Yoḥanan b. Torta, to say, "Grass will grow etc.," and we would be given merit for following the words of the sages.[14]

Sasportas's argument goes something like this: if Ben Koziva appeared so convincingly to be the Messiah but nevertheless turned out to be false, then is it not likely that Shabbatai Ṣevi, who exhibits nothing like Ben Koziva's strength and military success, is similarly false? And if R. Yoḥanan b. Torta had the courage to raise objections before even such great sages as Rabbi and R. Akiba, then is it not our duty today likewise to raise objections even in the face of majority opinion?

Nathan's discussion of Bar Kokhba constitutes, in part, a reply to an argument like that of Sasportas.

The Milui of the Tetragrammaton

Nathan of Gaza mentions Bar Kokhba in two letters that appear in *The Fading Flower of Ṣevi*, both of them written toward the end of 1665, and also briefly in his "Treatise on the Dragons" of 1666.

In the letters, Nathan adopts Vital's idea that Ben Koziva was an earlier *gilgul* of the messianic soul, but instead of basing his argument on Scripture and the roots of Hebrew names, as Vital did, Nathan bases it upon *gematria*, an interpretative system that treats Hebrew words according to the numerical value of their letters. In this way, Nathan proves that Ben Koziva manifested the "holy spark" of the Messiah ("the same holy spark" that was reborn in Shabbatai Ṣevi, whom Nathan calls "our Lord") and that in this sense, Ben Koziva truly was "the King Messiah," as R. Akiba perceived. For evidence, Nathan points to the fact that in *gematria* the numerical value of the name Koziva equals that of the name of God according to its *milui*. (*Milui*, as Nathan uses the term, is a method of counting so-called "hidden

---

14. Jacob Sasportas, *Ṣiṣat Novel Ṣevi*, ed. Isaiah Tishby (Jerusalem, 1954), 150–51.

letters" in a word.)[15] Sasportas records Nathan's first letter mentioning Bar Kokhba as follows:

> Ben Koziva had the same holy soul as our Lord, may His glory be exalted, and he was the King Messiah and therefore R. Akiba was his standard-bearer. But he did not attain to the level of YHVH; only the *milui* of YHVH has the same total as "Koziva," and the *milui* means Judgment, and therefore he was killed. But our Lord, may His glory be exalted, attained to the [full] name of YHVH; and there is an allusion in the name "Ṣevi": the sum of the letters in Ṣevi "ben Yud" amounts to 72 (YHVH) in all. This means that the name of the Existence [YHVH] in yuds amounts to 72, and the *milui* equals 46, and likewise the middle letters of Shaddai; and *ha-Mashiaḥ* (the Messiah) makes up the entire *milui* of Shaddai.[16]

Nathan's second letter referring to Bar Kokhba adds several details.

> Nathan the Prophet wrote that Ben Koziva had the same holy soul as our Lord, may His glory be exalted, and he was the King Messiah and therefore R. Akiba was his standard-bearer. But he did not attain to the level of YHVH, but only to the *milui* of YHVH alone, which equals the total of "Koziva"; the *milui* means Judgment, and therefore he was killed. But our Lord, may His glory be exalted, attained to the name of YHVH entirely, by means of good deeds. To this there is an allusion in the word "Ṣevi"—the *notariqon* [summation of letters] of Ṣevi "ben Yud" equals the total of YHVH [72]. There are innumerable further examples.[17]

The very names of Ben Koziva and Shabbatai Ṣevi reveal the inner nature of these men, explaining why one failed to attain full messianic

---

15. Specifically, to count the *milui* of a word, say "*ben*," one spells out the two letters in the name: bet = bet + yud + taf, and nun = nun + vav + nun; and then one counts the value of each letter except the letters in "ben" itself (bet and nun)—thus, yud + taf = 410, and vav + nun = 56. Hence, the *milui* of "ben" is 466. Its full value, counting the bet and nun, is 518.

Nathan uses the terms *notariqon* and *minyan* to signify the numerical value of the actual letters used in spelling a word. For example, the *notariqon* of "ben" is 52 (bet + nun). The *notariqon* of "Koziva" is 46, and the *milui* of the tetragrammaton YHVH using *yudim* (that is, using the letter *yud* to spell out the names of the letters he[y], va[y]v, and he[y] in YHVH, before counting its *milui*) is also 46.

16. Sasportas, *Ṣiṣat Novel Ṣevi*, 154.
17. Ibid., 156.

stature and the other succeeded. Ben Koziva failed because *Koziva* equals only the *milui* of the tetragrammaton, which is an incomplete spelling-out of the divine name. His soul never attained a high enough level, but reached only a level equivalent to the *milui* of YHVH—which, as Luria taught, alludes to the *sefirah* called *din* (judgment, the manifestation of God's wrath).[18] This means, in a sense, that Ben Koziva's soul, reaching only the inferior level of *din*, was destroyed there: "and therefore he was killed." Phrased differently, Ben Koziva had been judged deficient as a Messiah.

In contrast, the fact that the numerical value of Shabbatai Ṣevi's name equals the full spelling-out of YHVH proves to Nathan that Shabbatai Ṣevi had attained full messianic stature.[19] Nathan's second letter states that the reason Shabbatai Ṣevi was able to arrive at this highest level was that he performed "good deeds." In kabbalistic thought, this refers to works of *tikkun*—performing commandments, praying, doing penance, meditating, all with the proper kabbalistic intentions (*kavvanot*). What Nathan implies, therefore, is that Shabbatai Ṣevi had succeeded where Ben Koziva had not, because Shabbatai Ṣevi had accomplished a greater *tikkun* of his soul than Ben Koziva had. In other words, Ben Koziva had failed to fully purify and elevate the messianic soul.

We see, then, that both Vital and Nathan viewed Ben Koziva as a man who manifested the messianic soul in a deficient state. Vital blamed the soul's deficiency upon the inadequacies of Ben Koziva's generation, but Nathan ascribed it to Ben Koziva's own failure to purify his soul. Vital made redemption dependent upon the generation's success in effecting *tikkun*; but Nathan, expecting the Messiah to liberate his own soul, gave a much greater role to the Messiah in initiating redemption.[20] For Vital, the example of Ben Koziva taught a lesson of caution in respect to messianic movements; whereas for Nathan, the example of Ben Koziva conveyed a message of hope and even stood as proof that Shabbatai Ṣevi was truly the Messiah.

---

18. Isaiah Tishby, in his ed. of *Ṣiṣat Novel Ṣevi*, 154 n. 4, explains that the word "*milui*" amounts to the same sum as the word "*elohim*"—the divine name that corresponds to the *sefirah* of *din*; hence, the *milui* of a divine name indicates *din*.

19. Nathan computes the *notariqon* of "Ṣevi" written as a name, "Ben Yud," based on its last two letters, *bet* and *yud*. This name, fully spelled out, equals 72, and that is the total of the full spelling-out of the letters in YHVH with *yudim*.

20. See Scholem on Nathan's concept of the Messiah's heroic struggle to purify his soul sunk in the depths of the *qelippot* (the evil "shells") and to redeem them: *Sabbatai Ṣevi*, 301–8.

Nathan's Reply to Sasportas

How, then, does Nathan answer opponents like Sasportas who point to the example of Ben Koziva as a warning against Shabbatai Ṣevi? Nathan replies, first, that Ben Koziva was not in fact a false messiah, but merely an incomplete messiah, one who had not raised his soul to the necessary level of perfection. As such, his example demonstrates nothing absolute about messianic claimants but implies, on the contrary, the possibility that some future *gilgul* of the messianic soul would achieve perfection where Ben Koziva had failed. Second, Nathan turns the example of Ben Koziva's failure into a specific validation of Shabbatai Ṣevi. For exactly where Ben Koziva had failed, by not attaining the level of the full name of God, precisely in this had Shabbatai Ṣevi succeeded, as his name proved. By this reasoning, Nathan turns the anti-Shabbatean argument upside down, using it to strengthen his readers' faith.

Such reasoning made it difficult for Nathan's opponents to refute his claims for Shabbatai Ṣevi. As pointed out earlier, the kabbalistic Messiah cannot be identified by traditional forms of evidence. Vital, for example, considered Ben Koziva a potential messiah on the basis of his name alone, prior to anything he did in his life. Nathan invokes the same kind of evidence to prove not only that Ben Koziva possessed the messianic spark but also that Shabbatai Ṣevi had perfected that spark and was therefore the Messiah. It was not what Shabbatai Ṣevi did on the plane of ordinary history that proved this, but what he did in the hidden realms of the universe and what could be inferred by *gematria* from his name. Opponents like Sasportas, who looked only at Shabbatai Ṣevi's character and accomplishments in the world of history ("what deed did we see?" he asks of Shabbatai Ṣevi), could refute such claims only by overthrowing the whole system of Lurianic kabbalah. The same kind of evidence that was offered for believing that Ben Koziva had embodied the messianic soul in an unperfected state was offered as proof that Shabbatai Ṣevi had perfected that soul and become the Messiah.

Nathan's later "Treatise on the Dragons" (*Drush Ha-Tanninim*) demonstrates in similar fashion that Ben Koziva "had a spark of the soul of the Messiah ben David." The name "Koziva" itself points, through *gematria*, to the *sefirah* of *Yesod*, in the divine configuration of the "Father" (*'Abba*), which has a redemptive quality and is linked with Mordechai, also a spark of the Messiah's soul. There was messianic significance, too, in the rabbinic legend about Ben Koziva throwing catapult stones back at the enemy: it symbolized, Nathan wrote, "a wondrous *tikkun* that he worked in the upper regions." The Treatise also specifies the relationship between Ben Koziva and

R. Akiba. Both had souls from the heels of the primordial Adam, which were "the souls of the messianic advent"—those that would appear after the year 1575, during the last days before redemption. R. Akiba's soul, which was very high, "was the soul of the Messiah ben Joseph."[21]

We have seen, then, that Nathan conceived of Ben Koziva's relationship to Shabbatai Ṣevi as one of promise and fulfillment, of a process completed, a fruition. Just as Vital had activated Ben Koziva for the present generation, so, too, had Nathan—claiming further that Ben Koziva had been reborn specifically as Shabbatai Ṣevi. In this sense, therefore, the soul manifested as Ben Koziva was alive in Nathan's day, acting upon his world. Nathan's image of Ben Koziva had reclaimed him from the past. Ben Koziva's failure was no longer irreversibly final, nor was history closed and sealed. For the concept of *gilgul* dissolves historical boundaries into an ever-present flow of life moving toward its fulfillment. One aspect of Ben Koziva, the most important, the soul dwelling in him, had persisted through time until it had now, in Shabbatai Ṣevi, finally fulfilled its destiny. In Ḥayyim Vital's symbolism: Shelah had at last grown to become Shiloh.

The Kabbalistic Image of Bar Kokhba

The kabbalistic image of Bar Kokhba is an image not of a false messiah but of an unfinished messiah, the messianic soul unfulfilled.

As such, it comes surprisingly close to the view of Maimonides, since he too considered Bar Kokhba a potential messiah. Maimonides thought that R. Akiba was right in proclaiming Bar Kokhba tentatively the Messiah, which implies that Maimonides must also have thought that Bar Kokhba could actually have become the Messiah. The underlying idea that Maimonides and the kabbalists share, therefore, is that the advent of the Messiah involves a gradual process: God does not choose or send a man into the world fully empowered to redeem it; instead, people must struggle over time to achieve messianic redemption. Maimonides and the kabbalists disagree, however, on the realm where this struggle for redemption takes place. For Maimonides, it is the realm of political history; whereas for Vital and Nathan, the crucial events take place in a transcendent realm of invisible, inner

---

21. Nathan b. Elisha Ashkenazi, "Drush Ha-Tanninim," in *Be'iqvot Mashiaḥ*, ed. Gershom Scholem (Jerusalem, 1943), 44–45. See *Sabbatai Ṣevi*, 306–7 for Scholem's explanation of the reference to the *sefirah*, "*yesod* of the Father."

processes such as *tikkun* and *gilgul*, or in the hidden soul of a potential messiah. In looking at Bar Kokhba, therefore, Maimonides and the kabbalists discover his messianic potentiality in radically different areas of his life. In Maimonides' view, that potentiality is to be seen in Bar Kokhba's character and deeds—his righteousness, military success, and reestablishment of the monarchy; but for Vital and Nathan, this potentiality derived from the transcendent dimension of Bar Kokhba—his soul, as revealed primarily by his name itself. Correspondingly, Maimonides explained Bar Kokhba's failure from his sinful actions and inability to complete the political tasks of the Messiah, and the kabbalists explained it from the state of his soul—that it never attained full messianic stature.

This difference between the views of the kabbalists and Maimonides highlights one of the most important ways in which the kabbalistic image of Bar Kokhba diverges from the earlier images. By focusing attention on Bar Kokhba's soul and his place in the hidden drama of *tikkun*, Vital and Nathan discount Bar Kokhba's character and deeds in the realm of history. But the public, historical aspect of Bar Kokhba was exactly what was of greatest concern to the sages and all writers afterward whom we studied: they wanted to know whether Bar Kokhba was a righteous or wicked man, what political and military actions he took, and what consequences those actions had for the Jewish people. The kabbalists' nearly total lack of interest in these issues constitutes a radical transformation of the story.

Moreover, the kabbalistic texts introduce new modes of knowledge and argumentation into the story of Bar Kokhba in order to speak of matters lying beyond the reach of ordinary reason and the rabbinic exegesis of Scripture. Seeking the deepest truth about Bar Kokhba, Vital and Nathan turn to archetypal analogies, *gematria*, and a scriptural exegesis that unveils hidden references to kabbalistic realities. With other topics, kabbalists utilized occult techniques such as inducing visions and reading souls.

These changes in the story constitute just as serious a break with traditional rabbinic thought as did Azariah de' Rossi's introduction of foreign sources and standards of knowledge.

Yet the kabbalistic image of Bar Kokhba is clearly not a secular one. It clarifies sacred doctrine (the doctrine of the Messiah), and it speaks of holymen—in Vital's book, the story is linked to the life of R. Akiba, and in Nathan's letters, the life of "our holy Lord," Shabbatai Ṣevi. Moreover, both Vital and Nathan cite only internal, holy sources of information, and, most importantly, they present the story of Bar Kokhba as part of the sacred history of the coming of redemption.

Conclusion

In drawing general conclusions about the image of Bar Kokhba in the Jewish literature of our study, it is important, first, to recognize that the writings we examined were written by just a few of all the Jews who lived during the fifteen centuries between Bar Kokhba and the letter of Nathan of Gaza. Some of these writings were among the most influential and widely read books of the period: the Talmud and Midrash, Rashi's commentary, Maimonides' code, and, though less so, Ibn Daud's history; and the history books of Ha-Kohen, Ibn Yahya, and Gans were addressed to popular audiences. These books shaped the images of Bar Kokhba held by a large number of Jews. Other writings, however—those of Abravanel, Usque, Zacuto, Azariah de' Rossi, Vital, and Nathan—reached more limited audiences. But even with all the written evidence we have, the influential books along with the lesser-known, there still remain great gaps of population, time, and geography for which we have no indication as to what, or how much, Jews were thinking about Bar Kokhba.

In particular, there is little indication of what the lower, less-educated classes thought about him. The literature provides us with scant evidence for determining anything about a popular image of Bar Kokhba during the period under study. Gershom Scholem and Yigael Yadin cannot, therefore, substantiate their claims, mentioned in the Introduction, about a "popular" or "people's" image of him. Nor does the formal literature support Scholem, Yadin, and Harkabi when they speak of only one predominant image of the man—an image of a hero-saint (according to Scholem), a freedom fighter (Yadin), or an irresponsible, deluded general (Harkabi). We have seen that pre-modern Jewish writers remembered Bar Kokhba in a variety of different and often complex ways and that no single image asserted by these scholars predominates.

This is one conclusion that can be drawn from our study. A few other generalizations are possible.

First of all, we have learned that the various images of Bar Kokhba appearing in Jewish literature up to the seventh century derive from two distinct traditions about him in rabbinic literature—the tradition of the false messiah and that of the military hero. In the later literature, these two traditions usually coalesce into a single image, often that of a hero who was believed to be the Messiah because of his extraordinary military feats. In addition, Ibn Daud introduced a subsidiary tradition derived from the Christian chronicles; but this did not alter the two basic images of Bar Kokhba so much as give them realistic political and geographic features. In the sixteenth century, however, some writers began to separate the two traditions: Zacuto treated the two sides of Bar Kokhba as separate topics, Gans treated the rebellion as almost wholly a political event, and the kabbalists spoke of Bar Kokhba's messianic nature in a way that nearly excluded his political and military deeds. The history of the image of Bar Kokhba, then, can be understood as a development and interplay of these two basic views of who he was.

But as we also saw, individual Jewish writers set their own distinctive stamps upon the development of these two images. Thus, the legends of Midrash Lamentations gave Bar Kokhba the charisma and the virtues and vices characteristic of the rabbinic image of mighty warriors called gibborim. In the writings of Ibn Daud and Maimonides, on the other hand, Bar Kokhba assumed the features of a human king acting through natural (Aristotelian) political processes. Three centuries later, Abravanel thought of Bar Kokhba as a divinely appointed agent of vengeance wielding miraculous powers, perhaps an avenging knight of God. Sixteenth-century historians gave Bar

Kokhba, variously, the features of a Faustian scholar-magician, the ruler of an expanding city-state, a military power in world history, and (in reference to the Spanish expulsion) an avenger upon the Gentiles. Among the kabbalists, Bar Kokhba assumed the very different identity of *gilgul* of the messianic soul, an unfinished messiah representing one stage in the slow growth of that soul toward full messianic status. These distinctive pictures of Bar Kokhba, reflecting the visions of individual writers and the values of specific cultural settings, individualized his two basic images as false messiah and great gibbor, and endowed them with contemporary life and significance.

Some of the changes exhibited by the image of Bar Kokhba during its long history, however, are best described through the categories of sacred and secular.[1] From this perspective, the rabbinic legends told Bar Kokhba's story as sacred history, ascribing a theological significance to the events of his life and using the story to define messianic doctrine and bring about repentance. This interpretation then became itself sacred tradition to later Jews. We saw how, as subsequent writers retold the story, they removed certain elements of its traditional sacred framework, while other aspects of the story acquired new theological meanings. For example, both Ibn Daud and Maimonides eliminated the direct intervention of God from the story, explaining its outcome through immanent causality; but they seem also to have understood those immanent causes in the context of a transcendent process of redemption. Abravanel placed the story into the problematic context of Jewish-Christian debate, buttressing his picture of Bar Kokhba through the profane observations of the Latin chronicles, and yet he identified Bar Kokhba's wars more closely with God's will, as the execution of divine wrath, than any of the other writers we studied. Further secularization occurred in sixteenth-century historical writings. Images of Bar Kokhba came openly to include what non-Jews, the secular world, saw in him; he was portrayed as a political and military participant in secular world history; and he became an object of explicitly secular goals in historical study—the search for "pure" truth, a topic of conversation between Jews and Christians, or even a source of entertainment. Azariah de' Rossi's treatment of Bar Kokhba's name, in particular, as a topic in the realm of secular historiography, separated him distinctly from the sphere of sacred truth and authoritative doctrine. And yet most of these

---

1. Kees Bolle, in fact, has suggested that secularization is almost always accompanied by a reciprocal process of mythification: as secularization desacralizes some symbols, other symbols, newly felt to be sacred, take their place. See Bolle, "Secularization as a Problem for the History of Religions," *Comparative Studies in Society and History*, 12 (1970): 242–59.

writers were moved by intense messianic yearnings, and most continued to see Bar Kokhba's story within a larger framework of Israel's punishment for sin and Israel's eventual redemption. The kabbalists, finally, might be said to have desacralized the traditional historical and ethical aspects of the story while enlarging upon its sacred transcendent dimensions: it came to symbolize profound processes occurring at a level beyond normal human perception, in the hidden depths of the universe, even in the Godhead itself.

The image of Bar Kokhba, then, had a long and complex history in the literature of premodern Jews. That Bar Kokhba did have significance to Jewish writers is important to take note of: many times over the centuries they found meaning in his story. We have also learned just what it was that they found meaningful about him. The story conveyed a message to them about some of their deepest hopes, their hopes for the Messiah and their yearnings for national redemption, challenging these hopes as well as strengthening them. In addition, the story interested later Jews because it raised a range of crucial religious and political issues: it raised questions of messianic doctrine, rabbinic authority, and political policy; it posed the problem of identifying the Messiah; and it taught lessons about Israel's relationship with God, and about sin, suffering, and repentance. What is more, the story of Bar Kokhba spoke to later Jews about specific events that were occurring in their own day. We can distinguish at least three kinds of events that gave special import to the story of Bar Kokhba during our period of study—messianic movements, acts of Gentile persecution (especially the expulsion from Spain), and polemical attacks on rabbinic authority and Jewish messianic doctrine. When events such as these occurred, Jewish writers discovered particular meaning in the story of Bar Kokhba, as explanation, warning, consolation, or defense.

These are the issues and questions that Jewish literature associated with Bar Kokhba, but we can also identify a persistent pattern of answers to those questions, of specific lessons his story taught, and of attitudes, often a set of opposing attitudes, expressed toward him.

The primary political lesson that premodern Jewish writers drew from the story was the lesson of political quietism. When most writers looked for the story's political meaning, they discovered a warning: it warned Jews not to seek national power by their own political, military efforts. Bar Kokhba usually stood as an example of forcing the end. But this warning applied only to the present time; for the past and future, many writers found value in the power Bar Kokhba had wielded—value as a memory of Israel's past glory, or value as a foretokening of messianic triumph and power. The rabbinic legends, for example, while plainly taking pride in Bar Kokhba's military might, relegated it to the past. Rashi described Bar Kokhba's kingdom as the last brief glory of Israelite sovereignty. For Abravanel, Bar Kokhba's wars were a historical example of divine retribution rendered against Israel's persecutors, as well as a foreshadowing of the messianic vengeance to be wreaked upon Christian Europe in the near future. And even though Gans considered Bar Kokhba's wars just a political event of secular world history, he seems nevertheless to have hoped that, like other stories of the might of kings, Bar Kokhba's would move his readers to pray for future redemption. Nathan, in contrast, did use Bar Kokhba's example to build support for a contemporary messianic movement, but the story still did not urge military or political action and it retained a warning, one against mistaking messianic claimants whose names lack a truly messianic pattern. Maimonides, however, was something of an exception. In shifting the criteria for messianic authenticity from the realm of miracles to that of political success, he had to consider Bar Kokhba's political activism the necessary foundation for messianic fulfillment, despite the unfortunate consequences for Betar. Yet he, too, seems to have advocated a passive waiting: the community was to wait for such a leader to appear and prove himself beyond all doubt before it could join actively in his efforts. In all the literature we studied, then, the community's proper path to political power was never Bar Kokhba's path, that of immediate political and military endeavor, but the path of prayer, alert observation, and faithful waiting. We thus see two opposing political attitudes being expressed in relation to Bar Kokhba—extreme caution about political action, on the one hand, and on the other, yearnings for national power.

Hence, power was never seen as an evil in itself, and the ethical question, when it was raised, related to the manner in which Bar Kokhba had exercised power. The ethical concern is clearest in the rabbinic legends, where Bar Kokhba's blindness to the transcendent source of his power is linked with an arrogant and reckless employment of force that resulted in enormous suffering. The legends about Bar Kokhba, like those of other gibborim, express a distrust toward warriors (he is called a "worthless shepherd") while commending the sages as more responsible and effective leaders, and prayer and intellect as superior forms of power. Maimonides, too, lamented the loss of life resulting from the rebellion, but he also condoned the rebellion as a necessary concomitant of the gradual process by which redemption is finally realized. On the other hand, those writers who viewed the Bar Kokhba rebellion as an act of divine vengeance (Abravanel and

Zacuto) had to understand it as a holy war fought in obedience to God, perhaps in analogy to the divinely enjoined biblical wars against Amalek and the Canaanites. Yet even in this case, Bar Kokhba's war remained an exception to, not a model for, normal life: the divine participation in such a war distinguished it from wars initiated by merely human efforts for human purposes.

The religious teachings conveyed by the story of Bar Kokhba were of several kinds. First, writers used the story to clarify messianic doctrine for other Jews (Maimonides is the prime example of a writer doing this) or to defend messianic doctrine against polemical attack (here, Abravanel is the prime example). Second, writers turned to the story of Bar Kokhba to defend rabbinic authority. R. Akiba's mistake in proclaiming the wrong man as the Messiah appeared to undermine rabbinic authority as it was traditionally conceived. We saw that Jewish literature usually defended R. Akiba by trying to demonstrate from the story itself that Bar Kokhba had exhibited enough messianic features to (almost) justify R. Akiba's mistake. The story performed the further religious function, moreover, of reconciling Jews to the ways of God, theodicy. The story did this by explaining the justice of what Jews had suffered at Betar, the justice of the history that God had decreed for Israel.

In addition, the story was often told in a way that implied a call for repentance. The story was presented as a lesson in how sin leads to punishment, and showed what was sinful about rebellion in particular. Bar Kokhba was often presented as the epitome of this type of sin—the sin of distrusting God and taking too much pride in one's own powers. This is the sin that later Jews most often associated with the Bar Kokhba rebellion, although they also discovered transgressions specific to their own generations. Writers hoped that their readers, seeing Bar Kokhba's sins and their consequences, and how his sins delayed redemption, would repent of their own sins, especially those resembling Bar Kokhba's, and turn to heaven for salvation.

A final religious function to which writers put the story of Bar Kokhba was that of consoling readers and strengthening their faith in God's promise of redemption. One would expect the story to have had the opposite effect, raising doubts about the messianic hope. Indeed, the writers we have studied were apparently aware of this possibility and worked to prevent it from occurring. Bar Kokhba's failure was bound to raise serious doubts about the validity of the messianic hope: if Bar Kokhba had failed in spite of his great effort and the support of R. Akiba and many other people, then who could possibly succeed? If R. Akiba had been wrong about the Messiah, can the promises made by other rabbis be trusted? Had God rejected Israel forever? Would there ever come a Messiah?

In the course of this study, I have tried to demonstrate how the various retellings of the story can be understood as replies to these doubts. Jewish writers told the story of Bar Kokhba in such a way as to neutralize the effects of his failure and even to turn it into cause for new faith. These are some of the reasons for messianic hope that they discovered: Bar Kokhba's failure, because it shows the intervention of God, constitutes a promise that God will intervene in the future to redeem Israel when the nation merits it (Midrash Lamentations); the fact that Bar Kokhba was not the Messiah means that the Messiah is still promised for the future (Ibn Daud and Abravanel); the failure of messianic movements has a purifying effect and makes Israel worthier of being redeemed (Maimonides); the vengeance God wreaked through Bar Kokhba means that God will ultimately act to wreak vengeance through the Messiah (Abravanel); and finally, Bar Kokhba's failure means only that the messianic soul was as yet not fully grown, and indeed, its very incompleteness implies its gradual growth and final completion into a full Messiah in later days (Vital and Nathan). All these ideas served to turn Bar Kokhba's failure into a source of messianic hope. Jewish writers succeeded again and again in bringing new hope out of the ashes of Betar.

They were even able to discover something truly messianic about Bar Kokhba. As we have seen, a major reason why Jewish writers spoke about Bar Kokhba was that he represented to them the prototype of later false messiahs. By exposing Bar Kokhba's deficiencies and showing how easily appearances mislead, writers could warn their readers against the messianic claimants of their own day. This was one of the lessons most frequently taught from the story. Yet Jews could not totally dismiss Bar Kokhba. R. Akiba had declared him the Messiah, and R. Akiba was an important figure in Jewish tradition. Jewish writers therefore undertook to discover something valid in R. Akiba's proclamation, something about Bar Kokhba that had made R. Akiba think him the Messiah. What Jewish writers discovered were definite achievements, powers, and features of character that genuinely fit what they expected of the Messiah. In this sense, most of our writers, while fully recognizing Bar Kokhba's failings and deficiencies, never totally repudiated the messianic claims made for him. Indeed, the kabbalists went so far as to grant Bar Kokhba, explicitly and without qualification, the status of a potential messiah; and, though less explicitly, Ibn Daud, Maimonides, Abravanel, and the rabbinic storytellers all believed that Bar Kokhba had exhibited many of the essential attributes of the Messiah, so that in this sense at least, they, too, considered him potentially the Messiah. Thus, much of the premodern Jewish literature about Bar Kokhba, far from portraying him as totally false, tended to emphasize his messianic features. In relation to Bar Kokhba, "false messiah" (a term no writer actually applied to him) meant "partly the Messiah." These Jewish writings, then, not only salvaged messianic hope from Bar Kokhba's failure, but even discovered an aspect of Bar Kokhba himself that truly was messianic.

The literature we have studied certainly does not ignore the dark side of Bar Kokhba—his sins, his failure to achieve freedom for Israel, his falsehood as a messianic claimant, the disastrous consequences of his rebellion, or R. Akiba's mistake. On the other hand, no Jewish writer left Bar Kokhba wholly unredeemed. Amazingly, the literature was able to discover hope and value in an event, the Bar Kokhba rebellion, that was filled with despair, shame, and grief. Bar Kokhba had caused enormous suffering and impelled Israel into the state of exile in which Jewish writers now found themselves. They struggled to make peace with this man, to come away from him with new understanding, acceptance, and hope. And they succeeded. The image of Bar Kokhba in premodern Jewish literature reflects this struggle. It shows us how a people came to terms with the sins, the mistakes, the sufferings, and the disappointed hopes of the past.

Appendix:
Roman and Christian Writings on the Jewish Rebellion of 116–117 and the War of Bar Kokhba

1. From the *Roman History* of Dio Cassius

[LXVIII, 32] ... Meanwhile the Jews in the region of Cyrene had put a certain Andreas at their head, and were destroying both the Romans and the Greeks. They would eat the flesh of their victims, make belts for themselves of their entrails, anoint themselves with their blood and wear their skins for clothing; many they sawed in two, from the head downwards; others they gave to wild beasts, and still others they forced to fight as gladiators. In all, two hundred and twenty thousand persons perished. In Egypt, too, they perpetrated many similar outrages, and in Cyprus, under the leadership of a certain Artemion. There, also, two hundred and forty thousand perished, and for this reason no Jew may set foot on that island, and even if one of them is driven upon its shores by a storm he is put to death. Among others who subdued the Jews was Lusius, who was sent by Trajan. ...

[LXIX, 12–14] At Jerusalem he [Hadrian] founded a city in place of the one which had been razed to the ground, naming it Aelia Capitolina, and on the site of the temple of the god he raised a new temple to Jupiter. This brought on a war of no slight importance nor of brief duration, for the Jews deemed it intolerable that foreign races should be settled in their city and foreign religious rites planted there. So long, indeed, as Hadrian was close by in Egypt and again in Syria, they remained quiet, save in so far as they purposely made of poor quality such weapons as they were called upon to furnish, in order that the Romans might reject them and they themselves might thus have use of them; but when he went further away, they openly revolted. To be sure, they did not dare try conclusions with the Romans in the open field, but they occupied the advantageous positions in the country and strengthened them with mines and walls, in order that they might have places of refuge whenever they should be hard pressed, and might meet together unobserved underground; and they pierced these subterranean passages from above at intervals to let in air and light.

At first the Romans took no account of them. Soon, however, all Judea had been stirred up, and the Jews everywhere were showing signs of disturbance, were gathering together, and giving evidence of great hostility to the Romans, partly by secret and partly by overt acts; many outside nations, too, were joining them through eagerness for gain, and the whole earth, one might almost say, was being stirred up over the matter. Then, indeed, Hadrian sent against them his best generals. First of these was Julius Severus, who was dispatched from Britain, where he was governor, against the Jews. Severus did not venture to attack his opponents in the open at any point, in view of their numbers and their desperation, but by intercepting small groups, thanks to the number of his soldiers and his under-officers, and by depriving them of food and shutting them up, he was able, rather slowly, to be sure, but with comparatively little danger, to crush, exhaust and exterminate them. Very few of them in fact survived. Fifty of their most important outposts and nine hundred and eighty-five of their most famous villages were razed to the ground. Five hundred and eighty thousand men were slain in the various raids and battles, and the number of those that perished by famine, disease and fire was past finding out. Thus nearly the whole of Judea was made desolate, a result of which the people had had forewarning before the war. For the tomb of Solomon, which the Jews regarded as an object of veneration, fell to pieces of itself and collapsed, and many wolves and hyenas rushed howling into their cities. Many Romans, moreover, perished in this war. Therefore Hadrian in writing to the senate did not employ the opening phrase commonly affected by the emperors, "If you and your children are in health, it is well; I and the legions are in health."

Trans. E. Cary, *Dio's Roman History*,
Loeb Classical Library (London, 1925), 8:421–23, 447–51

2. From the *Ecclesiastical History* of Eusebius of Caesarea

[IV.2] While the teaching of our Savior and the church were flourishing daily and moving on to further progress, the tragedy of the Jews was reaching the climax of successive woes. In the course of the eighteenth year of the reign of the Emperor [Trajan] a rebellion of the Jews again broke out and destroyed a great multitude of them. For both in Alexandria and in the rest of Egypt and especially in Cyrene, as though they had been seized by some terrible spirit of rebellion, they rushed into sedition against their Greek fellow citizens, and increasing the scope of the rebellion in the following year started a great war while Lupus was governor of all Egypt. In the first engagement they happened to overcome the Greeks, who fled to Alexandria and captured and killed the Jews in the city, but though thus losing the help of the townsmen, the Jews of Cyrene continued to plunder the country of Egypt and to ravage the districts in it under their leader Lucuas. The Emperor sent against them Marcius Turbo with land and sea forces including cavalry. He waged war vigorously against them in many battles for a considerable time and killed many thousands of Jews, not only those of Cyrene but also those of Egypt who had rallied to Lucuas, their king. The Emperor suspected that the Jews in Mesopotamia would also attack the inhabitants and ordered Lusius Quietus to clean them out of the province. He organized a force and murdered a great multitude of the Jews there, and for this reform was appointed governor of Judaea by the Emperor. The Greek authors who chronicle the same period have related this narrative in these very words. . . .

[IV.6] The rebellion of the Jews once more progressed in character and extent, and Rufus, the governor of Judaea, when military aid had been sent him by the Emperor, moved out against them, treating their madness without mercy. He destroyed in heaps thousands of men, women, and children, and, under the law of war, enslaved their land. The Jews were at that time led by a certain Bar Chochebas, which means "star," a man who was murderous and a bandit, but relied on his name, as if dealing with slaves, and claimed to be a luminary who had come down to them from heaven and was magically enlightening those who were in misery. The war reached its height in the eighteenth year of the reign of Hadrian in Beththera, which was a strong citadel not very far from Jerusalem; the siege lasted a long time before the rebels were driven to final destruction by famine and thirst, and the instigator of their madness paid the penalty he deserved. Hadrian then commanded that by a legal decree and ordinances the whole nation should be absolutely prevented from entering from thenceforth even the district round Jerusalem, so that not even from a distance could it see its ancestral home. Ariston of Pella tells the story.

Trans. Kiropp Lake, The Ecclesiastical History,
(New York, 1926), 1:305–7, 311–313

3. From the Latin Version of Eusebius's *Chronicon*

Christ [A.D.]	Rome [Year of Reign]	
	Domitian	
95	14	Domitian orders those who were of the line of David to be killed, so that no one of royalty would remain of the Jews.
	Trajan	
106	8	Earthquakes destroy four Asian cities, Elea, Smyrna, Pytane, and Cyme, and in Greece, the two distinguished cities of the Opuntii and the Oriti.
109	11	The Pantheum at Rome is struck and burned by lightning.
110	12	Earthquakes destroy three Galatian cities.
116	18	The Jews who are in Libya fight against other aliens dwelling there. Likewise in Egypt and in Alexandria. In Cyrene and the Thebaid, they rush into a great rebellion. But in Alexandria, the side of the pagans triumphs.

		When the Jews in Mesopotamia rebel, Emperor Trajan orders Lysias Quietus to exterminate them from the province. After Quietus prepares an army against them, he kills innumerable thousands of them; and because of this, he is appointed Procurator of Judea by the emperor.
117	19	The Jews destroy Salamina, a city of Cyprus, after having killed the pagans there.

Hadrian

118	1	Hadrian rebuilds Alexandria at public expense, it having suffered damage from the Jews. Hadrian overcomes the Jews [who are] rebelling against the Romans a second time.
121	4	Hadrian sends colonies to Libya, which had been laid waste by the Jews.
133	16	The Jews, taking up arms, lay waste to Palestine, while Tinius Rufus holds the province, to whom Hadrian sends an army in order to crush the rebels.
134	17	Cochebas, head [*dux*] of the Jewish faction, kills the Christians with all kinds of executions [when] they refuse to give assistance against the Roman army.
136	19	The Jewish war that was conducted in Palestine reaches its conclusion, the problem of the Jews having been completely suppressed. From that time, they were forbidden even to enter Jerusalem, first

because of the will of God, as the prophets had prophesied, and secondly because of the Roman interdiction.

J. P. Migne, ed., *Opera Omnia*
(Paris, 1857), 1:754–760

4. From the *Seven Books of History Against the Pagans* of Paulus Orosius

[VII, 12] . . . At the same time [in the reign of Trajan], an earthquake laid low four cities in Asia, Elaea, Myrina, Pitane, and Cyme, and in Greece, the two cities of Opuntii and the Oriti. This same earthquake demolished three cities of Galatia. Lightning struck and burned the Pantheon at Rome, while at Antioch an earthquake laid almost the entire city in ruins. Then violent rebellions among the Jews broke out simultaneously in various parts of the world. The Jews acted as if turned into mad savages. Throughout Libya they waged pitiless war against the inhabitants and caused great desolation by killing the tillers of the soil. So merciless were they that if the emperor Hadrian had not afterward colonized the country with people from without, the land would have remained absolutely destitute and entirely without inhabitants. They disturbed all Egypt, Cyrene, and the Thebaid by sedition and bloodshed. In Alexandria, however, the Jews were defeated and crushed in a pitched battle. When they also rebelled in Mesopotamia, the emperor ordered war to be declared against them; many thousands of them were exterminated in a vast carnage. It is true that they did destroy Salamis, a city of Cyprus, after they had killed all the inhabitants. . . .

[VII, 13] . . . In one final massacre he [Hadrian] subdued the Jews who, excited by the disorders caused by their own crimes, were ravaging the province of Palestine, which had once been their own. In this way he avenged the Christians, whom the Jews, under the leadership of Cochebas, were torturing because they would not join them against the Romans. The emperor gave orders that no Jew should be permitted to enter Jerusalem and that only Christians should be permitted to occupy the city. . . .

Trans. Irving W. Raymond, *Seven Books of History Against the Pagans* (New York, 1936), 341–43

Bibliography

Abraham bar Ḥiyya. *Megillat Ha-Megalleh*. Edited by A. Poznanski. Berlin, 1924.
Abraham ben David Ha-Levi (Ibn Daud). *The Exalted Faith*, Hebrew ms. edited by Gershon Weiss. Translated with commentary by Norbert Samuelson. Rutherford, N.J.: Fairleigh Dickinson University Press, 1986.
———. *Ha-Emunah Ha-Ramah*. Edited by S. Weil. Berlin: L. Lamm, 1919.
———. *Ḥibburei Ha-Qronografiyah shel Ha-Rabad Ha-Rishon*. Mantua edition. Edited by H. H. Ben-Sasson. Jerusalem: Hebrew University, 1964.
———. *Zikhron Divrei Romi*. In *Ḥibburei Ha-Qronografiyah shel Ha-Rabad Ha-Rishon*, Mantua edition, edited by H. H. Ben-Sasson. Jerusalem: Hebrew University, 1964.
Abramsky, Shmuel. *Bar Kokhva: Nesi Yisra'el*. Tel Aviv: Massada, 1961.
Abravanel, Isaac. *Yeshu'ot Meshiḥo* 1861. Reprint. Jerusalem: 1967.
Adler, Elkan Nathan, comp. *Jewish Travellers: A Treasury of Travelogues from Nine Centuries*. New York: Hermon Press, 1966.
Aescoly, Aaron Zev. *Ha-Tenu'ot Ha-Meshiḥiyot Be-Yisra'el*. Jerusalem: Mossad Bialik, 1956.
Almbladh, Karin. *Sefer 'Emeq Ha-Bakha (The Vale of Tears), with the chronicle of the anonymous Corrector*. Introduction, Critical Edition, Comments by K. Almbladh. Uppsala, 1981.
Alon, Gedaliah. *Toldot Ha-Yehudim Be'Ereṣ Yisra'el Bi-tequfat Ha-Mishnah Ve-ha-Talmud*. 2 vols. Tel Aviv: Hoṣaat Ha-Qibbuṣ Ha-Menuḥad, 1956.
Applebaum, Shimon. "Points of View on the Second Jewish Revolt." *Scripta Classica Israelica* 7 (1983/84): 77–87.
———. *Prolegomena to the Study of the Second Jewish Revolt*. British Archaeological Reports. Supplement 7. Oxford, 1976.
———. "The Second Jewish Revolt (A.D. 131–35)." *Palestine Exploration Quarterly* 116 (1984): 35–41.
Avi-Yonah, Michael. *The Jews of Palestine*. New York: Schocken Books, 1976.
Azariah de' Rossi. *Sefer Me'or Einayim*. Edited by David Cassel. Vilna: Romm, 1864–66. Reprint. Jerusalem: Maqor, 1970.

Baer, Yitzhak. "Don Yiṣḥaq Abravanel ve-Yaḥaso el Ba'ayot ha-Historiyah ve-ha-Medinah." *Tarbiz* 8 (1937): 241–59.

———. *Galut*. Translated by Robert Warshow. 1947. Reprint. Lanham, Md.: University Press of America, 1988.

———. *A History of the Jews in Christian Spain*. Translated by Louis Schoffman. 2 vols. Philadelphia: Jewish Publication Society, 1966.

Baron, Salo W. *History and Jewish Historians*. Philadelphia: Jewish Publication Society, 1964.

———. *A Social and Religious History of the Jews*. Vols. 2, 5, 14. New York: Columbia University Press, 1952, 1957, 1969.

Barth, Lewis M. "Literary Imagination and the Rabbinical Sermon: Some Observations." In *Proceedings of the Seventh World Congress of Jewish Studies: Studies in Talmud, Halakhah and Midrash*, 29–35. Jerusalem: Perry Foundation for Biblical Research, 1981.

Barzilay, Isaac E. *Between Faith and Reason: Anti-Rationalism in Italian Jewish Thought, 1250–1650*. The Hague: Mouton, 1967.

Benjamin of Tudela. *Mas'ot shel Rabbi Benyamin: The Itinerary of Rabbi Benjamin of Tudela*. Text edited and translated by A. Asher (Elkam Adler). 2 vols. New York: Ha-Keshet Publishing Co., 1840.

Ben-Sasson, H. H. "Galut u-Ge'ulah be-Eynav shel Dor Golei Sefarad." In *Yitzhak F. Baer Jubilee Volume*, edited by S. W. Baron, B. Dinur, S. Ettinger, and I. Halpern. Jerusalem: Ha-Ḥevrah Ha-Historit Ha-Yisra'elit, 1960.

———. "Li-Megamot Ha-Qronografia ha-Yehudit shel Yemei Ha-Beinayim u-Be'ayotekha." In *Historionim ve'Ascolot Historiot*. Jerusalem: Ha-Ḥevrah Ha-Historit Ha-Yisra'elit, 1962.

———. *Peraqim Be-Toldot Ha-yehudim Bi-yemei Ha-Beinayim*. Tel Aviv: Am Oved, 1969.

———. *Trial and Achievement*. Jerusalem: Keter Publishing House, 1974.

Biale, David. *Power and Powerlessness in Jewish History*. New York: Schocken Books, 1986.

Bolle, Kees. "Secularization as a Problem for the History of Religions." *Comparative Studies in Society and History* 12 (1970): 242–59.

Bonfil, Robert. "The Historian's Perception of the Jews in the Italian Renaissance: Towards a Reappraisal." *Revue des Etudes Juives* 143 (1984): 59–82.

———. "How Golden Was the Age of the Renaissance in Jewish Historiography?" *History and Theory* 27 (1988): 78–102.

———. "Some Reflections on the Place of Azariah de Rossi's *Me'or Enayim* in the Cultural Milieu of Italian Renaissance Jewry." In *Jewish Thought in the Sixteenth Century*, edited by Bernard D. Cooperman. Cambridge: Harvard University Press, 1983.

Bowerstock, G. W. "A Roman Perspective on the Bar Kokhba Revolt." In *Approaches to Ancient Judaism* 2, edited by William S. Green. Chico, Cal.: 1980.

Breines, Paul. *Tough Jews*. New York: Basic Books, 1990.

Brenan, Gerald. *The Literature of the Spanish People*. Cambridge: Cambridge University Press, 1953.

Breuer, Mordechai. "Modernism and Traditionalism in Sixteenth-Century Historiography: A Study of David Gans' *Tzemaḥ David*." In *Jewish Thought in the Sixteenth Century*, edited by Bernard D. Cooperman. Cambridge: Harvard University Press, 1983.

Burckhardt, Jacob. *The Civilization of the Renaissance in Italy*. Translated by Ludwig Geiger and Walter Götz. Illustrated edition. New York: Harper and Row, 1958.

Cavendish, Richard. *A History of Magic*. London: Weidenfeld and Nicolson, 1977.
Cohen, Arthur. *In the Days of Simon Stern*. New York: Random House, 1972.
Cohen, Gerson D. *The Book of Tradition by Abraham Ibn Daud*. A Critical Edition with a translation and notes. Philadelphia: Jewish Publication Society, 1967.
———. *Messianic Postures of Ashkenazim and Sephardim (Prior to Shabbethai Zevi)*. New York: Leo Baeck Institute, 1967.
Cohen, Jeremy. *The Friars and the Jews*. Ithaca, N.Y.: Cornell University Press, 1982.
Cohn, Norman. *The Pursuit of the Millennium*. Revised edition. New York: Oxford University Press, 1970.
Dan, Joseph. *Gershom Scholem and the Mystical Dimension of Jewish History*. New York: New York University Press, 1987.
David, Abraham. "R. Gedalya ibn Yahya's *Shalshelet HaKabbalah* ('Chain of Tradition'); A Chapter in Medieval Jewish Historiography, Introduction." Translated by Bruce Lorence. *Imanu'el* 12 (1981): 60–76.
Degani, Ben-Zion. "Ha-Mivneh shel Ha-Historiyah Ha-'Olamit u-Ge'ulat Yisra'el be-Ṣemaḥ David le-R. David Ganz." *Ṣiyon* 45 (1980): 173–200.
Dio Cassius. *Roman History*. Loeb Classical Library. Translated by E. Cary. 1925.
Efron, Joshua. "Milḥemet Bar Kokhva Le'or Ha-Mesurat Ha-Talmudit Ha-Ereṣ Yisra'elit Keneged Ha-Bavlit." In *The Bar Kokhba Revolt: New Studies*, edited by A. Oppenheimer and U. Rappaport. Jerusalem: Yad Izhak Ben Zvi, 1984.
Elbogen, Israel. "Abraham ibn Daud als Geschichtsschreiber." In *Festschrift zum siebzigsten Geburtstage Jakob Guttmans*. Leipzig: Gustav Fock, 1915.
Eldad, Israel. *The Jewish Revolution: Jewish Statehood*. Translated by Hannah Schmorak. New York: Shengold Publishers, 1971.
Elior, Rachel. "Messianic Expectations and Spiritualization of Religious Life in the Sixteenth Century." *Revue des Etudes Juives* 145 (1986): 35–49.
Eusebius of Caesarea. *The Ecclesiastical History*. Translated by Kiropp Lake. Loeb Classical Library. New York: Putnam's Sons, 1926.
———. *Opera Omnia*. 4 vols. Edited by J. P. Migne. Paris: Petit-Montrouge, 1857.
Even-Shmuel, J., ed. *Midreshei Ge'ulah*. Jerusalem: Mossad Bialik, 1954.
Finkelstein, Louis. *Akiba: Scholar, Saint, Martyr*. New York: Atheneum, 1975.
Frankel, Jonathan. "Bar Kokhba and All That." *Dissent* 31 (1984): 192–202.
Friedlander, Gerald, trans. *Pirqei d'R. Eliezer*. New York: Hermon Press, 1965.
Funkenstein, Amos. "Basic Types of Christian Anti-Jewish Polemics in the Late Middle Ages." *Viator* 2 (1971): 373–82.
———. "Maimonides: Political Theory and Realistic Messianism." *Miscellanea Mediaevalia* 9 (1974): 81–103.
Gans, David. *Sefer Ṣemaḥ David*. Edited by Mordechai Breuer. Jerusalem: Magnes Press, 1983.
Gedaliah ibn Yaḥya. *Shalshelet Ha-Kabbalah*. Warsaw: A. M. Zisberg and M. Y. Holter, 1881.
Gilmore, Myron. "The Renaissance Conception of the Lessons of History." In *Facets of the Renaissance*, edited by William Werkmeister. New York: Harper and Row, 1959.
Ginzburg, Louis. *Legends of the Jews*. Philadelphia: Jewish Publication Society, 1962.
Glatzer, Nahum. *Essays in Jewish Thought*. University, Ala.: University of Alabama Press, 1978.
Green, Otis. *Spain and the Western Tradition*. 4 vols. Madison: University of Wisconsin Press, 1963.

Guttmann, Jacob. *Die Religionsphilosophischen Lehren des Isaak Abravanel.* Breslau: M. and H. Marcus, 1916.
Hadas, Moses, and Morton Smith. *Heroes and Gods.* New York: Harper and Row, 1965.
Harkabi, Yehoshafat. *The Bar Kokhba Syndrome.* Translated by Max Ticktin. Edited by David Altshuler. Chappaqua, N.Y.: Rossel Books, 1983.
Heinemann, Isaak. *Darkhei Ha-Aggadah.* 3rd ed. Jerusalem: Magnes Press, 1970.
Heinemann, Joseph. *Literature of the Synagogue.* New York: Behrman House, 1975.
Hillgarth, J. N. *The Spanish Kingdoms, 1250–1516.* 2 vols. Oxford: Clarendon Press, 1978.
Isaac, Benjamin. "Cassius Dio on the Revolt of Bar Kokhba." *Scripta Classica Israelica* 7 (1983/84): 68–76.
Isaac, Benjamin, and Aharon Oppenheimer. "The Revolt of Bar Kokhba: Ideology and Modern Scholarship." *Journal of Jewish Studies* 36 (1985): 33–60.
Kahanah, Abraham. *Sifrut Ha-Historiya Ha-Yisra'elit.* Warsaw, 1922.
Kerenyi, C. *The Heroes of the Greeks.* Translated by H. J. Rose. London: Thames and Hudson, 1959.
Klausner, Joseph. *The Messianic Idea in Israel from Its Beginning to the Completion of the Mishnah.* Translated by W. F. Stinespring. New York: Macmillan, 1955.
Klein, M., and E. Molnar. "Ha-Rabad be-Tor Ḥoker Divrei Yemei Yisra'el." *Hazofeh* 8 (1924): 24–32.
Kochan, Lionel. *The Jew and His History.* New York: Macmillan, 1977.
Kohn, Martin. "Jewish Historiography and Jewish Self-Understanding in the Period of the Renaissance and Reformation." Ph.d. diss., University of California, Los Angeles, 1979.
Kraemer, Joel. "On Maimonides' Messianic Posture." In *Studies in Medieval Jewish History and Literature,* vol. 2, edited by Isadore Twersky. Cambridge: Harvard University Press, 1979.
Kraus, Samuel. "Ḥayyalot Bar Kokhva." In *Sefer Ha-Yuval Likvod Alexander Marx.* New York: Jewish Theological Seminary, 1950.
Kristeller, Paul O. *Renaissance Thought.* New York: Harper and Row, 1955.
Kronholm, Tryggve. "The Vale of Tears: Remarks on the New Edition of Joseph Hakkohen's Sefaer Emaeq Habbaka." *Orientalia Suecana* 30 (1981): 149–71.
Lesky, Albin. *Greek Tragedy.* Translated by H. A. Frankfort. New York: Barnes and Noble, 1964.
Lerner, Ralph. "Maimonides' Treatise on Resurrection." *History of Religions* 23 (1983): 140–55.
Levey, Samson. *The Messiah: An Aramaic Interpretation.* Cincinnati: Hebrew Union College Press, 1974.
Liebman, Charles, and Eliezer Don-Yehiya. *Civil Religion in Israel.* Berkeley and Los Angeles: University of California Press, 1983.
Mallett, Michael. *Mercenaries and Their Masters: Warfare in Renaissance Italy.* Totowa, N.J.: Rowman and Littlefield, 1974.
Marks, Richard G. "Dangerous Hero: Rabbinic Attitudes Toward Legendary Warriors." *HUCA* 54 (1983): 181–94.
McGinn, Bernard. *Visions of the End: Apocalyptic Traditions in the Middle Ages.* New York: Columbia University Press, 1979.
———, trans. *Apocalyptic Spirituality.* New York: Paulist Press, 1979.
Melamed, Abraham. "The Perception of Jewish History in Italian Jewish Thought of the Sixteenth and Seventeenth Centuries: A Re-examination." In *Italia Judaica*—

"Gli ebrei in Italia tra Rinascimento ed Eta barocca." Atti del II Convegno Internazionale, Rome, 1986, 139–70.
Meyer, Michael. *Ideas of Jewish History.* New York: Behrman House, 1974.
Moore, George Foot. *Judaism in the First Centuries of the Christian Era.* 2 vols. 1927. Reprint. New York: Schocken Books, 1971.
Moses ben Maimon (Maimonides). *Epistle to Yemen.* Edited with introduction and notes by Abraham S. Halkin. New York: American Academy for Jewish Research, 1952.
———. *Iggerot.* Arabic original with translation by Joseph Kafih. Jerusalem: Mosad Ha-Rav Kook, 1972.
———. *The Guide of the Perplexed.* Translated with Introduction and Notes by Shlomo Pines. Chicago: University of Chicago Press, 1963.
———. *Ma'amar Tehiyat Ha-Metim.* Edited by Joshua Finkel. New York: American Academy of Jewish Research, 1939.
———. *Mishneh Torah.* Jerusalem: Mossad Ha-Rav Kook, 1966.
Muneles, Otto, ed. *Prague Ghetto in the Renaissance Period.* Prague: Orbis, 1965.
Nathan ben Elisha Ashkenazi (Nathan the Prophet). "Drush Ha-Tanninim." In *Be'iqvot Mashiaḥ,* edited by Gershom Scholem. Jerusalem: Hoṣa'at Sifre Tarshish, 1943.
Neher, André. *Jewish Thought and the Scientific Revolution of the Sixteenth Century: David Gans (1541–1613) and His Times.* Translated by David Maisel. Oxford: Oxford University Press, 1986.
Nemoy, Leon. *Karaite Anthology.* New Haven: Yale University Press, 1952.
Netanyahu, Benzion. *Don Isaac Abravanel: Statesman and Philosopher.* Philadelphia: Jewish Publication Society, 1953.
Neubauer, Adolph. *Medieval Jewish Chronicles.* 2 vols. London: Oxford University, 1887.
Neuman, Abraham. "Abraham Zacuto Historiographer." In *Harry Austryn Wolfson Jubilee Volume.* Jerusalem, 1965.
Neusner, Jacob. *A History of the Jews in Babylonia.* Leiden: E. J. Brill, 1965–70.
———. *Judaism: The Evidence of the Mishnah.* Chicago: University of Chicago Press, 1981.
———. *Messiah in Context: Israel's History and Destiny in Formative Judaism.* Philadelphia: Fortress Press, 1984.
———. *Our Sages, God, and Israel.* Chappaqua, N.Y.: Rossel Books, 1984.
———. "Religious Uses of History." *History and Theory* 5 (1966): 153–71.
———. *There We Sat Down.* Nashville: Abingdon Press, 1972.
Novak, David. "Maimonides' Concept of the Messiah." *Journal of Religious Studies* 9 (1982): 42–50.
Oppenheimer, Aharon. "Meshiḥiyuto shel Bar Kokhva." In *Meshiḥiyut ve-Eskhatologyah,* edited by Zvi Baras. Jerusalem: Hoṣa'at Merkaz Zalman Shazar, 1983.
Orosius, Paulus. *Seven Books of History against the Pagans.* Translated with introduction and notes by Irving W. Raymond. New York: Columbia University Press, 1936.
Patai, Raphael. *The Messiah Texts.* New York: Avon Books, 1979.
Pesiqta d'Rav Kahana. Edited by Bernard Mandelbaum. New York: Jewish Theological Seminary, 1962.
Ratner, B., ed. *Midrash Seder Olam.* Reprint. New York: Talmudical Research Institute, 1966.
Ravitsky, Aviezer. " 'Kefi Koaḥ Ha-Adam'—Yemot Ha-Mashiaḥ Be-Mishnot Ha-Rambam." In *Meshiḥiyut ve-Eskhatologyah,* edited by Zvi Baras, 191–220. Jerusalem: Hoṣa'at Merkaz Zalman Shazar, 1983.

Reeves, Virginia. *The Influence of Prophecy in the Later Middle Ages.* Oxford: Clarendon Press, 1969.
Roth, Cecil. *A History of the Marranos.* Philadelphia: Jewish Publication Society, 1932.
Rowland, Robert. *The Rhetoric of Menachem Begin: The Myth of Redemption through Return.* Lanham, Md.: University Press of America, 1985.
Sarachek, Joseph. *The Doctrine of the Messiah in Medieval Jewish Literature.* New York: Hermon Press, 1932.
———. *Don Isaac Abravanel.* New York: Bloch, 1938.
Sasportas, Jacob. *Ṣiṣat Novel Ṣevi.* Edited by Isaiah Tishby. Jerusalem: Mossad Bialik, 1954.
Schäfer, Peter. *Der Bar Kokhba-Aufstand.* Tübingen: J.C.B. Mohr, 1981.
———. "The Causes of the Bar Kokhba Revolt." In *Studies in Aggadah, Targum and Jewish Liturgy in Memory of Joseph Heinemann,* ed. Jakob Petuchowski and Ezra Fleischer, 74–94. Jerusalem: Magnes Press, 1981.
———. "Rabbi Aqiva and Bar Kokhba." In *Approaches to Ancient Judaism,* 2, edited by William S. Green. Chico, Cal.: Scholars Press, 1980.
Scholem, Gershom. *Kabbalah.* New York: Quadrangle, 1974.
———. *The Messianic Idea in Judaism and Other Essays on Jewish Spirituality.* New York: Schocken Books, 1971.
———. *Sabbatai Ṣevi: The Mystical Messiah.* Princeton: Princeton University Press, 1973.
———. *Von der mystichen Gestalt der Gottheit.* Zurich: Rhein Verlag, 1962.
Schonfield, Hugh, trans. *According to the Hebrews* (Toldot Yeshu). London: Duckworth, 1937.
Schürer, Emil. *The History of the Jewish People in the Age of Jesus Christ.* New English Version Revised and Edited by Geza Vermes and Fergus Millar. Edinburgh: T. and T. Clark, 1973.
Seder Olam Rabbah Ha-Shalem. Edited by M. Weinstock. Jerusalem: Torat Hesed, 1962.
Sedinova, Jirina. "Non-Jewish Sources in the Chronicle by David Gans, 'Tzemah David.' " *Judaica Bohemiae* 8 (1972): 3–15.
Segal, Lester. *Historical Consciousness and Religious Tradition in Azariah de' Rossi's Me'or Einayim.* Philadelphia: Jewish Publication Society, 1989.
Sharot, Stephen. "Jewish Millenarianism: A Comparison of Medieval Communities." *Comparative Studies in Society and History* 22 (1980): 394–415.
———. *Messianism, Mysticism, and Magic: A Sociological Analysis of Jewish Religious Movements.* Chapel Hill: University of North Carolina Press, 1982.
Shulvass, Moses. *The Jews in the World of the Renaissance.* Translated by Elvin I. Kose. Leiden: E. J. Brill, 1973.
Silver, Abba Hillel. *A History of Messianic Speculation in Israel from the First through the Seventeenth Centuries.* New York: Macmillan, 1927.
Solmon ibn Verga. *Sefer Shevet Yehudah.* Edited by M. Wiener. Hanover, Orient-Buchhandlungen, 1924.
Sprinzak, Ehud. *The Ascendance of Israel's Radical Right.* New York: Oxford University Press, 1991.
Strauss, L. "On Abravanel's Philosophical Tendency and Political Teaching." In *Isaac Abravanel: Six Lectures,* edited by J. B. Trend and H. Loewe. Cambridge: Cambridge University Press, 1937.
Tamar, David. "Ha-Ṣipiyah Be-'Italyah Li-Shnat Ha-Ge'ulah 5335." *Sefunot* 2 (1958): 61–88.

Twersky, Isadore. *Introduction to the Code of Maimonides (Mishneh Torah)*. New Haven: Yale University Press, 1980.
Urbach, Ephraim. *The Sages: Their Concepts and Beliefs*. Translated by I. Abrahams. Jerusalem: Magnes Press, 1975.
Usque, Samuel. *Consolation for the Tribulations of Israel*. Translated with an introduction by Martin A. Cohen. Philadelphia: Jewish Publication Society, 1977.
Vital, Hayyim. *Sefer Ha-Gilgulim*. Premisla, 1875.
———. *Sefer Sha'ar Ruah Ha-Qodesh*. Edited by Shmuel Vital. Writings of Our Teacher the Ari, Part 11. Tel Aviv: Eshel Press, 1963.
Walker, D. P. *Spiritual and Demonic Magic from Ficino to Campanella*. Notre Dame, Ind.: University of Notre Dame Press, 1957.
Waxman, Meyer. *A History of Jewish Literature*. New York: Bloch, 1933.
Weiss, R. "Learning and Education in Western Europe from 1470–1520." In *The New Cambridge Modern History*. Vol. 1, *The Renaissance*, edited by G. R. Potter. Cambridge: Cambridge University Press, 1957.
Wertheimer, A., ed. *Yosippon*. Venice and Mantua editions. Jerusalem: Hominer, 1956.
Yadin, Yigael. *Bar Kokhba*. New York: Random House, 1971.
Yeiven, Shmuel. *Milhemet Bar Kokhba*. Jerusalem: Mossad Bialik, 1952.
Yerushalmi, Yosef Hayim. "Messianic Impulses in Joseph ha-Kohen." In *Jewish Thought in the Sixteenth Century*, edited by Bernard D. Cooperman. Cambridge: Harvard University Press, 1983.
———. *Zakhor: Jewish History and Jewish Memory*. Seattle: University of Washington Press, 1982.
Yosef Ha-Kohen. *The Vale of Tears*. Translated by Harry S. May. The Hague: Martinus Nijhoff, 1971.
Zacuto, Abraham. *Sefer Yuhasin Ha-Shalem*. Edited by Zvi Filopowski. Frankfort-am-Main, 1924.
Zinberg, Israel. *A History of Jewish Literature*. Translated and edited by Bernard Martin. Cincinnati: Hebrew Union College Press, 1974.

Index

Abraham ben David Ha-Levi. *See* Ibn Daud
Abravanel, Isaac (1437–1508), 63, 99, 137, 145, 153, 158–60, 171, 183, 201, 202, 203, 205, 207
   ideas of, about Rabbi Akiba, 111–17
   polemical concerns of, 102–7
   social and intellectual environment of, 101–2, 127 n. 50, 123–34, 132–34
   vengeance in writings of, 121–25
   writings of, 100–101, 125
Akiba ben Joseph, Rabbi, 6–7, 14–16 (rabbinic texts), 17–18, 20, 25 (text), 30–31, 58 n. 2 (text), 69, 81–82 (text), 82–83, 87, 88, 89, 103, 105–7 (with text), 107–8, 108–11 (text), 111–14, 122, 131, 146–47, 156–57 (with text), 163, 165, 169–170 (text), 170–73, 174–75 (text), 177, 187 (text), 189–90 (text), 188–93, 194–95 (text), 195, 196 (text), 198–99, 206–8
   defense of, 78–80, 90–91, 112, 116, 121, 131, 157, 206–8
Almbladh, Karin, 150 n. 41
Applebaum, Shimon, 5, 7, 8
Aristotle, 39, 44, 72–73, 79, 96, 202
Avi-Yonah, Michael, 49
Azariah de' Rossi (1511–c.1578), 161, 172 (social conditions), 182–83, 200, 201, 203
   analysis of Bar Kokhba's names by, 162–63, 168

   historical methods of, 164–69
   Light to the Eyes, 160–61, 162, 164, 165–69
   meaning of Bar Kokhba to, 163–64, 166–67

Baer, Yitzhak, 77, 119 n. 32, 127 n. 50, 129, 132
Bar Kokhba in Greek and Latin writings (translations), 209–14
Bar Kokhba in Jewish literature (translations of Jewish texts), 14, 20, 23–25, 47, 58, 59–60, 81–82, 86, 106–7, 108–11, 115, 138, 150–51, 152, 156–58, 161–62, 169–70, 171–72, 174–76, 187–90, 194–95, 196, 199
Baron, Salo, 48, 159 n. 57, 161 n. 58, 164
Barth, Lewis, 53
Begin, Menachem, 2, 9
Benjamin of Tudela, 140, 142
Ben-Sasson, H. H., 123, 135 n. 1
Betar, 8, 32, 85–88, 115, 140, 151, 169, 171
   Betar organization, 2
   destruction of, 41–43, 51, 60, 75, 80, 138, 145–49, 152–154, 158, 161, 170–73, 174–75, 178, 181
Biale, David, 49
Bolle, Kees, 203 n. 1
Bonfil, Robert, 136, 164, 167 n. 2
Breines, Paul, 2, 9 n. 18
Breuer, Mordechai, 177, 179–80

224   Index

Christians, 76, 100–6, 122–23, 125, 129, 136, 138, 144–45, 147, 156, 157, 159–60, 168, 178–79, 182, 203, 205
Cohen, Arthur (*In the Days of Simon Stern*), 3
Cohen, Gerson D., 63–64, 65 n. 15, 68 n. 21, 70–71, 78, 79
    theory of, about Ibn Daud's story of Bar Kokhba, 61–62
Cohen, Jeremy, 100 n. 2
Cohen, Martin, 145, 146 n. 29
Cuthean, 23–26, 36–38, 44–46, 49

Dio Cassius, 4, 8, 119 n. 33, 146 n. 29, 176, 209–10 (on Bar Kokhba)

El'azar, Rabbi, 34–36, 37–38, 39, 42, 44–45, 45–46, 48, 55, 87
Eldad, Israel, 5 n. 7
Eusebius of Caesarea, 8
    Chronicon (world chronicle), 64, 67, 69, 69 n. 22, 119, 130, 157–59, 212–14 (translation)
    Ecclesiastical History, 14, 36 n. 51, 161–63, 176, 211–12 (translation)

Funkenstein, Amos, 84, 100

Gans, David (1541–1613), 173, 182, 201, 205
    historical methods of, 176–78
    meaning of Bar Kokhba to, 178–81
    social environment of, 178, 179–80
    Sprout of David, 173–74, 178–80
Gedaliah ibn Yahya. *See* Ibn Yahya, Gedaliah
gibbor, or mighty warrior, 27–31, 32, 37, 38, 40, 42 n. 61, 44, 49, 50–51, 59, 82, 119–20, 122, 132–34, 159–60, 205
Glatzer, Nahum, 48
Greek heroes, 31, 43

Hadrian, 8, 32, 40–41, 42–43, 50, 66–67, 80, 138, 147, 151, 152, 153, 157–58, 161–62, 163, 169–70, 172, 174–5, 176, 178, 209–14
Ha-Kohen, Yosef. *See* Yosef Ha-Kohen
Harkabi, Yehoshafat, 9–10, 202

Ibn Daud, Ibrahim (Abraham ben David Ha-Levi, c.1110–c.1180), 57, 59, 86, 95–97, 119, 126–27, 150, 158, 163, 169, 170, 175, 177, 179, 201, 202, 203, 207
    social and religious concerns of, 73–81

    sources for story of Bar Kokhba, 63–72
Ibn Yahya, Gedaliah (1515–1578), 169, 179, 181, 182, 201
    The Chain of Tradition, 169, 170, 172
    social environment of, and image of Bar Kokhba, 170–71, 172
    theme of Jewish suffering, 181
image of Bar Kokhba
    as cause for hope, 55–56, 80–81, 90–91, 125–26, 150, 180–81, 192–93, 198–99, 206–7
    as false messiah, 20–22, 56, 77–78, 86, 114–18, 122, 140–43, 146, 151, 155, 163, 171, 181–82, 191, 208
    as *gibbor*, or mighty warrior, 26–31, 33–34, 37, 38, 40, 43, 44, 46–48, 50–51, 55–56, 58–59, 89, 118–22, 126, 132–34, 159–60, 179–81, 191, 202–3, 205
    as national leader, 58, 61, 72, 86–88, 89–90, 95, 152, 171, 179–181, 204–6
    as potential messiah, 88–92, 121, 187–93, 195–97, 199–200, 207–8
Italy, 101–2, 124, 136, 142, 144, 149 n. 34, 152, 164, 167, 171, 172, 181

Jabotinsky, Vladimir, 2
Jacob ben Abraham (twelfth century), 58–59, 126
Jewish historiography, sixteenth-century, 135–37
Jewish history as suffering, 137–38, 147, 149–50, 153–55, 171–73, 181
Jewish revolts of 116–117, 65, 69, 119, 159, 163, 176, 178, 211, 212–13, 214
Josephus, Flavius, 127 n. 50, 129

Kabbalah, Lurianic, 185–87
    concept of *gilgul*, 186
    concept of Messiah, 186–87, 190–91, 192–94
    concept of *sefirah* (*sefirot*, plural), 189, 197
    concept of *tikkun*, 186–87
Kabbalistic image of Bar Kokhba (summary), 199–200
Kochan, Lionel, 126–27

Maimonides, Moses (Moses ben Maimon, 1135–1204), 57, 79, 81, 95–97, 114, 115, 116–17, 121, 126–27, 157, 169, 171, 187, 199–200, 201, 202, 203, 205, 207

concept of the Messiah and messianic age, 83–85, 88–92
  The Guide of the Perplexed, 83, 84, 91, 93
  Mishneh Torah, 81, 83, 85–86, 93–94
  relation of, to messianic expectations of his time, 82, 88, 93–94
Messiah, 3, 17–20, 30–31, 77–79, 83–85, 88–92, 95–96, 103–6, 117, 120–21, 145, 150, 186–87, 189–91, 193–94, 197, 198–99
  Messiah ben Joseph, 82, 88, 112–13, 120–21, 193 n. 10, 199
  as warrior, 18, 19–20, 30–31, 82
messianic expectations, messianic movements, 17–20, 76–77, 82, 90–91, 93–94, 101, 114–18, 143–44, 145, 148–49, 150, 151–52, 165, 180, 182, 192, 194, 197, 199, 204, 206–8
  warnings against messianic movements, 47–48, 75–77, 97, 146, 152, 155, 165, 191–92, 193–94, 194–95, 204, 207
Meyer, Michael, 135 n. 1, 136 n. 3
millenarian expectations, Christian, 101–2, 144–45
Muslims, 76, 115, 117, 123

Nathan Ashkenazi of Gaza (1644–1680), 185, 194, 200, 201, 207
  ideas of, about Shabbatai Ṣevi, 195–97, 198–99
  meaning of Bar Kokhba to, 195–97, 198–99
  messianic concept of, 197–99
  reply of, to opponents, 198–99
Neher, Andre, 173 n. 87
Netanyahu, Benjamin, 102, 124, 127 n. 50, 132 n. 55
Neusner, Jacob, 15, 49
Ninth of Av, 51–56, 85–88, 95–96, 170
Numbers 24:17, 14–21, 30, 77, 156, 161–63, 174

Oppenheimer, Aharon, 4, 5

Paulus Orosius, 63–67, 119 n. 33, 161, 162, 214 (translation)
polemical contexts of the story, 75, 78–80, 95, 100–102, 103–7, 114, 128–29, 138, 156–57, 194–95, 198–99, 203, 204, 206
political implications of the story, 45–49, 76, 79–80, 92–95, 132, 171, 180–81, 204–6

Prague, 136, 144, 173, 178, 182
Pugio Fidei, 100, 103 (image of Bar Kokhba), 116

rabbinic authority and leadership, 48–50, 74–75, 78–80, 90–91, 94–95, 103–5, 107, 111–14, 126, 128, 156, 157, 165–66, 204, 205–6

rabbinic stories of Bar Kokhba
  audience response to, 44–45
  in Babylonian Talmud, 21–22
  as *gibbor* (heroic warrior), 26–31
  as impostor, 20–22
  in Jerusalem Talmud and Midrash Rabbath, 14, 20, 22–43, 47
  as messianic figure, 16–20, 30
  political implications of, 45–51
  religious implications of, 56
  two traditions of, 56
rabbis (as characters in the stories of Bar Kokhba), 21–22, 32–33, 37, 109, 111, 194–95
Rashi (Rabbi Solomon bar Isaac, 1040–1105), 57–58, 59, 86, 109 n. 18, 126, 201, 205
repentance, 52–56, 85, 87–88, 95, 126, 148, 150, 192, 203, 206

Safed, 144, 185, 190, 192
Sasportas, Jacob (1610–1698), 194–95, 198
secularization (or secular aspects) of image of Bar Kokhba, 4, 73, 96, 128–31, 156, 157–60, 166–69, 173, 178–81, 182–83, 203–4
Segal, Lester, 136 n. 1, 161 n. 51, 164, 166, 167 n. 2, 168
Schäfer, Peter, 6–7, 8, 42 n. 61
Scholem, Gershom, 10, 47 n. 66, 82, 93 n. 77, 187, 190, 197 n. 20, 202
Shabbatai Ṣevi (1626–1676), 194, 195–99
Spain, 59, 75, 76, 80, 95, 99, 100, 102, 123–25, 129 n. 52, 132–34, 137, 143, 145, 149, 152, 154, 155–156, 181
Spanish expulsion, 99, 123–25, 135, 137–38, 149, 154, 181, 203

traditional aspects of image of Bar Kokhba, 4, 96–97, 126–27, 128, 132, 156–57, 168, 173, 180–81, 181–82, 200, 203–4
Twersky, Isidore, 84, 93

Index

Usque, Samuel (c.1492–1547), 137, 155, 168, 179, 181–82, 201
   Consolation for the Tribulations of Israel, 137–38, 145–46, 148
   relation of, to messianic movements, 139, 141–42, 143–45, 146–47
   relation of, to problem of Portuguese conversos, 148–49
   response of, to Gentile persecution, 147
   sources for story of Bar Kokhba, 139–42

vengeance, 121, 123–25, 131–32, 133–34, 147, 150, 153, 150–60, 172, 182, 202, 205, 207
Vital, Ḥayyim (1542–1620), 185, 195, 197, 200, 201, 207
   meaning of Bar Kokhba to, 191–93
   messianic concept of, 188–91, 191–94
   Sefer Ha-Gilgulim, 187
   theory of, on relation between R. Akiba and Bar Kokhba, 188, 191–92, 193

Yadin, Yigael, 5 n. 7, 10, 202
Yerushalmi, Yosef Hayim, 126–27, 135, 136, 150, 152
Yosef Ha-Kohen (1496–1578), 149, 168, 179, 181–82, 201
   additions of, to story of Bar Kokhba, 151–54
   theme of Jewish suffering, 154–55
   The Vale of Tears, 149–50, 153–55
Yossipon, 68, 129

Zacuto, Abraham (1450–c.1515), 63, 64, 119, 155–56, 168, 171, 174, 177, 182–83, 201, 202, 205–6
   Book of Genealogies, 156, 159
   citation of "Christian chronicle" by, 157–59
   defense of R. Akiba by, 157
   interest in chronology, 158–59
   theme of revenge, 159–60

www.ingramcontent.com/pod-product-compliance
Lightning Source LLC
Chambersburg PA
CBHW031549300426
44111CB00006BA/233